S PERRY

THE UNIVERSAL SINGULAR

PIERRE EMMANUEL

THE
UNIVERSAL
SINGULAR

*Translated
from the French by
Erik de Mauny*

THE GREY WALLS PRESS

*First published in England in 1950
by the Grey Walls Press Limited,
6 & 7 Crown Passage, Pall Mall,
London, S.W.1*

*Printed in Great Britain
by the Northern Publishing Company,
Liverpool*

AUSTRALIA
The Invincible Press
Sydney, Melbourne, Brisbane, Adelaide

NEW ZEALAND
The Invincible Press, Wellington

CANADA
The Falcon Press
263-7 Adelaide Street West, Toronto

SOUTH AFRICA
M. Darling (Pty.) Ltd., Cape Town

This book
is dedicated to two of the living
PIERRE CROZIER
martyr under the barbarians
and ALBERT BÉGUIN

He who is with himself dissatisfied
Though all the world find satisfaction in him
Is like a rainbow-coloured bird gone blind,
That gives delight it shares not.

THOMAS HARDY, *The Dynasts*

Frère, je ne puis vous donner mon coeur, mais
où la matière ne sert point vaut et va la parole
invisible

Qui est moi-même avec une intelligence éternelle.

PAUL CLAUDEL, *L'Esprit et l'Eau*

CHAPTER ONE

I LIVED to thirty on a few truths, and a good number of errors, nearly all acquired during my childhood years. Certain particular characteristics arising from my upbringing, the not always felicitous circumstances which often strengthened them, and the practice of a speculative art whose source lies in the obscure part of being, prevented me up to then from finding my feet, if not in reality, at least in existence. But at thirty I was seized with uneasiness at a life slipping through my fingers without having been lived. From the outside, and judged by visible works, it appeared as a grand design: *work in progress,* an attempt to elucidate through symbols those permanent conflicts of mankind from which modern man suffers most. God forbid that I should renounce such an ambition! But I have yet to make it truly my own. I must inevitably be judged by the sentiment which I uphold. And yet I am like a stranger before my own books: the dramas they evoke are merely things I imagined; and even for those that I felt, and which spring from my own flesh, I provided only an ideal solution. Boldness of mind has nothing to do with the defections of the heart. And if there emerges from my work an ethic, a metaphysic, or that universal form of love which is called the religious spirit, I must state clearly to those who draw their conclusions about the man from his works: on the scale of greatness as I conceive it and feel it to be real, my life is that of a pygmy. Living on two different planes, that of art and that of life, in the long run harms both the man and the artist. I still believe there is a common salvation for these two beings who must exist as one. I have even begun to think that the humblest human existence, when it attains a rounded whole, is more beautiful than the work of the greatest artist. Our work is only an aspect, and not the whole of our life. There comes a time when it must be brought into harmony with the whole. Or else we are forced to the craven admission that our life belies our voice—then the poet in us becomes a personage whom we will not carry much further. We become mere peddlers of literature, or fall into plain despair. Personally, if I fail in the task I have given myself, to regain possession of my totality, I still prefer this latter alternative: I would rather find myself guilty than remain empty and satisfied.

*   *   *

Like a dreamer who breaks free from a long dream and becomes aware of the wind on his face, or like a man in love with night whom dawn surprises in the midst of his ruins, I have woken from these thirty years: and for the first time I am truly alone, for I recognise my solitude. Yet not alone—isolated rather, lost in the desert of my own footsteps, a stranger before the hostile faces, the mythical carved panels, that for ten years I have disinterred from my slumber. The lines I wrote a year ago:

> *Être seul est un grand courage. Donne à l'homme*
> *La force de s'aimer assez pour être seul,*
> [*To be alone is truly brave. Give man*
> *The strength to love himself enough to be alone*],

speak to my understanding now, and order me to act. Between isolation and solitude stretches all the distance of charity. I contemplate and measure the distance: but it cannot be spanned by mind alone. Pure mind, wishing to be eternal and free from all attachment, is in reality inert before life: the ubiquity of the spectator before the object is an intellectual lure only, so long as knowledge does not become experience. Nothing is more

8

deceptive than this faculty of moving while remaining immobile, or the willed detachment on which the mind prides itself, when it abstracts itself from its very existence. And what do the most sublime thoughts matter to me, if I make them reverberate in a void, or the subtlest ventures into analysis if deliberately they lead to nothing?

In ten years I read a great many books, particularly those to whose authority the contemporary mind refers. What intelligence I discovered—and nothing but intelligence! Here, everything serves as *pretext* for thought. The initial impulse once given, the fabulous machine feeds solely upon itself, a grasp of words being sufficient: secreting its ideal metamorphoses in a purely imaginary realm. What role is left to the feelings—the feelings of everyday and of all time? What happens to the unfathomable capacity to suffer, to love, to enter into communion with life itself, through which the humblest of mortals and the greatest spiritual seeker alike discover the true measure of their dignity? It is one's sensible nature that suffers, being forced into twisting ways, and seeking an outlet through some path of least resistance, on one of those escape routes that eternal man always finds in himself the moment he loses faith in the unity of his own nature and the world.

Like so many others, I fled: being concerned only with my intellectual progress, and ignoring my own feelings. But am I to continue in this mental trance? Must I abandon any longer my everyday man's life to alternating desire and boredom, to the intermittent fevers of the body forsaken by the spirit? I am weary of living like a beast and feigning to think like a pure intelligence. What is the man of isolated moments, of disconnected fragments, but an animal pulp? Discontinuity is chaos, not possibility: the possible is what *I* may do. If I do not 'hold together', in the absolute sense of the striking popular phrase, if I do not integrate each moment in a total awareness of my fate, what can I do? Can I call it a virtue to surrender to every passing hazard? What is there in common between the taste for adventure, which conjures up an unknown but real space, imbued with characteristic force, coherent and self-sufficient, and this being dragged from one episode to another, these automatic *adventures* that the least image, the least external sign release? The first is like a challenge the adventurer makes to himself, a risk indeed, but which he feels sure enough of himself to face: and whether he succeeds or fails does not greatly matter, for he attains to his true stature through his extreme awareness of himself, which is only fortified by being threatened. In the second instance, a chaos of impressions invades the seat of the soul: and now one impression, now another, the most persistent or the most recent, manifests its sway upon the vacant being. The intellectual swaggerer meanwhile escapes into fine phrases: he expects others to take his notions seriously, and imagines himself a master at the art of living. We have seen latterly how far this folly can go: and will see it even more tomorrow, when the same men who were wrong about the very substance of man are summoned back as advocates for the man they have denied. If I should ever fall into such a contradiction, let every word I have uttered be considered null and void: my work is nothing if I do not sign it with my life. I am not a mind *plus* a body, being one or the other according to the way the wind blows, but inextricably both together, a man who owes it to himself to be entire. The moment has arrived—and it is a serious moment—to grasp the meaning of Jouve's admirable lines:

> *J'aimerai comme un homme*
> *Non plus comme illimitée une chair.*
> [*I shall love like a man*
> *No more as some carnality unbounded.*]

*   *   *

Isolation is the purest discontinuity; isolated, I am wholly exterior; I may enter into any combination of interchangeable elements, without being anything more than contiguous to them.

Anything may contain me, and only the resistance of my surroundings determines my form. Proteus drew the power of metamorphosis from himself, and for all his supreme mobility, remained coordinated to his centre: his guises were not at all without reason. But I myself, isolated, am the protean matter of the moment: it is not an exuberance of form, but its absence, that makes me plastic. I adapt myself to that which shuts me in: my false freedom is that of a prisoner changing his prison indefinitely. This sort of ubiquity embraces nothing: having no density of my own, I sprawl in the void and take up the volume of a moment; and the very next moment deflates and reduces me to nothing without encountering any substantial resistance to check this return into nothingness.

To resist, one must be erect within one's being, defining oneself within the situation according to multiple coordinates. Thereafter, there is no movement but that which is willed: while pure non-attachment, linking up with pure fatalism, moves within the anarchy of hazard, true freedom inscribes itself in a history which bends hazard to its law. I wish to be free: to make my life. But my life does not begin or end in myself: what little I know of it shows it to be connected. I am a focal point of various relationships, whether I am aware of them or not: the centre of a double impulse, centripetal and centrifugal; and it is in the balance of these forces, some converging, others radiating outwards, that I confirm a presence which is constantly being challenged. If I cease to radiate outwards, the pressure of diversity tosses me about like an empty shell: but I cannot radiate outwards if the world does not rouse me with its innumerable stimuli. These actions and reactions are the warp and woof of duration: the pattern which they bring to light at a given epoch in my life has already been evolving for a long time, and its groundwork may go back to my childhood.

How many books have been written, and are still to be written, on the mystery of time! Of all I have read on this theme, which has barely ceased to obsess me, I remember above all the lordly vision, so shocking to reason, conjured up by Léon Bloy. I shall doubtless return to it in this book, for it provided me, at a point in my reflections, with the illumination I lacked. I now perceive that I am contemporaneous to myself, that all my actions, past, present and future, are inter-related in a mysterious simultaneity, whose still shadowy pattern becomes clear if I but for a moment turn my attention on myself. During the past few months I have felt the repercussions of certain major phases of my adolescence. I had thought them long since terminated; but on the contrary, what I have lived through since invests them with a new significance. My equilibrium is therefore not in the instant: the convergence and irradiation continue through duration. And doubtless the same simultaneity which forms my basis despite the flood of time is found also in the whole course of the universe. Hence the impression of true ubiquity which the man of action and thought must feel when he grasps the universal in its plenitude.

For the moment, I have the more modest desire to gather into one sheaf the components of my history; to link myself with this past which is always present, to elicit from it that image of myself which perhaps still animates me, to judge it by its strengths and weaknesses; and through it also to come for the first time to a full realisation of having lived too long in an imperfect form, prevented from maturing by strange interdicts; to measure the split these interdicts have created between the living world and myself; and finally, to try to break off a painful soliloquy and initiate, as a man, the dialogue I was incapable of starting as a youth. To take my bearings, certainly: and perhaps also to recognise my limitations. Or rather, to recognise my centre, and the energy it sustains. Energy has no absolute limit, unless it be its own centre. Everything proceeds from this focal point, and everything returns to it. The following pages will show whether this postulate is dictated by egoism, or whether it is on the threshold of charity.

CHAPTER TWO

I was a solitary child, although by nature I felt no leaning towards solitude. My parents lived far away: and their letters, infrequent as they were and not addressed directly to myself, told me very little about them. I have no memories of my earliest childhood years: yet from the ages of three to six I lived in America, where my parents had settled. Even now I do not know whether they kept me at home with them: apart from a scattered image or two, my memories begin with my return to France, whither I was sent back in the care of some obliging passengers.

I saw my mother again two years later: my brother was born in France. A few months after that she departed once more, leaving him in the care of the aunt who was already bringing me up. I was ten when my parents came back again: they had decided I was to go to college, and sent me to live with a paternal uncle. Then, having done what they considered to be their duty, they left France, not to return until fifteen years later. I was thus separated from my brother, whom I saw only in the summer holidays.

In short, I never knew my parents: as a child, I did not spend six months in their company; and when they settled in France (the war came, and held them back longer than my father wished), my life had begun without them, and our lack of understanding was mutual. Yet from the time I was six until I was twenty, I never received an admonishment which was not prefaced by something in their praise; people spoke of their sacrifice, and of their exile far from their children; I looked for an echo of this in their letters, but did not find it. Doubtless I was wrong to judge by the absence of effusiveness in their letters: my father, as I learned later, gave no outward show of sentiment. When I saw him again on his final return, there was a reserve about him which at first I found chilling, but later infinitely attractive, for it concealed a kind and sensitive heart. If my father did not show his feelings in words, my uncle showed them too much: sententious and given to moralising, he worked himself up with his own harangues, and the tears came into his eyes at the thought of all that my parents were doing for me. I listened to his homilies with an air of compunction that merely concealed my perfect indifference. As I grew older, the unreality of my parents became more obvious: by comparison with my companions, I felt like an abstract being: I was hurt, but not deeply unhappy, for at that age one's feelings are too spontaneous to allow one to realise what is really lacking.

My father is dead, and all I really knew him by was his smile, and his fine eyes which were clear like those of a child, and a prevailing air of quiet suffering, or of lurking sadness, on his sensitive features. During the last years he came to see me often: in my house he behaved with all the discretion of a guest. Our timidity had always been a reciprocal thing, but we were happy to understand each other, almost without words. And in a few months I learned to love him more than in almost thirty years: what gave our affection all its value, all its nostalgic *charm*, was the regret we both felt that so many years had been lost before.

I shall explain in a moment why the absence of my parents (of my father particularly) isolated me harshly within myself. Moved by the best intentions, my father lived solely for his sons: they were his pride and his justification. He worked for them, even before they came into the world. Of humble parentage, yet endowed with an intelligence far above the average, he had a craving for knowledge which the accident of his birth made a dangerous luxury; he went on learning, however, right up to his death, and I was often astonished to see him venturing with a fine discriminatory power into many an entirely modern field of science or art. But this self-acquired learning was by no means the end: his only thought was to perpetuate himself through his children, and to furnish them with means of access to that knowledge from which he himself was excluded. He worked, built up a little fortune, lost everything, and started again. Full of ideas, building castles in the air, he combined in a curious fashion, which was not always to his advantage, dream and reality.

His great mistake, and perhaps his fault, was in cutting himself off from his sons: while being Americanised himself, he wanted them to be brought up in France, content to summon them back to him once their education was complete. But his reckoning had terrible consequences: my mother, deprived of an outlet for her maternal feelings, was afflicted with melancholia which clouded her reason: she held up my father's enterprises, and made him vegetate while he was in the prime of life. Worse still, without realising it, he remained a stranger to my brother and myself; absorbed by the picture he built up of us, he knew nothing of our true development; there was no tenderness between us, no freedom of sentiment in our letters. He must have led a terribly lonely life, lost in his dream of the future he was making for himself and for us. He had the joy, in his later years, of having my brother back with him, and of inspiring his affection: but he lacked paternal experience and the knack of wielding authority; my brother was brought up in anarchy (although, it is true, his education up to then had been anything but coherent).

As to the relationship between my father and myself, I cannot look back on it without sadness. When I was twenty, and he asked me to follow out his plans, I was already fixed within myself, and several personal tribulations had made me extremely aggressive on the subject of my integrity. I refused to leave for America: it was a country that meant nothing to me. He played a trick, and had me informed by wire that he was on his deathbed. I went to New York to see him, and found him waiting for me at the landing stage. Instead of awaking pity, this piece of pusillanimity made me more obdurate. Added to that, my father, afraid of talking to me alone, employed a cousin to read me a lecture on his behalf. Blackmail on a small scale followed, but did not last: what it amounted to was, that I was not to return to France, but must think about finding a job for myself on the spot. I gave all the necessary promises, then, as soon as the storm had died down, with infinite relief took the boat back to France. My father's behaviour left me filled with nothing but resentment. An inner conviction, unspecified, but how strong I then realised, had been shattered. Parents, even when they are most distant, never realise how deeply their children's lives are rooted in their own. It seems strange that at thirty I should feel like an orphan, and that this should cause me grief.

*   *   *

The guardians of my childhood, until I was ten, were a sexagenarian aunt, rather brusque in manner but infinitely kind, my grandmother, a pretty, blue-eyed little old woman with very delicate features under her black, peasant shawl, whose memory was a treasure-house of stories, and a great-aunt, older than the hills, but whose astonishingly youthful voice brought back to life the old airs of our local patois. Needless to say, they had no notion of education; but my good aunt was obsessed by the fear of illnesses and accidents of all kinds. Nothing could have been more fatal for my hardening up.

At school, I soon forged ahead not only of boys of my own age, but even of the biggest ones. This effortless progress was made possible by a fortunate technique of memorising things, which I have since lost. At eight, I was in the 'certificate' class with boys from four to six years older than myself. To my misfortune, I came first: but the meagre pride first place afforded me was counterbalanced by the persecutions heaped upon me by my jealous companions. At the age when children begin to play games together and discover the meaning of friendship, I was an exile, too weak to join in the older ones' games, and cut off from the young ones for whom I was a big boy like the rest. The three old women were the only company I had, and they pampered me, stirred up my sickly resentment, and dangerously fanned my pride.

My apprenticeship for life began badly: and I find it easy to trace the reason for more than one subsequent setback in my childish failure to fit into things. There arose, first of all, my leaning towards solitude: I liked my aunt's fond attentions, but they did not console me for not being able to join in the older boys' fun, which she forbade from fear of their being too rough. Furthermore, the approaches I made to my school companions and the platitudes I uttered trying to be agreeable to them were mostly met with a rude rebuff. I was the master's white-haired boy, an ignominious position: and many thought me a spy. 'Dirty tell-tale' is a serious insult, and the schoolboy code of ethics (on this point, as on many others, the same as that of grown-ups) is justly severe where talebearing is concerned: the mere idea of informing against a companion filled me with horror even as a child, and I often wept bitterly at feeling myself suspected without just cause.

Isolated as I was, and shut in on myself to be as little vulnerable as possible, I found my passion in books, and from Erckmann-Chatrian to Jules Verne, from Hector Malot to George Sand, not forgetting the Russia of the *ispravniks* and of General Durakin, I let my imagination run riot. But this universe where all was plain sailing, which momentarily avenged me for the other, made me lazy about action, incurious about my body, and timorous as a girl. Far from shaking me from my inertia, my aunt encouraged me in it, for it protected me from those ambitious escapades during which so many catastrophes may arise. A fall from the top of a tree, a ducking in the river, an encounter with a snake or a savage dog—these and heaven knows what besides were the frightful visions conjured up by my aunt, for whom I was more fragile than glass. Her life became a torment when I was not near her; and had she dared, she would have followed me every step.

Wild perfume of childhood, odour of blood and dust and damp grass, of stolen fruit and spring water glistening on the body, bitter scent of perspiring scuffles and scrapes, and the vast delights one conceals at the bottom of one's pockets between a dirty handkerchief and three clay marbles—I was never able to savour your heady charm: it even meant much to look on the honey-suckle encountered in spring on the way to school as a friend. But what of the mysterious palavers, the elaborately planned expeditions, the finds that set the heart leaping, the moments of brusque and tongue-tied recognition, the games that develop into battles, the battles that turn into play? What triumphs reward the strong in this little world which seasons one so well for the world of men! I knew I had no place in it; if I did slip into it, I was tacitly regarded as a nobody: and yet I admired from afar a world more fabulous than that of books. The worst little hooligans were my heroes. They have since become estimable family men, and must cuff their offspring for the same escapades of which they themselves were so proud. I sensed clearly that the strongest are sometimes the most cowardly, because they discover soon enough how easy tyranny is, and because their tyranny degrades and softens them with success, but disarms them at the first setback: I did not envy them their power, but their self-confidence, their animal freedom. Had I been older, and among equals, I should have known how to use my fists just like any other: but it must be remembered that I was eight or nine, in the midst of boys of thirteen and fourteen; I had no other defence against force, no other safeguard against the fascination of force, but my inner pride, which, though still undeveloped at that period, the teacher and my aunt did all they could to foster. The idea was instilled in me that my companions were jealous: in reality, it was I who was jealous of them, seeing nothing in myself to excite their envy.

It was only slowly, and under the pressure of a sort of antiphonal adulation, that pride took root in my heart. The moral effect was disastrous, and I suffer from it still. This first split between mind and reality was to become aggravated throughout my adolescence, without my once being warned against it by any of those who pampered me until I was twenty.

When I look at myself as I am, I discern the features of a child who did not have his fill of childhood. I suffer now from that earlier deprivation as if from a wound: forgetfulness lulls but does not heal it, and it is ready to open afresh at each new encounter. Let parents remember the fact: childhood is the crucial period in the formation of character, and it is they who bear full responsibility, for the child, however rich he may be by nature, has neither the willpower nor the understanding of things to be able to bring to light and above all to fashion the riches within himself. Later, no doubt, the pangs of awareness may sometimes, but not always, pierce the dense wall of experience which blots out a lost childhood. But this path has many pitfalls, without any softening certainty, and the undertaking seems more chimerical at every step. The spirit of childhood, for those who have never known it, can only be revealed at the end of a drawn-out exhausting effort, like a mirage, or of a slow fulfilment, as an act of grace. Some grow like the grass, at the first shower, and all their lives preserve the spring scent of the earth. Others close in upon themselves, weary of waiting for the propitious dew which would make them open out; and when the dew does come, often enough their arid soil will not receive it; time, for them, is hard like granite, and they are haunted by the odour of stone.

Oh what isolation, what inner obscurity, wait for the child who knows no childhood! There was a young and attractive woman, no doubt full of affection in her innermost being, but somehow spurned by life, or herself spurning it through some personal unhappiness, who said to me recently: 'I feel as though I were

19

three hundred years old. I never knew what it was to be a child'. Daughter of a White Russian, she had gone through the horrors of the civil war: in her, the divine instinct of hope had become atrophied; it was as if she dragged her whole life behind her, or as if her terrible experience had walled it up at the very threshold—she endured without existing. I think of the Jewish children, confined in the German concentration camps, with piled up corpses for horizon; of the millions of children in the bombed cities who, year after year, have seen nothing but ruins all around them. I think of the Russian boy Malaparte talks about: captured as a sniper, he is taken before the officer. The latter, having lost one eye in the fighting, is very proud of his glass eye which he pretends is indistinguishable from the other. On a savagely humorous impulse, and having anyway decided to hand his victim over to the soldiers, he offers to spare the boy's life if he can distinguish the artificial eye. 'It's the only one,' the boy says, 'that looks human.' An unfathomable reply, coming from a boy of under twelve.

That such truths should come from the mouths of children is a sign of the terrible anguish of history, for the child's being is more open to influence than any other, lacking intellectual structures to shield its mystery; unhappiness marks it permanently, in the manner of an indestructible habit; and scarcely are they born but these innocents already curse their father and mother; a glimpse of man as he really is leaves them inconsolable for their own existence. When I think that some error, made in good faith but which wounded me in my being, implanted unhappiness in my childish soul, how should I not shudder—and it is something which should make us all shudder—at the sight of innocence with extinguished eyes accusing life itself? 'And whosoever shall offend one of these little ones that believe in me, it is better for him that a millstone were hanged about his neck, and he were cast into the sea.'

*   *   *

It is not good for a child to be brought up by old women: age turns their thoughts to death and makes them timorous of everything; they imagine that the frailty of the child is identical to their own feebleness, created by length of years. With their senile terror of taking risks, they are alarmed by the impulses of the child, those gestures of violence that already challenge the universe. If the child under their care lives in normal surroundings at school, emulation in games and battles will provide an excellent antidote to the hothouse atmosphere in which fondling and pampering and advice to be careful are designed to keep him. But if he is, as I was, out of his element among much older companions, and a prey to their open or lurking hostility; he will retire into himself, abandoning himself to those tender attentions which may easily deaden his powers.

A precociously active intelligence is by no means an unmixed blessing: and if it is accompanied by facility, there is an even greater danger of a rupture with the real world. I believe that the most gifted child suffers less if his potentialities are allowed to remain latent than if, through haste to mature what time will reveal in due course, he is familiarised too young with the abstract aspects of the mind. Knowledge is nothing without experience, which modifies and strengthens it. When the child fails to come face to face with concrete reality, his knowledge merely feeds his dreams. For the children of intellectuals, well and good—safeguarded from outside circumstance, the beautiful mechanism gets into its stride, ever more supple and smoothly lubricated; but when intelligence is grafted on to a sensual or sensitive nature, the disadvantages of too narrow an upbringing only become more marked with time; and no matter how vast the intelligence may then be, it never achieves a perfectly normal functioning.

I was certainly both sensual and sensitive: my body would have found exhilaration in being exercised within the limits of my strength; and I was so naturally inclined to open out and to love that the least object stirred me beyond measure. But, being inactive and too well fed. I sank into physical sluggishness. Later, I was haunted by sensual visions which bodily exertions would have dispelled. But in the closed world in which I lived, my sensibility discovered only things of mediocre essence: a false family, rolled in upon itself like a porcupine, and making a principle out of its egoism—this was the universe which claimed my unique allegiance between the ages of ten and twenty. When scope is denied it, sensibility revolts or goes underground: between it and the uselessly vegetating body, an obscure complicity is formed. Most of our neuroses, our perversions and failures derive from a few initial errors, for which the guardians of our childhood bear entire responsibility: a certain physical space, and a complex moral background are equally necessary to us, failing which thwarted energy ravages the depths of our being.

I had a quick brain, as I have said: under the guidance of a good teacher, I would rapidly have absorbed all, and more, that a primary school can give. My master was of the old school, one of those Jean Costes that Péguy so lovingly described: he had a great respect for language, and the syntax he taught, though a little lacking in flexibility, was admirably sound. I derived from him a certain taste for exactness, which he was always at pains to make clear to us in the mechanism of sentences: he never produced an explanation which was not clear, whether in the analysis of a problem or in the examination of a well-constructed period.

Having a kind heart as well as a good brain, he spent his time protecting me from the older boys' malice: and as persuasion was scarcely enough, he dealt with them severely, which did not exactly endear me to my companions. His solicitude was only equalled by the hopes he placed in me: when I was ten, and my father took a hand in deciding my future, my teacher told him I was a prodigy of learning. Already they both saw me becoming an engineer: they flung wide before me the doors of the university colleges; they calculated possible expenses, and envisaging me emerging fresh from college, enumerated all the openings there would be. I knew no more of the colleges than the uniform worn by the students, which I had seen in the *Petit Larousse Illustré*, and such dreams had never entered my head. It was decided that I should leave my kindly aunt: we wept on parting, for my whole childhood centred on her. My father's brother was a professor in Lyons, and it was to him that my father entrusted me. My uncle was married, with one son the same age as my brother. Thus, at ten, I entered a strange family: but perhaps my father thought that this family atmosphere would make up for my own parents being so remote.

A college was soon chosen for me, and I was sent to the Lazarist boarding-school, which was run by the Brothers. This establishment had a sturdy and partly justified reputation for getting pupils through the competitive exams for the science faculties: my uncle had connections there, and got me placed in the fifth class in spite of the fact that I was only ten. My uncle looked on classical studies with great disdain: for his part, and with good reason, my father held no opinion; I was not asked what I thought about it, but for that matter, what could I have said? I was ten, but was already regarded as if I were twenty: and what I needed at twenty was a good *position*. A position meant a sure and automatic safeguard against hazard: my uncle's ideal was a regular monthly salary, and a respected professional standing; and in a world dominated by technical processes, it seemed to him that only the technician could command such security. Such wisdom was Greek to me: but my future was too important for my child's opinion to be consulted. My uncle, who had read nothing and looked on literature as mere school drudgery, felt no compunction in debarring me from a sphere which he considered superfluous. The idea never entered his head that I might derive some benefit from classical studies: he had the poorest possible opinion of other Jesuit schools in Lyons where classics took first place; he thought they were made for idlers, for the sons of the rich, and reiterated that their teaching of the sciences was lamentable, which is not always the case; as for the *lycée*, it was a thoroughly worthless institution, where one might be exposed to the worst influences.

Thus I studied neither Greek nor Latin, which showed my uncle's total lack of perspicacity. This was all the more so, since in that school the teaching of French and of modern languages (the only teaching that might have nourished my feelings) was abysmally mediocre, thoroughly academic, and devoid of the least preoccupations with the inner life or with beauty. My uncle, it is true, did not give a fig for either: in all the time I spent with him, he showed no other concern but for mundane matters, for his own conception of comfort, and no other obsession but for the *old days*. But this obsession assumed metaphysical proportions, and was largely the basis of the family ethic and the family relationships. My uncle was kind in an unexceptional way, honest and respectable; but in his case these virtues became almost prejudices. He felt no spiritual lack: his wisdom did not go far. He was unaccustomed to the notion of thinking for its own sake: common sense and habit were enough for him, and he lived entirely within their domain. If he had some faint conception of the plurality of worlds, their inhabitants seemed as bizarre to him as those of the planet Mars. He never took up a book: literature for him was a dead thing; the only value in knowledge was a practical one.

It may be asked, what use would such fusty things as Latin and Greek have been to me? I see their value clearly now. The thought of the ancients is still apposite to-day: freed from academicism (and any fairly lively intellect discards such trammels in order to find nourishment) it puts order into our modern chaos and reinstates the eternal. It accustoms us from childhood to think in a continuity of space, in which mind, heart and senses are in harmony. In a non-classical education a high proportion of the things taught refer back to classical thought, of which the pupil thus gains only a piecemeal and second-hand conception. What is

24

more serious is that such an education is, by definition, fragmentary and disjointed: it possesses neither centre nor perspective; and having pursued it to the end, the mind remains uncultivated as before. Perhaps this is too absolute a judgement, and the fault was in part due to the spiritual indigence of my teachers: however that may be, I derived nothing from my secondary studies which allowed me to make a single step forward, in the spiritual sense. Having laboured since to discover what I lacked, and partly to acquire it, I am convinced that the moral genius of the ancients, their fabulous imagination, their powerful, balanced vigour, would have progressively revealed me to myself: while on the other hand, the barrenness of our French manuals, the absence of stimulating reading, and the lifeless commentaries of the teachers, all made literature insipid for us. All one needed was a fairly good memory, for even had we had the urge to demonstrate some subtlety of style or feelings, our teachers would not have understood. We were allowed such subtleties in mathematics : but intuition in mathematics is wholly bound up with the mechanism of the intellect; what the heart invents is quite different, something in which we had no practice.

Where the head of the family is concerned, is there one in ten who pauses to consider the moral importance of the subject taught? My uncle had satisfied his conscience by entrusting me to the care of the Brothers: their religion, if I may say so, was his guarantee that later I would have *principles*; he clung to this word, one of the noblest in the human vocabulary, and one of those which are most maltreated. My uncle used it so often that in the end I no longer recognised it, which scarcely put me on the way to becoming a man of principles. In another mental atmosphere, I should have found these principles in myself, and they would have grown with me: on the contrary, they were loaded on to me like chains, without explanation. And not only principles, at that, but the whole educational programme. I was never able to have a living dialogue with my books. My solitude was thereby

25

strengthened, and the progress I made, which earned me the reputation of being a model pupil, was a soulless business, rooted in nothing.

*   *   *

The Brothers in the Christian Schools had been banned from teaching at the time of the 'wicked laws'.* In order not to lose their profitable establishments, they had abandoned religious garb, while still maintaining some semblance of religious rule. However advantageous it was to the Order, this arrangement necessarily led to a falling off in its religious character: these counterfeit monks were for the most part merely old egoistical bachelors, imprisoned within the double routine of an obsolete system of teaching and a devotion which held them in obeisance. They led niggardly lives, and pined for their cassocks: they were jealous of the world, which they touched on but dared not look in the face, and of the priests, whose ministry they secretly envied. Apart from scraps of gossip, which with clerical malice they cheerfully turned to acrimony, they took small notice of events: brought up in the seraglio, they had remained eunuchs. Their newspaper did their thinking for them (it was an infamous reactionary rag, the *Nouvelliste de Lyon*, which stank of high-minded hypocrisy; that was in the days when M. Francisque Gay was the Devil, and *L'Aube* the paper of the Christian 'Reds'; but *Action Française* was also read in secret, doubtless with qualms of conscience because of the sentence against it). They had no gloss of culture, or even of courtesy; their attainments were mediocre, except for a few, mostly mathematicians; their lack of curiosity was so ridiculously naïve, so ridiculously in good faith, as to be almost admirable. There were few that I ever saw reading, even for their own instruction.

* These were laws passed under the Waldeck-Rousseau and Combes ministries in the early 1900's, providing for the separation of Church and State, and the dissolution of the orders. Translator's note.)

As the Institute gained few recruits, or kept the best products of its noviciates for its missions, the professorial body included several lay members. Some were resident teachers grown old in harness, miserably exploited, and having nothing, not even old vows, to justify their existence; the others, non-resident, and often married men, were few in number but of a high standard, teaching the senior classes and winning for the college its renown. It was they who brought in from outside the little air that circulated among the ruins. To this heterogenous crew must be added several needy students, given all the dirty work but unlearned in the arsenal of punishments, whom their colleagues despised for their youthful candour, without the case-hardened urchins put in their charge being correspondingly endeared to them. In addition, there was many a weird bird of passage, some unsuccessful inventor or other decrepit failure, promoted professor in the school year to fill a vacant post. There was no doubt about it: we were in good hands.

But the method was carefully calculated to produce results, irrespective of the teachers. As in many religious establishments, the important thing was to maintain and, with a bit of luck, to improve the statistics. In good and bad years alike, the machine guaranteed a minimum percentage of successful exam candidates: the parents were entirely satisfied! Better still: the college had the reputation, which may seem a rather dubious one, of retrieving lost sheep. All the hardened failures at the school-leaving certificate, all the inveterate dunces, came there to have one more try: the anxious parents knew it, and passed the word around; and every year, a contingent of veterans, drained from all the South-East, came to swell the ranks of the upper forms.

As to the children it had suckled from the lower classes on, the College had them firmly in hand: it was they who bore its stamp. We were treated like pieces of clockwork, the mechanism constantly being taken apart, checked, and perfected. The statistics were based on us in advance: there was almost no danger of a falling-off. The reason will be more easily grasped when I have explained the method. It may be summed up in this principle: give the child no peace. From eight-thirty to midday, and from one-thirty to six-thirty, sometimes seven, the class went on uninterruptedly except for a half-hour break morning and afternoon. Lesson followed lesson without a pause. There was no free study, and no initiative. The lessons were learned in class, and repeated on the spot. In this way, one's memory was constantly kept alert, but one's intelligence had neither the time to get into motion nor to turn back and assimilate what had been acquired. The aim, as can clearly be seen, was to form reflexes: the whole procedure, besides, was utterly monotonous. To the credit of certain of the masters, who nearly all came from outside, I should say that some of the mathematics lessons (at almost all levels) and French lessons (in the upper forms) were worthy of the name: such masters were an exception, and inspired affection.

Before leaving this subject, I must add a word about the textbooks. I am still shocked, when I think of the ones we had for French. There was one in particular, compiled by a 'Group of Professors'. In this, the authors were given marks for conduct and religion, and the number of pages assigned to them was determined by their value as apologists: by which curious yardstick Louis Veuillot was the greatest of French writers. It may be judged from such textbooks what the corresponding 'passages for reading' were like. I may add that the 'Group of Professors' was none other than an anonymous Brother, delegated to the task by the Institute: that it was compulsory for us to procure these textbooks from the College shop: and that we thus lived, on the material as on the spiritual plane, in the strictest economy.

My memory has since grown rusty. I find great difficulty in summoning it back nowadays. But at College it was supple enough to deal with everything: learning became simply a technique. I came first six years running: I recorded and returned the answers. People boasted of my intelligence: looking at it now, I see merely a rather mediocre facility. In order to develop properly, the mind needs obstacles to overcome, not by the trick of circumventing them, but by experience which sees through them: in order to be truly first, one should not always be first. The whole art of the teacher is to raise obstacles: my teachers, however, followed the textbooks to the letter. We neither raced ahead of an idea nor lagged behind it: and what did it matter if the words remained veiled to us? The only criterion of our progress was our capacity to remember things, not to understand or explain.

In mathematics alone could intelligence play a part. In this, the logical sequence is so close that memory always stumbles: one must either mentally follow each step or become more and more lost, so that apparent feats of memory can always be unmasked. Look at the young hopeful who has just been triumphantly trumpeting forth his theorem, ask him how he arrived at his answer, and you will see him redden to the roots of his hair, unable to retrace his steps; the memory seizes up as soon as it is forced into a contrary direction. In mathematics, knowledge increases and becomes unified all in one: it is present in its entirety in each new proposition; any given problem which I have to solve presupposes a simultaneous apprehension, even more, a ubiquity of relationships. How different then is this organised knowledge from the disparate spoils of memory! No other science gives one more of a taste for exactness: this art of speaking in few words, but each one just and necessary, links style with proof: it has a sober, wholly intellectual beauty, perceptible only to the mind, marvellous as a desert flower, and no one can ever have perceived it, however fleetingly, without feeling that clarity lay claim to his allegiance. Even in a worthless education, mathematics are a unifying factor. Doubtless, by themselves, they only free the mind within their own domain; but the mind becomes accustomed to their rhythm in the analysis and synthesis of ideas, and strives for coherence first and foremost, and hence perceives more clearly the servility of memory. Nevertheless, they are dangerous in such measure as the mind only discovers itself through them: a counter-balance is needed to their study.

Mathematics reigned supreme in the College: the rest was a mere hotch-potch. The claim of mathematics was the over-riding one: the merest problem to be solved excused a scamped piece of translation or a badly learned history lesson. Mathematics polarised our activities, but exerted no influence outside their own sphere: as a subject they still seemed to us merely a set of strict processes, not a permanent orientation. The idea did not occur to us to apply them in other spheres—or if it did, it was merely in passing, as a sort of caricature. None of our teachers took the trouble to show us the mathematical idea in operation, in other forms and more diversified terms, in thought and in life itself: or even to compare it with other methods, taking as basis, for example, a proposition by Descartes or an aphorism by Pascal. I have quoted these two great men on purpose: without under-standing them, we chewed over Descartes' rules for the proper conduct of thought, and Pascal's famous distinction between subtle minds and geometers. For the rules and the distinction alike to have become real to us, it would have sufficed to encourage us to apprehend our thought in action, to suggest that we reflect on our own moral experience: and to point out to us the difference between the logical progress of reasoning, which moves between like points without ever leaving the mind, and the affective movement, which goes from the same to something other, resolving the intellectual theme in a sudden flash or in nuances, according to the mutual positioning of the soul and its object.

For we had an inner life, however rudimentary it might be still: we had projects, and memories, and virtues and vices in embryo, and we practised examining our own consciences, at least in confession. But I do not think we were ever led to confirm, by reference to what we already knew about ourselves, that every man carries within himself the integral form of man. We lived outside our studies: our minds were crammed without being moulded. The only branch of learning which seemed alive to us (mathematics) isolated us in the abstract: and among those who knew no other mental atmosphere but that created by their studies, their sensibility lay fallow—some being abandoned to a chaos of instincts which their parents understood only too little, others being forced by a senseless repression to cultivate their instincts hypocritically, like inward-turned abcesses.

As for our teachers, their hearts and feelings had grown rancid in a mediocre asceticism without any true background: the renunciation which demands a constant vigilance of the truly spiritual was in their case merely an adaptation to a few low and comfortable virtues, and as they were never put to the test, filled them with a pharisaical vanity. Or it may have been that many of them had no temperament at all. They hated the promptings of instinct: any sort of vitality was necessarily bad; and they were ready, besides, to detect infinite perversions behind the small intrigues that any school discipline gives birth to. I know only too well what fantasies fill such vacant heads: the humbled but unmastered flesh obsesses them continually. And as they dare not speak with healthy frankness, they wallow in clerical allusions, until they manage to implant the idea of evil where it was hitherto unknown. Ignorant of what they teach, with no knowledge of the real struggles of the world, and haunted by the image of one sin alone—a fine lot of teachers! Yet these are the sickly beings who have to educate the young: and a man in his right mind has only to protest, for parents to be up in arms, with outcries about political bias and the murder of religion!

*   *   *

My uncle had been one of their products, before returning into the world. They gain their following in the country, where

31

families overburdened with children are happy to send them one of the young ones. From the Brothers' school to the noviciate, the noviciate to the college, the college to the cloister, they live and die for the most part without leaving the walls of their Order: they travel across the seas, work in the apostolic field, touch upon twenty strange worlds, but their eyes remain riveted on their task; their lack of curiosity preserves them from learning anything or asking themselves questions.

Above this mass with their multiple tasks a few great administrators uphold the vigour of the Order. Intelligent, hostile towards speculation, which is frowned on under the founder's rule (or which is mistrusted by it), all their boldness of mind is centred on business matters: they direct the Order's establishments and wealth, and try to increase both; keep a look out for subsidies; administer carefully that sacred power, money; build, balance budgets, and check the provincial balance-sheets; beg among the wealthy and stir up people's compassion because, if they have thriving establishments, they also have poor ones which must be wholly or almost self-sufficient so as not to encroach on the wealth of the whole. In addition, they spend as little as possible, constrained by their vow of poverty, and live on a miserable pittance. When they employ laymen, they pay them as little as possible, except where paying them more ensures them some benefit: and thus retain distinguished men, whose presence among them causes astonishment. But their money-bag morality has all the eloquence of a loftier one, and to hear them, they are all sweetness and light. The poor sheep (and the few great souls) who make up the mass of the Order therefore live in the conviction that the whole Institute is composed solely of lilies of the fields and birds of the air; but the young school assistant, sitting up late over his books and earning reproaches for keeping his light burning after ten o'clock, is not perhaps of quite the same opinion.

My uncle, after all, owed nothing to the Brothers: a more flexible mind would, on leaving them, have shaken off the fetters they had imposed. But from having lived too long under the domination of superiors, he had remained dependent, and all his thinking was merely an echo, a set of prejudices many of which he had acquired from the Brothers. As I must speak harshly of him elsewhere, I must say at this point to his credit that he maintained throughout the war the sanest views and, by a paradox which strikes me as peculiarly amusing, was never for a moment taken in by the moral tirades of Pétain, in which, however, his own language was given free rein. He had innate good sense, limited it is true, but unwavering. And rectitude as well: he stuck to his 'principles'. If his virtues were lacking in imagination they were not less scrupulous; his prejudices were open to argument, but none of them were base; and he was just in his way, insisting that sentiments and deeds should match. Despite all my reasons for condemning his limitations, certain features redeem him in my eyes, and fill me with affection for him. For example, throughout my adolescence, I never heard him utter a single word, even in jest, against the Jews: I lived until nearly twenty without ever dreaming that there might be racial barriers. A man was simply a man: ethics dispensed with distinctions. The solitary but insuperable barrier was that which separated 'respectable' people —meaning those who lived by my uncle's canons—from the rest, whose existence seemed to him quite inconceivable. Wisdom consisted wholly in strengthening one's defences against the unknown, against the temptation of a life other than that which 'everybody' led. His prejudices became fiercely militant the moment they seemed to be threatened: and as he sensed any threat from afar, he sprang to the alert for every trifle. All things considered, dividing up the sheep and the goats is a racial division like any other: and I had full opportunity to see to what intolerance it leads.

My father was overjoyed that I was being brought up in a family circle: and in fact, my uncle and aunt soon regarded me with affection as their own child, and made no distinction between my cousin and myself. But from the first days on, I felt that I was in a prison without windows. My uncle, when he began to talk of the family, was quickly carried away: outside the family, there was no salvation, he would reiterate, and one must live in the family, find one's amusements in the family, and do nothing without the family. The family was the repository of all experience: it would have been sacrilege to feel cramped in it. But the family circle is essentially a circle of ideas: my uncle had a few, limited notions, which according to him should be sufficient for all of us. He staked these ideas on the eternal verities in the same methodical way he polished his shoes: each one was final, having the force of law.

I lived continually beneath that fatherly eye. My least actions were censured by the family standards. I had only to hazard a personal judgement, or some suggestion beyond the family ken, to be immediately crushed, and in a tone which brooked no reply. I was supposed in all things to think like my uncle, and never to answer back. He was doing it all for my own good, and knew how to set about it better than I did. In the early days I argued hotly, and even did things on my own initiative: but it cost me dear. After that, I was content to make suggestions: might I do this, or go there? My uncle saw that I was chafing at my bonds, and reproached me with not finding the family enough: he spoke of ingratitude, a form of blackmail to which I always surrendered. Under this regime I would quickly have lost all spontaneity. I curled up into myself: forced to dissimulate, I lived under the cover of that apparent self in which my uncle thought he was following the progress of my education.

Thursday and Sunday were dreadful days! I was entirely under his domination. Those were the occasions of family excursions, in jolting trams which made me feel sick, through sinister suburbs dotted with vacant lots, with an imaginary 'countryside' behind

34

the high walls of the villas. On Sundays, we visited cousins: my aunt had complicated family ties in the immediate neighbourhood; and, lunch over, the tribal sense drove us out into an allotment-strewn landscape. Uncles, aunts, male and female cousins—there were so many I became confused, and kept on my guard: once home again, my uncle accused me of being 'stuck-up'. For, according to the ritual, there was much mutual embracing: but something stopped me joining the happy chorus. After these effusions came the harmless little family jokes, which never varied: the tribal sense of humour in a petrified mould. As to this vast horde of kith and kin, they were all estimable people, mostly elderly, who asked me kindly questions about myself to which my uncle replied: for a child, even when questioned, has to let the grown-ups do the talking. I remained in a state of docile boredom, sitting for hours on my chair, or standing about in some minute garden, listening to them discussing the progress of the plant life with my uncle. I was forbidden to go into the workshop or the washhouse or any of those places where friendly objects beckon to you, and seem to ask to be played with. I had to be careful of my nice college uniform, of a hideous blue material that never wore out. Had I been one of those consummate numskulls who stay at college till twenty, I would have worn the uniform until I was twenty, day in, day out. It was an idea which haunted me often, and gave me nightmares. For the uniform was a symbol of that stifling constraint, making it plain for all to see, and filling me with deep shame : I cannot think of it even now without a sudden qualm.

For several days now, I have been trying to continue this chapter, the most painful of all. I would like to be rid of it, but the past holds me still: and I am seized by an insurmountable disgust, a lassitude like that which fell on me when I was nearing seventeen. The holy rage, the sacred revolts of adolescence—all these I repressed, simply to have some peace. And now *I feel their lack*:

I am still locked up in the old stubborn silence. Never for a moment since then have I ceased to feel ill at ease with myself: each memory is a wound, as though I must be constantly reminded of my cowardice, as though I must bear forever the weight of some unpardonable disgrace. I remember the homeward trek on Sunday evenings: I was loaded up with badly tied parcels, from which emerged bundles of greens, and no sooner had I taken them than the parcels began to come undone. Tomatoes, spinach and black salsify were scattered in all directions, completing my humiliation. In the middle of a crowded tram, I was the butt of shrill reprimands and jests, whose poor taste made me squirm. I might have forgotten such a trivial mishap, if it had not occurred a hundred times. But that was the basis of my obsession: the same circumstances and the same reproaches were repeated day after day.

Against the monotony of this servitude which bowed me down, I took refuge in a growing inertia. Paralysed as I was by an unending watchfulness, I sank into total indolence. Incredible as it may seem, I lived for eight years (apart from the vacations) without leaving the family circle for an hour. I was often invited by friends from college to visit them, but always declined their invitations under my uncle's pressure: he alleged that they came from a different background to mine, but the real reason was that he did not want to lose sight of me. Once only, a friend came to visit me at the house: I had invited him in fear and trembling of my uncle's reproaches. My friend was subjected to a thorough examination, and the whole time we were together my uncle remained in the next room, spying on our conversation. Finally, he came in and joined us, and the talk became so tedious that I determined never to invite anyone again. When my friend had gone, my uncle pulled him to pieces: he excelled at finding something bad everywhere. And whatever came from outside was bad.

Two or three times I made a strong plea to be allowed to join a boys' club or a boy scout troop: I was always refused, on the score that my uncle was responsible for me, and must watch whom I associated with. It was added that those kinds of team games, usually poorly supervised, were rough and dangerous, and sometimes led to serious accidents: and as in my uncle's imagination disasters were always imminent, he immediately saw me in hospital with a broken leg, or languishing in a sanatorium with pleurisy. Other objections were advanced when I voiced a desire to go in for sport. My claim, for all that, was a very modest one: I had been good at gymnastics. From the third form on, gymnastics classes ceased and there was only private tuition: I wanted to take lessons. My uncle opposed to this the time I should lose from my studies. He had a very poor opinion of boys who were keen on sport, who, in his opinion, were nearly all dullards. I will not mention many of the arguments he used, although some were really piquant: I was so clumsy, he said, that in wielding the dumb-bells, I might easily let them drop; swimming is a fatal exercise, because every swimmer sooner or later tries to be too clever, and meets his end. These arguments were illustrated by a host of examples, and my uncle seemed to discover a smug satisfaction in the accidents that confirmed his theory. Like all people who avoid taking the slightest risk, he hated vitality. So much so, that in the end he deprived me of my own, and I have never found it again since: any sustained effort exhausts me, although I despise myself for growing tired so quickly, and having so little perseverance in my projects.

As the physical and the mental are interdependent, my indolence perpetuated my boredom: neither my body nor my mind ever had to cope with any difficult task. I have a quick brain, a faculty for taking in much at a glance, and a deep-rooted intuition: but I have no system, being repelled at the outset by the routine grind of knowledge; I have a few happy flashes of insight, but little sustained curiosity. It may well seem hasty to blame all this on a lack of athletic background, where the lack is, furthermore, merely one aspect of a graver absence of contact with life: but it is of major importance in my opinion, for my body, ignorant of its own rhythm, is incapable of disciplining itself for a given action; it never achieves either true concentration or relaxation, and has never known the pleasure of a successful physical effort; and is thus a sorry support for the mind, which it lets down half-way. In addition, neither my mind nor my body have the notion of competition.

Without a friend until I was eighteen, without the least idea of the team spirit, without any physical training, doing everything with a vulgar facility, joylessly and without any sense of triumph, and living in a solitude devoid of experience, upon the narrowest of precepts, with the most petty-minded thrift for law, if not for ideal, I grew old before beginning to live. My uncle and aunt were perpetually worried over my physical well-being, feeding and clothing me, and avoiding every risk. With too many clothes, I was always catching colds, but they only swaddled me all the more. These added precautions only made me more susceptible: but flannel was a religion in the family, and any protest from me at these attentions would have seemed like sacrilege. It is the same obsession which swaddles our bodies with clothes and our minds with inhibitions.

When the family sets itself up as the focus of all reality, in imagination it is immediately surrounded by enemies, and spends all its time fighting on its own frontiers: any trifle, a new face, a fall in the temperature, sets the alarm bell ringing. And all in defence—of what? A void! For after all, what my uncle called 'the family' had neither soul nor centre, no other justification but the animal one of existing. Its talent was buried underground: one knew it was there, and thought oneself rich, but one let it gather rust for fear of wasting it. If it had been a true family, at that! But between its members there was no exchange, no contact: it was a physical aggregate, under the authority of unyielding prejudices. There were four of us, four minds, four hearts: four mutes who dispensed with converse, some not even knowing what it was. We lived in a vaster community: we were French, we were Catholics, we were surrounded by the world. So it seemed. . . . But repercussions from the outer world rarely reached us. We revolved in our orbit, indifferent to the universe of men, or rather, secretly afraid of it, as one fears fate.

My uncle, with unconscious humour, loved repeating that the family is the cell of society. There cannot have been many as fiercely asocial as ours. Admittedly, our morality was the common one, whose principles, soulless as they were, remained universal: my uncle had contracted them like a set of habits, or reflexes, which he transmitted to us in his turn. Thanks to them, we were sure of being utterly like everyone else, anonymous and without history, in keeping with our background. We were to live on our habits—nothing offered greater security! But not once must we come face to face with life itself, the problem which fell only to the individual to solve. We must pass through life without hearing life murmur our name: we were deaf in advance to any behest from outside in which we caught no echo of certain principles and prejudices. We were supposed to live in society, without having received any social upbringing: we were planted in it, without participating. Our duties were hollow things, which we thought of as a rent which we had to pay scrupulously in order to be left in peace. But we had no heart in these things: our virtues were all turned in towards ourselves. And my uncle was so sure of being a paragon of ethical behaviour that he gauged the solution of every individual and social conflict by his own very mediocre standard: he was just without imagination, merciful without love, knowing nothing of the immense sufferings of the social body and the hidden anguish of the soul. He clung to the letter of the Law, to its formal universality. But he never dreamed for an instant that the Law must be ceaselessly revised, lest it become in fact a dead letter. He took nothing from experience but such examples as supported his principles: the rest remained chaotic. In his mind, the world of workers, of machines, of vast economic interests, and the international predicament, were reduced to a few gross generalisations: while his vision of the inner world was if possible even more paltry. If he did not manage to isolate me entirely from everything, that was because my inner life escaped him: he set a high fence around me, but could not prevent me from thinking for myself and from realising how much I was shut off from the world—which was already a way of communing with it, and all the more essential for being held in check.

I could not avoid fate: some of my aspirations were vast, and burst from me in spite of censure and the discipline of silence I had imposed on myself. Nothing shocked my uncle more: he put all originality down to pride. We had come from nothing, he used to say. No one in our family had risen above the mediocre, and according to his logic, I should remain there too. I was crushed to the very marrow by his crazy desire to see everyone on the same level, and he excelled at humiliating me with a perfectly cheerful conscience in the very thing I held most dear—my ideas. Although I was obstinate, he attacked them in such a way that it was futile to contradict: he looked on sentiments and ideas as luxury articles, beyond the scope of an average purse. Before thinking for myself, I should find myself a job.

Such reasoning sickened me, and filled me with shame: I learned to keep silent more and more, and soon could do nothing else. The sort of reticence I acquired then has made it impossible for me since to unburden myself naturally, even to those most dear to me. I developed the habit of wearing a mask to such an extent that I find difficulty in recognising my true visage. At the period of which I am speaking, I often took refuge in the absurd: a burlesque humour served me both as a loophole and a defence. This is a quirk I still have: I spend my time poking fun at myself, and catching myself in the act of being serious. Right in the middle of a discussion in which I thought my own arguments were coming from the heart, the demon of comedy creeps into

40

me, and I have a sensation of diving through paper hoops: at once I am in the circus, quick, subtle, making a play of everything, dividing every word against itself. Spurred on by an implacable irony, my mind flexes and springs. I no sooner feel a conviction than I want to seize it and shatter it entirely: I have a sensation of not having earned it, and I treat it as unworthy of me. Abruptly, in the midst of my dream of destruction, I wake to a feeling of futility, and melancholy grips me again.

This determination not to be serious, when taken to such an extreme, is the sign of a metaphysical sadness, of a carefully hidden and deeply wounded *seriousness*: and the further I go, the less able am I to shake it off. Everything shows me my own void, and my void annihilates everything: I exist in reference to nothing. The reasons for this psychosis of failure are not all family ones: but I am not sure that my uncle, thinking he was curing my eccentricity, did not turn it into something unhealthy, which it was not to begin with. By shutting me up in an unbreathable atmosphere, and forbidding me all outside encounters or attachments, he condemned me to a soliloquy which found no confirmation in reality. By infering, from a poverty of origin, a corresponding mediocrity of intellect, he made me proud and timid.

Pride is a vice of the isolated. By nature, I was rich and generous. Once brought face to face with the world, I would have certainly had enough inner strength to defend and assert myself without arrogance. But my uncle was afraid of the world: his principles ensured him against all risks, and he thought it his duty to make me share that security. I can only praise his intention, though hardly his perspicacity. The problem between us was wrongly stated: and now, if he taxes me with ingratitude, how can I tell him it is nothing of the kind? One does not condemn the blind solely on the score of their blindness.

CHAPTER THREE

I PASSED my two *baccalauréats** like everyone else, and won the prize for best work during the year, given by the Old Boys. Three months later I had already forgotten a good deal, and of all the encyclopedic knowledge of the exam candidate, retained only fragments. Of literature, I recalled virtually nothing, except, perhaps, the extraordinary *Jugement Dernier* of d'Aubigné. Of history, a few striking scenes, inspired by the Revolution. Geography appealed to my imagination: but it was so arid, so drily statistical, so deprived of its true social content that I could not manage to learn it. I did not have a gift for languages: I was moderately fond of English, and German interested me more, with its rich syntax and complicated internal structure; but the texts, presented without imagination, were merely examples of grammar. As for philosophy! . . . We gave the worthy priest who taught it plenty of headaches. (The Brothers, with their scorn for ideas, considered philosophy useless. They did not teach it themselves, and decried it openly, which scarcely made the poor man's task any easier. Well pleased, besides, at seeing a priest fail to maintain his authority, they made little effort to quell the uproar, but merely shook their heads and smiled among themselves.) But the teacher, a rather colourless and dreary person, did not greatly matter. The textbook was a recent one, and good, rich in matter even if confused: lacking sub-headings and clear divisions, it made little concession to the memory, and could not be learned by heart, like the other books used in class—one had either to

* The *baccalauréat ès lettres* and the *baccalauréat ès sciences* are the school-leaving certificates, giving access to the University, etc. (Translator's note.)

use one's brains on it or abandon it for some mere list of formulae. Thanks to it, I learned one essential thing: that thought is created by its own movement.

Until then, I had depended above all on my memory: I learned something merely to repeat it. Here, I no longer thought from memory but from experience: these problems were a part of life, and touched on my deeper needs, my impulses, my inner difficulties. Not long ago, I re-read some of my school essays in philosophy. Most of them are very poor, crammed with formulae: but occasionally I can catch the authentic note of my own voice. These examination questions became something that affected me personally: and even had I forgotten all I had learned, I should still have been able to solve them, simply through the struggle of awareness alone, bent on elucidating its own mystery. And in fact, that was all I learned in philosophy: each must decide for himself whether it was a trifle, or rather, the essential.

Finally, there was science, the only part of the school curriculum for which we felt any real respect. I have already mentioned what I owe to mathematics: they saved my mind from the bastard processes of memory, and taught it to be self-sufficient once their laws were known. Physics and chemistry appealed to me less. They were taught in wholly academic fashion. Once a year, in the second and first, we were shown experiments, many of which had a flavour of magic. In elementary mathematics we made a few practical experiments in chemistry, but apart from the discovery that acid burns, they taught us little. I had recourse to a convenient memory, which was beginning however to be less reliable. But this gave me no pleasure, and I was put off in advance by those subjects to which I was supposed to devote my time.

In all this, it is easy to discern the most serious flaw in the education I received, and no doubt in all our secondary education. Each subject is presented as something separate and unconnected. It is treated in the abstract, without reference to the real world whose form it is supposed to convey: thought remains divided into watertight compartments, and there is thus no inter-penetration between these worlds which seem to exist each for its own sake. Such and such a period of history, and the literature it contains, are studied in parallel fashion, but the relationship between the social background and the thing written is never given more than a brief mention. The language of mathematics is used as an instrument in physics: but before he can sense that both these sciences derive from a single method of perception, the pupil must wait until his year of philosophy. Even then, it is from the philosophers, not the scientists, that he discovers the fact. The theory of the human mind is one thing, the exercise of the mind another.

The adolescent taught in this way does not think, he records. Without a higher ethic, without a real synthesis of the soul, education is merely a gratuitous activity, whose results are lost the moment it ceases. We do not know what we want to make of our youth: and this absence of a deep finality is only the echo of a material crisis, which brings into question again the entirety of human relationships. For, having become abstract, these relationships no longer subtend intellectual development. When communion of minds disappears, culture loses its true purpose: knowledge, when it no longer *yields* anything, is simply a luxury of the intellect, which treats it as a purposeless diversion.

How little we learned, on the school benches, to think of ourselves in relation to the world which we were soon to enter! In the primary schools, some time is given up to the teaching of civics: properly done, it does awaken a social awareness at the same time as an understanding of institutions. The child, who has an instinctive feeling for justice, learns to recognise it in the laws: free, he understands that the freedom of all is the guarantee for his own. Used to co-operating in his games, he sees the pattern of a larger co-operation emerge in the nation: a continuous chain is established between his everyday responsibilities and his duties as a citizen. From childhood on, he belongs to the social body: and whether through the prestige of history, or through the exercise of the civic sense within the scope of his understanding, he feels the very life of the nation beginning to pulsate in him.

But once these conformations and elementary virtues, the axioms and postulates of the political and social universe, have been recognised, one must go, by a double process, from the simple to the complex: the first, historical, the second, in the present day. History is merely a succession of episodes, however vividly they may speak to the imagination: it is the labour undertaken by the whole community upon itself. The evolution of social forms gives purpose to the apparent discontinuity of events. Even more, its perspective is contained in its progress: history should be the study of the future. Seized in movement, it would provide a vindication of the complex texture of the modern world, showing it as a becoming. There is a continuity in time between the communities of the Middle Ages and the regime of trades unions and parties: in a certain sense, the forms of yesterday and to-day are contemporaneous. To link them explicitly is to bring to light the constant factors of civilisation, to bring history to life, and the men who never cease making history: it is to integrate each individual effort within the exigency of one vast effort.

All well and good. . . . But, on leaving primary school, the aspiring student (the aspiring engineer, lawyer, diplomat, professor) does not hear another word about civic training. He will learn less about social problems than his less favoured companion, who has become an apprentice, then a worker, and as a very young member of a trades union organisation, is moulded *by* and *in* the real world. Yet this common-sense fact continues to escape those who draw up the school curriculum. And what is the result? The students, crammed with family prejudices, either accept or reject their teachings, as their instinct dictates, but without any critical instrument to appraise them: and as they are full of energy, and eager to find outlets for it, they allow themselves to be lured by factions, which launch them into the political whirlpool, and into pure action, which has no doctrine but is born of the hollow and pompous slogans by which the engineers of the *coup d'état* canalise it.

I knew these factions in their palmy days, from 1927 on until the war: two-thirds of my companions, from the age of fifteen upwards, belonged to *Action Française, Jeunesse Patriote,* or the *Croix de Feu,* whose vaunted insignia gave them a social personality of which they were deprived by their hidebound education. Theirs was, on the whole, a boy-scout totemism, but more aggressive, and sometimes ferocious. The few ideas they were given along with the badge puffed them out with an idiotic dogmatism, and a discussion with them quickly turned to blows. Our teachers made the best of it, and found no other solution for bringing them back to reason but banning the wearing of badges in class: their pupils wore them in their hearts, and assumed the air of martyrs. The masters, besides, were too inclined to venerate all outward show of order not to accept the slogans of the extreme Right as some new gospel. In their usual oblique way, in the crab-like fashion with which they approached reality, they allowed their sympathies to be glimpsed: among some of them, it even amounted to open flattery, which did not for an instant take in the extremists, already aware of the foibles of the weak before the strong. The only fairly sensible, and at the same time revealing, words I heard at that time on the burning topic of politics came from a lay teacher, an old anarchist who loved moralising about everything and sometimes created a scandal. Having led the discussion on to the leagues (it was about the time of the famous 6th of February, 1934),* he shouted amid a great

* On this day, a new Government headed by Daladier was to make its first appearance. But public temper was aroused by the Stavisky Scandal and the blunders and indecision of the preceding government. Extremist groups of both Right and Left turned out in force. There was rioting before the Chamber of Deputies, and a number of people were killed or injured. Daladier was forced to resign. (Translator's note.)

uproar: 'Gentlemen, we live in a Republic, let us be Republicans!'
This opportunist argument was not followed by any proof, and
as such concepts remained empty for us, we were never made any
the wiser on the Republic and Republicans.

We played with words as though they were marbles: in a flash,
order knocked *workers* out of the game. Certain words were
banned, and called forth shouts of derision: *socialism* was one of
them. The word *communism* unleashed elemental furies: it flung
us into blind panic, ourselves, our families, our teachers, welded
into one by class hatred. The thought did not enter our minds that
behind these words might lurk suffering and hope, a touching and
powerful faith, an historical need to be fulfilled; a hatred no doubt,
but a lucid one, made legitimate by the blindness of another
hatred; an instinct, but one borne up by life, leaping to the assault
of senile systems. More immediately, we did not dream that there
might be problems to be solved, relationships of forces in movement, in which it is the role of social justice to establish a balance
and uphold progress. We judged things according to words, and
not words according to things. There were certain words which
were the totems of the clan: while the opposing clan had another
set. Our class, our clan, deserved to perish for its own stupidity:
it is enough to point out what violence it did to language, and
with what exclusive claim to the truth.

As the bourgeoisie at the present time lives in a state of uneasy
aggressiveness, undermined by the strange resentment of the rich
man towards the poor one whom he has robbed of his inheritance,
it throws out challenges to prove to itself its own strength, of
which it feels less and less sure: and while challenging, pretends
to be itself challenged. The nation is no longer its element, but the
strife of parties. Its sons have long since lost the notion of the
State, which should be the instrument of the national will, but for
them is merely a tool for their own domination. The worst of it
is that the bulk of the bourgeoisie, which is quickly transformed
into proletariat, is blind to its own interests, and upholds the

monopolies which ruin it but form an integral part of it, like a cancer. It might perhaps be sufficient to give the intelligent young members of the bourgeoisie an outline of social science—at the school stage, when the historic sense would help—so that reflection could work its curative virtues on their prejudices. But is it not ridiculous that a regime which claims to be founded on the enlightened awareness of its citizens should take that quality for granted, and make no effort to cultivate it from childhood on? Or that it should pay so little attention to the moulding of its picked elements in the heart of the collectivity, but bring them up remote from the major currents of national life, without providing them with any means, even theoretical, of judging the divergent views and conflicts which it attempts to reconcile?

It is true that everything has a place in the mind: each new idea is a point of reference, and reason, whether it is exerted in mathematics or in history, remains the same. Had our teachers taken the trouble to teach us to think correctly, through a proper wedding together of intelligence and facts, to look upon our thinking as the instrument and witness of our presence in the world, and to diversify our power of reflection in the manner of a nerve centre which gradually makes experience perceptible—this in all the subjects we were obliged to study—we would soon have understood that in politics as in the sciences, knowledge precedes opinion. We would have understood, too, that knowledge grows stronger the more it is nourished with facts, and that absolute honesty should be the major virtue of intelligence. But as I have said, our sole object in studying was to get a diploma: learning lay on one side, life on another. For many of us, thinking was only a piece of drudgery, fortunately mitigated by memory: and politics the sphere of action above all others in which thought could be dispensed with. This system, I believe, is still in force. But I doubt whether it can continue so for long.

*   *   *

One of the boys, having suddenly gone mad, had been put in a cubicle in the infirmary. His father or guardian were expected, and nothing would have leaked out about the affair had not the boy, after being taken for a cold shower, escaped, naked and dripping wet, into the corridor. He ran straight into one of the worthy Brothers who, thunderstruck at this unwonted nudity, could find no other gesture of exorcism but the timeless and ridiculous one of the farmer's wife chasing the chickens into the henroost, nor words other than the 'Shoo . . . shoo . . . shoo . . .' with which these gesticulations are always accompanied. The funny part was that the victim, who took himself for Chanticleer and was declaiming Rostand without drawing breath, entered so fully into the spirit of the thing that he marched back docilely to his cubicle. The incident must have become a school legend by now. But surely there was something symbolic in chasing that naked boy like an animal, without daring to touch him, or address him in human speech! The worthy Brother was gripped by a panic fear, and his instinctive reaction was a primitive one. I sensed the same fear, lurking silent and oppressive, behind the prohibitions, the pieces of advice, even behind the way of presenting certain subjects: a fear of the flesh, of sex, and a sacred horror of all that recalled life's workings.

My uncle was a pastmaster at concealing such things. But in fear and trembling that I might stumble across them, he gave the game away by the very awkwardness that his silence created between us. How shall I describe all his manœuvres and precautions? There was in his library a *Guide Bleu* to the South-West, and to prevent me reading about Jeanne d'Albret in child-bed, or some insignificant anecdote on the mistresses of Henri IV, he had stuck the offending pages together with the gummed paper one finds round sheets of stamps. While I was under his authority, I never went near a cinema or theatre: he dismissed them roundly as immoral. Once, however, he did take us to see *L'Aiglon*, an occasion which was long talked about in the family. I remember having once (I was just over eighteen) so deeply shocked my uncle, that he flew into a towering rage. I was beginning to discover the poets, and in all innocence was reading Eluard's *La Rose Publique*. My uncle picked the book up, skipped through it, and did not understand a word—a first cause for complaint! But some of the images seemed to him so directly allusive that he flung the book in my face, declaring that it was more immoral than the stories of La Fontaine: the latter, which he had read, having seemed up to his discovery of Eluard the height of immorality. When at sixteen I received as a prize one of the big Larousse volumes on *Man*, a fairly condensed anthropological synthesis, but in which the role of sex in primitive life was dealt with quite straightforwardly, he had long debates with my aunt as to whether to take it from me. It was a perplexing situation for his conscience, the book having been given to me by the Brothers (who were doubtless unaware of the contents): it was difficult to impound it without some explanation, and to start explaining things to me at that age was what my uncle dreaded most. I kept the book.

Fortunately, I never saw any girls (our relations did not count). I had a first cousin a little older than myself, whom we saw once or twice a year; she was very beautiful, or at least so it seemed to me. Brought up more freely than I was, but still very respectably, she was a minor source of scandal for her relations, whose greatest pleasure was to make moral reflections on her conduct. Her brother and I were of the same age: the three of us could have gone out together; but my uncle, mistrustful and jealous of his hold, would never consent. They themselves thought us supremely tedious.

One last incident, and the portrait of my uncle will be complete. I was nearly nineteen, and had been at the university for six months, after two years in higher schools. Coming into contact with this new environment had opened my eyes on the world.

I was among the first in Lyons to become interested in the review *Esprit*. With a few friends, we wanted to found a centre for *Esprit* in the town. One of the people most attached to the idea was a young widow, related to one of the leading figures of Lyons. One day, she had some urgent reason for sending for me, and did so by a rather long *pneumatique*.* My uncle had never seen one before, and mistaking it for a telegram, opened it: the message meant nothing to him, and all he understood was that a woman was asking me to meet her. At once he began to think the worst, and all my explanations only deepened his suspicions. The *Esprit* centre must be a mere excuse! What was I doing in some movement, instead of preparing for my exams? What proof was there, besides, that either I or the young woman were telling the truth? I pointed out her name and social standing, any argument in fact which he might be capable of understanding. For him, the thing was clear: this trollop (the higher her social status, the more she was one) wanted to seduce me, pervert me, and Heaven knows what besides. I was beside myself with rage: honour impelled me to defend her. So much narrow-mindedness, ill faith, stupidity and base suspicion amounted to an insult which I have never forgotten. But now I see the inevitability of it all. My uncle was true to his nature. He had been taught at an early age to see the Evil One everywhere: and had he ceased even to believe in God, he would have gone on believing in the Devil. For him, Woman still vied with the old Serpent.

I have been keeping to the facts: they are quite damning enough by themselves. From a distance, I find them laughable, although I see also how senseless they were. But it is not my intention to stir up indignation against a system which lingers on, but whose real death is imminent. The sooner it is liquidated, without any further discussion, the better, for it is dangerous for the young. A hundred stories spring to my mind, whose humour

*Express letter transmitted by pneumatic tube. (Translator's note.)

would be lost if I adopted the tone of a public ministry. The old anarchist whom I have already mentioned (despite his vanity, blessed be his memory) one day got himself into a scrape, which was brought to the ears of the cardinal, for having spoken of love in class, while talking about—Racine! Some rather simple-minded pupil had taken back Heaven knows what ridiculous stories to his parents who, being even more stupid, became so flustered that an enquiry was made, and the professor hauled over the coals.

But such scandals were rare, for the simple reason that the subject was taboo. There was less reserve in the students' own conversation, and the boarders, in particular, had a supply of pornographic magazines: these circulated in great numbers, disappeared at a given moment, and were never discovered in searches. As everywhere, masturbation was practised with zest. There were also stories of depraved masters, and harems organised in the attics. For all that, illicit friendships were rare, idyllic for the most part, and of a chasteness which invited gibes. Those who really took their pleasure that way kept it to themselves, without mixing sentiment with it: they formed an underground fraternity who hated the lovers, and were feared by them. The first group guarded their secret closely, since they ran a risk: the second unconsciously flaunted it, and only grew more mutually fond to feel themselves persecuted. The fact that they were under surveillance was a great help to the others, who did not fail to watch their moves and even to report them. But neither group was very large: I do not think that pederasty is as widespread in France as some people assert. The great majority of these adolescents thought much about women. The most daring used to break bounds, and their exploits, whether true or false, swelled a growing chronicle. Much has been said about *Les Amitiés Particulières** in which critics without experience of college life have claimed to recognise the atmosphere of religious colleges: but this novel was written by a man whose own leanings leave

*A novel by Roger Peyrefitte. (Translator's note.)

52

no room for doubt, and who colours the universe of adolescence with his own particular nostalgia. The truth is much rather between *Sainte-Colline* and *Dedalus*.

The sermon on Hell, as conceived by Joyce, is certainly in the manner of clerical pedagogy, in which morality does not scruple to use terror. I will speak shortly of our chaplains. They had experience of life, and some were remarkable men; but their influence on us was nil, being thwarted by the jealousy of the Brothers. It is not a question of them in this instance. They had no control over the retreats (which were held at the beginning of the year, and for students finishing their studies) : the Brothers had their preachers, with their own favourite methods. One of these preachers had acquired a certain fame: he had been preaching for thirty years, through the length and breadth of France, and almost without respite. The Pope had rewarded his labours by appointing him Apostolic Protonotary. He wore violet, and was addressed as *Monseigneur*. It was a mark of distinction for a college that he should consent to catechise the pupils. Monseigneur Saint-Clair was a monumental if somewhat shapeless figure, whose bulk, however, adorned in its vivid soutane, was not lacking in majesty. He had an episcopal air, the summit of dignity in an ecclesiastic: an air reminiscent, in passing, of an obese dowager and a new-born baby. With all of which he had a boundless vanity, speaking of the Holy Father as though he were his confessor, and claiming honours to which his, after all, not very weighty office of prelate gave him no right. The new members of his retreat each year were primed on the ritual before meeting him, but quaked in advance for fear of making a slip. He might easily have been taken for a pompous imbecile, lost in the vapours of incense: but, clever quack-doctor of souls as he was, always rushing from one fair to the next, he had built himself into a personality which paid him well, even while he seemed dazzled by his own eminence.

53

Each retreat produced more than just moral benefits. Monseigneur kept the statistics of conversions up to date: they increased quite regularly, by a certain infallible method which will soon be seen. But he did more than that: he sold everything, from soup to indulgences. Four whole days were spent in a religious establishment in the heart of the Dombes, and each participant of the retreat paid a reasonable but not too high price for his board. The food was good, but the invitation to fast so urgent and the appeal for self-mortification so eloquent that it was only hardened reprobates who refused to obey. Monseigneur was the author of a little book of spiritual exercises, the bulk of which consisted of dots and exclamation marks, and which he sold us as a prompt-book the evening of our arrival. He had in addition founded two fraternities, one devoted to the Virgin, whose sign was a religious picture, very modestly priced despite its miraculous powers, the other to the Sacred Heart, whose sign was a medallion. There were three models of the medallion: in gold, silver, and some base metal. The spiritual benefits doubtless remained the same, whichever model was bought: but Monseigneur, handing the medallion round to be admired, did not fail to point out that, worn on a watch-chain, 'it was a jewel as well as an act of faith'. This last argument clinched the matter: there was a brisk demand for the gold and silver models, as no one wanted to admit he was too poor to buy any but a lead medallion.

His hawker's tray once more folded up, the profits having come up to expectations, Monseigneur next turned his attention to our souls. The real show began—pure *grand-guignol* from start to finish. Thirty young men were about to embark on life: these four days of meditation were perhaps the chance to face up to the problems of the world. At least so some of us—the best—no doubt dreamed that first evening, in the silence of their cells. Monseigneur Saint-Clair however didn't give a rap: these thirty youngsters were not future men to be guided, but hardened sinners to be converted. His experience had taught him this simple equation: conversion = commotion. He had a whole battery of the most terror-inspiring tricks: and having tested them a thousand times, he never bothered to renew them, like an actor who has found the part of a lifetime. I later met several who had been to his retreats, and we compared memories: they were always the same tricks, neither more nor less, and always produced in the same order.

His method of provoking terror was a simple one—he held forth on the one thing that naturally troubles young people most: sexuality, the *flesh*. We had all masturbated once or more, or had wanted to: there were few whose sexual experience went beyond the solitary pleasure. But generally, with the exception of a few who were really depraved, our moral health was average, and some of us were completely chaste, either unconsciously or by willpower. That did not matter: Monseigneur found it more simple and effective to regard us all together as inveterate masturbators, and in order to cure us of masturbation, to transform it into a veritable obsession. The central theme of all his exhortations was the awfulness of the solitary sin, and incidentally, of pederasty. This sin was punished sooner or later by divers scourges, which rose in a crescendo with implacable certainty—disease leading to madness, madness to death, death to eternal hellfire.

Monseigneur had a rich store of examples which, to make them more vivid to us, he drew from earlier members of his retreats, who had turned out badly: for a certain number turned out badly, as if on purpose to bolster up his thesis. As often as possible (yes, he remembered now!) they were former pupils of our College. I will not lower myself to reciting all the fine yarns he spun us: but will note only one, which shows what the rest were like. Well, there was a certain student (from our College) who had turned out badly, shortly after the retreat he made on finishing his studies (at which he had shown great piety, but too little perseverance). I will skip the details: they were extremely precise, although veiled by a richly unctuous style. He fell dangerously ill, and his mother in despair sent for Monseigneur, who, in spite of hastening there at once, arrived too late: the wretched man was dead. (Here followed a description of Death himself in all his pomp, knocking, knocking at the door. . . .) In short, his client was dead, in a manner which few of my readers will be able to credit, but which the high authority of Monseigneur Saint-Clair does not permit me to doubt. I remember his exact words: 'He was dead, my children, with a book by Zola in one hand, and a photograph of a woman of ill repute in the other. When he was dead, his body went quite black.' This last was a masterly touch, well calculated to inspire terror—the idea that the black soul of such sinners, in its struggle to escape from the body, suffused the epidermis with a sable hue.

Need I add that the mimicry of the narrator reinforced the uneasiness produced by his tale, that Monseigneur had all the declamatory art, leaving his words in mid-air at the crucial moment—an art, incidentally, from which his written style suffered. Or that he used certain tricks of the theatre, calculated to strengthen the effect of terror: the sermon on death, for instance, took place in the evening, with all the lights out except for one flickering candle. The shadows yawned around us, the devil brushed us with his wings, and we began to have night-mares. And Monseigneur, that pure soul, pursued in us his own demons.

The man of God opened the abyss before us, and summoned up all its vapours. He had a medieval imagination, viscous, chaotic, swarming with monstrous apparitions: his sermons projected, in the manner of a magic lantern, a procession of infernal images with a full 'sound track' of groans and cries and bestial laughter. It might all have sounded like cheap melodrama, had there not been a curious regard for realism in the details. Purgatory might not be his strong point, but Monseigneur had

56

borrowed from it one of his most striking effects: the proof that the flames of the lower world are real and not figurative. A man had a brother, he related, whom he lost and soon forgot about. One day when this man was at mass, just as the priest arrived at the *memento mori*, a hand of fire descended on his book, and he heard the voice of his brother, saying to him: 'Your prayers have forsaken me, and I suffer the fire of Purgatory'. Then, drawing from his pocket a photograph showing a half-burnt missal, Monseigneur passed it round, with the comment: 'When the man picked up the book, he saw that the bulk of the pages had been eaten away, and the charred portion was in the shape of a hand. This book exists, and is preserved in the Vatican library: the proof is thus incontestable'. And off he went on other miracles, which would have filled Voltaire with glee.

When we all seemed to be in danger of burning for our sins, Monseigneur deigned to offer us a reprieve: the Virgin was brought on to the scene, the Universal Helper, whose goodness reached out equally to the sinner on his deathbed and the future exam candidate poring over his books. The very Holy Mother of God, whom the worthy prelate cherished with a touching devotion, took the place in fact of an Insurance Company against all material or moral risks. It was sordid and naïve at the same time, mixed up with the basest superstition. Moral consciousness gave way to mumbo-jumbo, and religion became a recipe book. It provoked no great change in us, however.

Flayed, bludgeoned, torn limb from limb by all the devils, in two days we were the stuff of which converts are made. The closing exhortations poured the water of grace upon us. But there was never a word of our duties to society, nothing to remind us that religious truth is a whole which unites the impulses of the heart and the sustained efforts of the mind: instead, merely a few threadbare pieces of advice, and a soulless bourgeois ethic, whose major precept seemed to be: 'Thou shalt not sleep with anyone outside wedlock'. One must admit that, after two thousand years of Christian truth, it was little enough.

Laying the accent on 'purity' of the flesh deforms the very idea of purity: for instead of being, as it should be, a fundamental aspect of one's being, an uncompromising loyalty towards oneself, one's neighbour, the universe and God, it becomes a sin-obsessed terror, a secretly repressed desire. It becomes a hatred of the body, a Pharisaism which falsifies all values, which the malediction of Christ against whited sepulchres has stigmatized in vain throughout the ages. It strengthens the demons rather than exorcising them. And it often happens that a young man, wanting to liberate himself from a wretched education, throws himself into debauchery from defiance: he is the unwitting slave of the prejudices of his teachers, who label everything they themselves are not, debauched.

After these four days spent breathing in Hell's atmosphere and its specific *odor di femina*, there were many general confessions: penances, reciting of the rosary on the knees, holding the arms in a cross. The masturbators promised the Virgin not to masturbate again, the budding fornicators to fornicate no more, and the pornographers to burn their books. In his farewell sermon, Monseigneur evoked the ship of life setting out from port with all sails spread. On the way home in the train, everyone told their beads. Then everything returned to normal, and each slipped into his old habits, with the shame of having let himself be hoaxed. The serious part was that those who were really inwardly troubled returned from the four days with several new obsessions: the 'tough nuts', having fallen momentarily under the spell, took their revenge in blasphemy, and forthwith threw religion overboard. Finally, a very few among us, more phlegmatic or younger than the rest, received a dreadful awakening. Monseigneur conducted fifty retreats a year, with an average of thirty adolescents at each retreat: and had been doing so for thirty years. A professional public malefactor might well go green with envy!

Was this, then, all our religion, and had we none but buffoons to guide us? Not at all. The College had two chaplains, but they were kept apart from their young flock by the Brothers: the archbishop, having no illusions on that score, appointed active priests who exerted a great influence by their ministry, and whose true sphere of work lay elsewhere: their position as chaplains gave them a niche, but left them with their full freedom. They said mass, preached on Thursdays and Sundays, took confessions, and shared six half-hours of religious instruction each week. The rest of the time, it was our own masters who taught us religion, and anyone, the professor of mathematics or the professor of Spanish, could undertake the task. We never saw our chaplains, although in theory we had the right to visit them outside class time. Those few among us who took advantage of this right were systematically spied upon. The Brothers had good reason to mistrust these priests, who were so far above them in intelligence and virtue. The Abbé Devert and the Abbé Monchanin, who occupied the position during my time at school, are among the people who have most influenced me. The former, for a long time, was all the real family I knew. The latter, at a later date, introduced me into a mental world for which I still feel a regret. One is now dead, the other is still alive, in India, lost upon the heights of contemplation. But neither their thoughts nor their prayers have left me: they lived and still live in the eternal. And it is not my least source of pride that I was once their friend: as I was the friend, a short time later, of another priest, both father and teacher to me, and dearly loved companion.

After the arid and often bitter pages that I have just written, praise leaps up in me like a spring in the middle of the desert. As soon as the four o'clock break arrived, I used to run to the Abbé Devert: I could tell him everything, and I knew it. When he first came to us, many of the boys, I don't know why, were hostile to him: that great-souled man was lacking in eloquence, and spun his sermons out with '... you see ...', which played into the hands of already bored listeners. He never hurried over his confessions, unlike the other priests, who worked like conveyor belts without even stopping to listen. As it was, we went to confession rather as a diversion from class-work than as an examination of our moral state. The Abbé Devert thus had few customers. It was by chance that I went to him with my faults.

Confession had up to then seemed to me a tedious duty, and a rather painful one at that: I was scrupulous in my attitude, but preferred to confess to a deaf person who would send me off, absolved, with two dozen rosaries to recite. For the first time I encountered a man who felt that the confession is a diagnosis: a true doctor of souls, not one of those who hand out their prescriptions at random, but a man who weighed up carefully every word; and with delicate insight at the same time, reducing to their true proportions those sins that our anxiety magnified. Finally, he was a man of prayer, who knew that prayer is not in the words but in the meditation which the words awaken and, above all, in the free disposition of a loving heart: he was a true director of conscience. There is no sacrament without joy: and the sacrament of Penitence is in a sense the most joyful of all, since it gives a soul to God: it should be a festival sacrament. The Abbé Devert had the genius of transforming humiliation into an offering, and restored to the eternal an act which for many had become mechanical. He made us feel that, in freeing ourselves of our faults, we were replying to the gift of God with another gift: not the immediate offering of a man who suddenly feels a weight lifted from him, gives thanks to God, and thinks of something else; but a gift which should be perpetuated, directing our least gestures, becoming a continuous and open-hearted dialogue with Christ.

In a few weeks, confession instilled the religious sense into me: from it I learned that the Kingdom is present in the depths of the heart, where the salutary act releases those fountains of the lost

Eden that Christians call grace. To the Jansenism, to the very Manicheism of my uncle and my teachers, was opposed the Catholic universe, wholly animated by the Presence of God. The meaning of the Beatitudes was the concordance of our presence with His, the creation of an eternal harmony in a world slowly emerging from chaos. Thus, confession taught me that spiritual vigilance is the striving after self-knowledge, the detection and examination of inner energies, and finally, mastery over these energies which consciousness, permeated with the divine, canalises towards their highest expression. I had adopted this discipline in life even before I understood it: it had already moulded me, when I discovered its true greatness, and realised that it united the omnipotence of God and the free will of man. Had I known only that discipline! Others, unfortunately, warred against it: the monsters of my Jansenist adolescence rise once more to the attack, and I see them grimace in the words of priests, gesticulate in the egoism of Christians. The image of God which they use as exorcism is not the irresistible lodestone of the mind, but a doll of wax and bran, the nice-young-man whose virtues are all passive, the same Christ who might serve equally well as emblem of Saint-Sulpice and as tailor's dummy in a drapery store. It is hardly to be wondered at if the monsters have the advantage. Hell is piquant, Heaven insipid.

The Abbé Devert was a worthy subject for a painter, and had that distinction which comes only from the heart. I have since met many men of fine feeling, whose mind and actions were one: but rarely, except among a few elect beings, such moral transparency. He was tall, with a dignified bearing, and measured both in voice and gesture. His prematurely white hair added to the serenity of his face, which showed a peace won from suffering. For the Abbé Devert, a hero of the first war, who wore with modesty almost invisible decorations, had been gassed at Verdun, and would have died at fifty of the delayed effects had he not overcome them by his resolute apostolic vigour. From his experiences in the front line, he had brought back a horror of warlike rodomontade, and viewed with disgust the development of exorbitant nationalist feelings at that time. He gave proof of this on the ceremonious occasion at the College when the tablet commemorating Those who Died for France was to be unveiled and blessed. The president of the Old Boys' Association, the model of a self-satisfied business man, had given an address full of jingoism, which was almost a propaganda speech for the leagues then being formed. Without being invited to speak, the Abbé Devert replied, denouncing in the strongest terms 'this war-horse patriotism with blaring trumpets'. In a few words, he outlined the true conception of France and her destiny. No one understood him at the time, and his attitude created a scandal. But he was not one to shirk a struggle, and nothing could defeat him, for this upright man was not alone in the Church. His activity made itself felt in circles to which only he had access. He was one of those rare pastors who can talk to the working class, and all the calumny and class hatred which his enemies stirred up against him were powerless to outweigh the esteem in high places for his apostolic labours. Those who would have been only too glad to see him fallen from favour and sent to some distant post were themselves forced to see reason. He did not express triumph, but knew admirably how to keep his own counsel.

He was a man who understood modern life, and the working of its laws. His views were concrete, he lacked all fanaticism, and was always ready to give and take: stupidity alone aroused his wrath. He never allowed himself to judge a thing lightly: he studied his apostolate, continually comparing his own ideas with those of others. But he was one of those who have devoured the Book, and who know that the Word of Christ is the fountain of eternal youth in the world. The life of society had been shown to me as a jungle, in which the workers are the wolves. He spoke to me of these men whom he knew well: of the gravity of their problems, which the paternalist order evaded, the modern feudal system which they fought against, the wider pattern which governed their struggles, and the socialism in which may be seen the shape of a higher communion. For if nothing seemed to him more essential than the reign of Christ on earth, he nevertheless believed that man lives first by bread: and the reign of Christ was in the first place in the urgent present, in bread for all, not that which is doled out by the hand of a master, but that which you have gained from the wheat you yourself have sown. The bread of your freedom and of your personal responsibility: the common bread which all may eat together, since it comes from the labour of each and of all.

For the Abbé Devert, it was not a question of sharing out bread in a more equitable fashion, but of giving the people the power of making their own bread, and the joy of watching their own harvests ripen. The Abbé Devert was neither more nor less than a collectivist, partly by evangelical propensity, but also by a deep knowledge of the social reality. That was in 1930, and the socialist concept has made much progress since: at that period, the Abbé Devert scandalised everyone, the more so as he had taken the trouble to study what he was talking about. He discussed it, besides, so simply, and with such disarming clarity, that his adversary, the wind taken out of his sails, could only fume with rage. He had an unrivalled power of persuasion over young minds, and that was why our teachers feared him: with an equivocal air, they treated him as a revolutionary, even while they pretended to praise the greatness of his virtues.

*   *   *

The Abbé Devert had greatness of another kind, a radical greatness upon which was based his action as a militant. His praying was a continuous thing and entered even into his bearing.

Tireless in action, still he cherished the contemplative virtues: one man's prayer, he used to say, resounds through the whole universe. He did not like those sentimental effusions which the soul takes for the language of love: but the unceasing purification of the spirit, the golden rule of the monastic state, seemed to him the most desirable of vocations. Born for the struggles of the world he humbly accepted the fact that the prayers of a single monk on the path of perfection might have more influence upon men than the whole of his own life. He taught me therefore to pray, and to stand in the presence of God. Prayer became a dialogue: he who addressed himself to God received a reply in the very words of his prayer, which came back to him mysteriously charged with significance. The dialogue of which I make myself the voice, is shared by every living being through my utterance. In the same way as the social body, in its fumbling search for unity, is the shadowy outline of the mystical Body, so the prayer of a single being, poor as it may appear, outlines the pattern of the Communion of Saints: these are two aspects of the same reality, superimposed one upon the other. The Abbé Devert would readily have echoed the words of La Tour du Pin in his XIVth Psalm:

> Voici que j'ai compris que la plus belle prière
> —ne devait pas être dite en mon nom, mais au nom de tous . . .
> C'est ainsi que j'ai compris la liturgie intérieure,
> —que je demeure en moi sans rester isolé.

> [Now I have understood that the finest prayer
> —should not be uttered in my name, but in the name of all . . .
> And thus I have understood the inner liturgy,
> —that I dwell within myself yet suffer no solitude.]

In this specific act of adoration, the man of deepest inner life is at once the nearest to his fellows: but the poet, lured on by his images, is in danger of prefering the 'inner liturgy' to reality.

The Abbé Devert, who was no more than a man, and little inclined towards angel-worship, thought that the modern cathedral in which all would pray together, each in the silence of his heart, should have for foundation a wholly new and unparalleled social structure, in which the workers, without knowing it and perhaps without wishing it, would labour for the furtherance of God's design.

* * *

I began to dream of saintliness as one dreams of love or fame. The Abbé Devert soon perceived that my prayers came more from impressionability than deep feeling, and without rebuffing me, but firmly, he tried to lead them into the right path. But my dream was the stronger, and so persuasive that the Abbé himself fell into the trap. I had only to look at him to evoke the perfect image of the ministry, and while he was too modest to recognise himself in it, he recognised his own impulse. He tested me in a thousand ways, but my dream remained unshaken. I can see it all clearly now: with the narrow and restricted life I then led, the inner world was the only one in which my freedom was unopposed. My intellectual background was nil, and I had no other mental sustenance but religion: so full a sustenance, thanks to the charity of the Abbé, that it was an incomparable viaticum in the spiritual indigence in which I lived.

If I fortified myself so young against mediocrity—and had I not done so then, it would have been too late afterwards—it was because my mind, like a thriving plant, spread wide its moral roots and gave them a nervous sensibility. Plunging into affective depths, it founded new sources of sap: this nourishment was all its own, drawn from my secret resources; still poor in ideas, but rich in images and energy. The plant needed a support if it was to shoot up towards the sky, and if the vigour derived from its many roots was to be concentrated in a single effort. My religious feeling and the certainty it gave me, not without a taste for the singular which strongly resembled the craving for fame, gave me the impetus to grow into an already designated shape. It is the fault of poetic natures to confuse aspiration and fact: they wish to accomplish everything by themselves, and be the demiurge of the highest reality. From this arises the difference, which later becomes a contradiction, between the aesthetic and the religious. But for poetry to come into being, aspiration must reveal itself. Thus, I was mistaken in calling my first self-generated impulse religious: I thought I was living the religious symbols which helped me to express myself. Quite naturally, I took the Abbé Devert as a model. I wanted to be exactly as he was.

Lacking a language of his own, the adolescent imitates what he admires. His native resources are not thereby diminished, but on the contrary are exercised, on condition that he does not harden in a mould essentially alien to him. The form of another person, however deeply we may have entered into it, is never more than the outward sign of an identity which escapes us. No two souls are alike, and whoever strives to resemble another ends only by annihilating himself. Later, in my first efforts at verse, I imitated Pierre Jean Jouve: he strongly discouraged me, and I have not forgotten the lesson. A short time ago, I read some verses by a young poet who copied Jouve so closely that a clever person might have been deceived: all that was lacking was that which makes Jouve like nobody else—not the style, but the essence, the inner determining factors of the style, the intangible something which separates actual experience from even the most deeply-felt mimicry of that experience. In the master's case, the form is charged with experience: in the disciple, it awakens some presentiment of what he himself is. But he takes this appeal from his future being as a self-contained experience, and thinks he recognises the field of life tilled by another person as his own. Imagining the labour is all his own, he drives an already existing furrow: but the blood that reddens the soil has not been wrung from him, and although he glories as if at the torment, his martyrdom is imaginary. His hour is still to come. He translates his potentialities, his indeterminate energies which already long for direction, in the gestures, words and attitudes of another who has long been adjusting and balancing them in terms of his own form and substance: he himself, however, is still unaware of his own form and substance.

If he is not careful, such mimicry may become a mental habit, detrimental to his being as a whole. In art as in life, many live on example, instead of on their own foundations. That may continue as long as no obstacle is encountered which challenges the whole person: then other arms are needed than a borrowed language. When uneasiness is aroused in the very core of language, there is no image of the self to satisfy the evolving personality. Narcissus has lost his fountain, and is no longer what he thought he was. But the experience whose reflection he has made himself, if he must now abandon it, has at least shown him henceforth autonomous potentialities, and depths of feeling no longer contained in the language of his masters. Let him then no longer strive after the example of the master. He must accept the formless anguish of having been born. For the preconceived forms that he but lately adored are henceforth no more than stately sepulchres.

People need a great mutual affection to know how to part when the time comes. When I realised that I had been mistaken, I was filled with shame, and saw myself abandoned in the Abbé's mind. Rather than explain my conduct, I preferred to disappear. I was then nearly seventeen, and felt a deep remorse at having abandoned through cowardice what I had thought was my path. But I must admit that it was not only spiritual reasons that diverted me from it at that time. The period of puberty is marked by terrible storms: and having lived up to then lost in admiration of myself, having become self-righteous through the excess of indulgence, and above all emotion, which religion had heaped

67

upon me, I fell, as so many have done, into the sad emptiness of the flesh. My education, which kept my body enslaved, had done nothing to make me respect it. Had I been given to sport, joining in my companions' games, I should have understood the nobility of the body, the beauty of its instincts, and the time they need to ripen. But being alone and a stranger to physical effort, I fell a victim, like all indolent people, to the claims of a vitality repressed until that moment. I thought myself pure, having never experienced temptation. When it did arrive, and my falsely lulled mind fastened on particular images, I found myself both physically and morally unprepared. 'Sport excites the senses,' they had dinned into me at home and in the classroom. Poor fools! It diverts sensuality, and canalises it in different directions, and our experience of the world thereby becomes more varied.

I did not know how to expend my energy, nor how to distract my body from sexual feelings. In pseudo-Catholic terminology (which in fact could not be less Catholic), the body meant the flesh, and the flesh meant vice. Troubled as I was, the upheavals of puberty flung me into all sorts of adolescent fantasies: but they were underhand, oblique, hidden beneath my everyday behaviour. Such fantasies are of little consequence in an adolescent whose surroundings enable him to free himself of them: he is caught by other attractions, more consistent with the diversity of his desires. But I lived in an empty world, peopled to no purpose by chimerical absolutes: my soul was without resilience, its purity unexercised. The voluptuous sense of perfection fostered by my religious dream was followed abruptly by a still more voluptuous terror, rendered fascinating by the sixth sense I had inherited from my teachers, the sad and equivocal sense of sin. I have experienced nothing so wretched as the shameful delirium in which I wallowed for two years: its pleasures were poor and coarse enough, and it was my imagination rather than my body which got something out of them: they were inspired by reading, by the sight of the warm streets, by the brushing past of a prostitute. And above all,

I lived in an immense solitude, with a panic fear of any real physical contact. The blood rushed into my face, my pace quickened, and I walked and walked for hours, my mind a blank, my body exhausted.

With a sincere effort, I might have come back to my senses: a few words from the Abbé Devert would have awoken my will. But I was terrified by the idea of confession, although not for its own sake, for during those two years, I went to confession several times, but always confessed very badly, and to chance priests whose exhortations always lacked force. I knew that these lamentable attempts were mere trickery with God. Anyone could give me absolution, but only one man could guide me: and, forgetting his priesthood, I was afraid that he would be ashamed of me, and could not imagine myself standing before him. Without courage, without any positive taste for goodness, I had lived up to then on the image another had made of me: the image crumbled up, and that man remained my judge; but his divine power had ceased. I had taken the affection I felt for him as a movement towards God, whereas God was only the pretext for it. It was a man, and not Christ, that I felt I was betraying. If a man carries God in his heart, and later drives Him out, God continues to live in him as a terrible and salutary absence; but the image of a man, even one whom we love dearly, only fills us with remorse for a time. I had left the Abbé Devert without saying good-bye. As I was in danger of meeting him every day, I shrank from passing before his door, and invented a thousand childish detours. But never once did I see him. We had friends in common, but never once did he summon me through one of them, or try to find out how I was. He had guessed everything, as I discovered later: he waited, and prayed, and did not abandon me in his thoughts.

I was unhappy and a coward: not daring to go thoroughly to the bad, I languished in a febrile state. I was caught in my own degradation, and sickened by it. I lived within a system of habits, the worst of which would seem puerile to me now: it was a vice surely enough, but a paltry vice, lacking depth, and without that force of moral conviction which one sees in the aberration of great souls. Total vice demands greatness: it is a challenge addressed by the spirit to itself, and is sustained by an astonishing moral perception. Few young people are capable of such vice. One must have lived long, loved much and despised much in order to seek the absolute in demoniac depths. It can happen that the profligate, clutching his demon by the throat and regarding it with a lucid eye, is suddenly struck as if by lightning with a sublime enlightenment, which unites him with the greatest saints, and sometimes hurls him from the furies of vice to the furies of holiness. But most of those whom their vice holds enslaved are vicious only on the surface—poor lunatics whose vice lacks any spiritual content. Mine did not even have a physical content: I was guilty in thought, that was all. I could look at nothing without soiling it. Fear and desire waged an abject struggle for possession of my heart—and both triumphed at once. I was less immoral than many of my age, but in a more unclean way: I spied out evil rather than committed it. These words are weighty to describe my actions of that time, which were of slight material gravity, and committed by others, in another moral context, would scarcely be noticed. But what does matter—their very intention was bad, and I took a foul pleasure in catching myself at fault, and unclean. These mental essays in evil put the finishing touches to all that my teachers had taught me. Having lost all spontaneity, my body reduced to larval gestures, I was rapidly slipping into their camp, and becoming a sort of perverse Jansenist. A fortunate encounter saved me, and I emerged again into the light, but the indelible mark can never be forgotten.

When the miracle had happened, I was astonished at myself: I was naked, my clothes at my feet. I ran to the Abbé Devert, impatient to see him again, and at the same time full of fear. He received me as if I had left him only the day before: he spared me all explanations, and our conversation was resumed at the point I had reached in my life, as if he had accompanied me silently through the mist of two years. Even death has not interrupted it, so true is it that in the spiritual world and in the universe of the Communion of the living, the bonds of time disappear. Being outside the moral shape of the world, they are overstepped by a loftier and freer consciousness in the vision of the eternally simultaneous Presence. Such was the lesson, through his life and his death, that the Abbé Devert left me: there is a ceaseless continuity between my mind and every other mind, and whether I wish it or not, my utterance fills the world. Even in the silence in which I sometimes take refuge, I hold a dialogue despite myself: I make my greatness and my perdurable essence truly mine when I elevate this dialogue to the highest awareness, and when I sustain in all its compass my relation to the universe. O priestly heart, that was your morning oblation! You might have exclaimed, in the words of Father Teilhard de Chardin: 'Accept, Lord, this total offering that creation, moved by your attraction, presents to you with the new dawn. This bread, our striving, is no more in itself, I know, than an immense disintegration. This wine, our suffering, is now, alas, but a dwindling draught. But at the heart of this shapeless mass you have placed—I am certain because I feel it—a sanctifying desire which makes us all cry: "Lord, make us ONE".'

CHAPTER FOUR

W HEN I had left the Father, my isolation became complete. The upbringing I had received was alien to my feelings: but it was all I had, and only one path lay open to me—Higher Schools, as they are called. Thus, at sixteen, I entered the Mathematics faculty, where I remained until eighteen. Only those who have followed the same course will understand into what a blind-alley I had been thrust. I can think of nothing more barbarous and more opposed to the laws of intelligence than the education I received there. This curious procedure, which continues to addle the brains of several thousand young men every year, consists of acquiring in the shortest possible time the maximum number of reflexes, driving from the mental horizon every consideration except that of competition, gulping down a whole programme in three months and brooding over it for three years, professing scorn for everything outside the language of the sciences, and knowing of the latter nothing but the jargon. It may be imagined what this did to a sensitive temperament: I saw several ruined by it. I myself was gifted with a good mental mechanism—the recording machine still worked— and apart from what I have said, these two years passed without event. They would merely have plunged me deeper in my ignorance, had it not been for my chance encounter with several books from which I derived various benefits. Three books in particular held my attention: the *Selected Writings* of Nietzsche, published by Albert at the *Mercure*, the *Nourritures Terrestres*, and Pascal.

The first became a sort of breviary for me: I was continually adding fresh notes in the margin, with the pretentious naïveté of those who, never having learned to think, look upon thought as something that works of its own accord. I am astonished when I look back on these scribblings now, and hard put to it to make any sense of them. The book must indeed have been important to me, to show so many signs of our past friendship: but however much I rack my brains, the reasons for that friendship are a mystery to me now. If I read Nietzsche subsequently, I certainly did not study him: he holds little attraction for me. What impulse made me buy the book? For it was the first I could call my own. Was it through talk among students, the prestige of revolt attached to the author's name? In all honesty, I no longer remember, and am grieved at my own forgetfulness. Skipping now with complete indifference through the pages of this arbitrary and ill-found choice, I see the tracing of paths that seem to lead nowhere. Was it really I who traced them? What was I searching for in these pages, what colloquy did I pursue there, and with whom? In my immature state, I could only have taken Nietzsche's thought, with its abounding paradox, his powerful irony which fashions an optimism from despair, in its literal sense, identifying it with the mask it assumed.

I should like to think, for the sake of the man I later became, that the powerful poetry of destiny, whose singer that obscure yet limpid genius was, acted as a spur upon my still unrevealed potentialities. But if I was stirred in the depths of my being, there was little change on the surface. It is not, after all, impossible to work on one's own evolution in a way not formulated consciously yet sustained by consciousness. No doubt it is more rare, at the end of a protracted effort at self-awareness, not to be able to discern the earlier self which a certain encounter inspired, after twelve years, and perhaps for ever, to be blind to the significance of that encounter. In the warp and woof of my mind, this discontinuity troubles me: it opens within my past (or, perhaps, in my future?), but upon what?

I know perfectly well what I got out of *Les Nourritures Terrestres*.
I know also that, when I read Gide later, he irritated me more and
more, and that, under the dictates of my own experience, I even
conceived a strong hatred for one of the books I had loved best,
down to the very inflexions of its music. It is nevertheless true
that I was, as many adolescents still are, that Nathaniel to whom
the caressing voice spoke.

Just after I had turned seventeen, I knew the first springtime of
my life. There was a long break at mid-day which left us free to
our thoughts: outside, the weather was beautiful, and the deserted
games room would soon be more sultry than a hothouse. I did
not feel inclined to go into the gymnasium, nor into the close
labyrinth of rooms. There was a broad avenue, planted with fine
trees, which offered scope for meditation: few people came there,
besides, as some were swotting for their last lectures, and others
sleeping, to be able to stay up later at night. I was alone, and I
walked in the May weather with its gusts of fragrance, dreaming,
a book in my hand. I walked to the inner rhythm of the book:
for me, it was sunlight and landscape, a fountain of delight,
manna in the midst of my aridity. It gave me vague and beautiful
intimations, which seemed to burst upon my understanding with
such sudden clarity that I wanted to shout them aloud until the
echoes rang. For several years, I used to murmur to myself these
two sentences, which seemed to me then as limpid as certain
verses from the gospel of St. John:

> *Et tu seras pareil, Nathanael, à qui suivrait pour se guider une*
> *lumière que lui-même tiendrait en sa main.*
> *Où que tu ailles, tu ne peux rencontrer que Dieu.*
>
> [*And you will be like a man, Nathaniel, who guides himself*
> *along his path by a light which he himself holds in his hand.*
> *Wherever you go, you can only meet God.*]

It seemed to me that the book loved me: I plunged into it
ecstatically, and took the shudders of delight it gave me for

conquests of the mind. For such a book operates by its charm, which excludes thought when it grows too powerful: yet the mind, enchanted with these imaginary landscapes, these effusions and paradoxes of feeling, accepts as laws the frailest maxims, clothed as they are in such richly sensual language. 'To act without *judging* whether the action is good or bad. To love without worrying whether it is good or bad'—such pseudo-Nietzschean banalities, reduced to their naked essence, are barely coherent propositions. Each word must be invested with much more than the author claims to be saying, before the whole reveals any virtue at all. The act, to love, to judge; good, bad, anguish: nowhere in the *Nourritures* did I find these words defined—nor a hundred others of equally magical effect. The effect is produced by their emotive charge, through the effulgence of conjoined images: the *Beyond good and evil* which, in Nietzsche's case, resolves itself into a Promethean ethic and shakes history to its very foundations, does not in this instance go beyond the aesthetics of sensation. The latter is thus carried on into literature, and sensual life with its dramas gives way to the harmonious arrangement of words.

The fallacious liberation offered so lightly by these aphorisms, which reveals through the book the dance of desire ever fulfilled and ever new, takes no account of the tragic side of instinct, and the vast decisions which each step in experience makes more weighty. It is as if neither the soul nor the world had any density, and mind alone, the highest peak of enjoyment, were the most subtle spirit in the alembic of pleasure. A pernicious, false air of freedom, and the world within one's grasp, full of fruits and fleshly delights; the art of always being ready to absorb it the very moment that the possible presents itself; never to encounter an obstacle which may not be transmuted into an object of pleasure; and the absolute diffused in all things, with the mystique of sensation supplanting the striving towards unity: in these things, certainly, a young, fresh mind discovers an egoistic exaltation of its own presence in the universe. I became intoxicated with this strange *religion*, whose only binding link is pleasure.

But my intoxication was entirely imaginary: the practice of pleasure demands an austere devotion of which this book gives no idea. It suggests luxuriant images, but without the terrible negative which turns sensual pleasure into the conflict of the mind against itself. It contents itself with words, and in reality gives food only for dreams. And the young man who loved it yesterday, when he compares it to the bitter demands of life, soon either hates it or laughs at it. When I reopen the book now, I cannot read the word *fervour*, which abounds on every page, without feeling something like wrath. Does desire upheld as an appetite deserve such an exalted word? And must the word *love* be attached to it, as if to corrupt the sense further? At the summit of passionate love, when the immense unifying effort resolves itself into a single, infinitely extended thought, and when the lover and the loved one at last hold their converse in silence, ardour gives way to fervour, the hot flame to light: the senses and the soul are balanced in the serene heights of the mind. But to call a suspended emotion fervour is to prostitute the spiritual to the sensible, to flee all determining factors, and to be constantly seeking a fresh agitation of the senses: for an entirely free disposition, when it remains for too long unattached to anything else, does not possess sufficient inner resource to avoid the chaos of boredom. A free disposition is furthermore a luxury that our condition as men does not permit, unless we slip from reality into a dream world. I see little difference now between the state of continuous fervour which *Les Nourritures* offer us, and the sad soliloquy of the flesh which others have since exploited. The evasion is the same, if the aesthetic is different: in Gide, it is still only the dawn of our false liberty; in others, the late-comers, we have reached the evening of lassitude, surrounded by the mechanical gestures of pleasure. But the whole road has been travelled, and the literary milestones are there through two generations.

For all that, whatever future judgement I was to pass on *Les Nourritures*, I was for a long time under their spell. It was only a book, but one whose music captures the unformed soul and the senses: upon an exquisite underlying melancholy, the emotions, in the absence of real objects, become iridescent with imaginary nuances, following the caprices of daydream. One learns to feel without the aid of tangible things, and more fully perhaps than by contact with them. But how is one to pass from a world lacking opacity and offering no resistance, in which sensibility, like a hothouse plant, is bounded only by the limits of the imagination, into the real world, whose rhythm is slower, whose tangible expanse is less dense? In the desert in which I lived and in which my desires found no roots, the same impulsion drew me towards the musical pleasure of these mirages and the morose delights of evil. I passed imperceptibly from one intoxication to the other, my will extinguished, my mind elsewhere.

I began to savour words and to claim for them much more than the essence they reflected: I cultivated an exorbitant sensibility which was based on nothing. Without being in the least a poet, I already had all the faults of a poet: I sensed that language can metamorphose the visible in the invisible and create a substitute life for us from which the everyday struggle has been banished. I had only to discover those singular ecstasies that hermetic art reserves for its chosen followers, in order to lose once and for all the sense of reality, and become a perfect Narcissus like those who, diverting the very sources of language to their own advantage, glory in blaspheming against its universal character. If I had ever known it, I was on the way to forgetting that the Word is the daily bread of all men. Life, thank heavens, reminded me of the fact: all the dignity of the creator lies in making and blessing the bread, all his anguish in failing in this simple vocation.

It would be unjust, however, if I were to ignore the role that *Les Nourritures* played in my poetic awakening: if it was not of supreme importance, it nevertheless had its hour. It was certainly

77

the first book that aroused my appetite for language: before having read it, I knew nothing of the savour of words. And if, after having left it, I had no further chance for some time of refining my appetite, at least, without my noticing, it had so much influenced my taste that I could make a list here of the books in which I rediscovered its fragrance. Why should I not admit it? Even in *La Jeune Parque* itself, when I came to read it a year later, I projected the shadow of *Les Nourritures*. Still to-day, its suavity comes back to me at times, like a nostalgic regret.

We had an hour of philosophy on the school syllabus, and for two years an episodic personage had been reading select passages to a drowsy class. He came to Pascal, whom I knew only from slices of literary history. I was tired of myself and of my dreams. This powerful voice, which made itself felt by the sheer fascination of the facts, found me a willing listener. I have re-read the *Pensées* a dozen times, as I re-read all the books I like most, not so much to remember their structure, as to saturate myself in their spirit. My memory is nearly always defective. If I ever entertained ambitions of becoming a philosopher, I had quickly to abandon them. I have to console myself with intuitive syntheses, which I consolidate as best I can within a personal system. I have therefore no critical apparatus for my knowledge of Pascal: which is, however, close enough to deserve being called a friendship.

The Jansenism of the *Pensées* freed me from another Jansenism, that of my teachers, in which I was foundering. Up till then I had been living in the midst of a dream, wilfully humiliating myself in evil, or glorifying myself in the simulation of mirages. Pascal made me recognise my true condition. Neither Satan nor demiurge, but capable at the same time of the demon and of God. In the narrow sphere of my experience I had quickly perceived that the potentiality of evil is not infinite: evil repeats itself, rearranges but does not invent, and it is boredom finally which puts the cap on its baseness. Hell is dull and flat, but the man

78

obsessed with hell, to achieve that illusion of the abyss which he needs if he is to retain some semblance of greatness in his own eyes, gives way to frenzied gesticulations as he feels inertia creeping upon him: he is a circus all by himself, but without an audience. Should he wake suddenly, he is filled with nausea at his own spectacle: that it is nausea rather than shame, I know from having experienced it. My teachers were assiduous in linking the image of sin with the reflexes of shame. But the blushes they provoked remained on the surface, and lasted only roughly as long as the confession. True shame, that which we feel when alone with ourselves, is a self-examination of consciousness in evil: blinding in its lucidity, it calls to our whole being; gathering together and unifying experience, it poses the question of both the ultimate and everyday meaning of our lives. Those who have once known it have found their lives changed, for its judgement is without appeal. But we never feel this burning and salutary shame, we never utter this cry of the spirit recognising its own treason, until we are at grips with the absolute: we may live for years disgusted with ourselves and with the world, sickened by the vanity of our gestures, delivered over in advance to the fatality which obsesses us, and powerless to perceive our capacity for our own truth.

But let a Pascal urge us to accept the paradox of our situation: 'What a chimera then is man? What innovation, what monster, what chaos, what vessel of contradiction, what prodigy! Judge of all things, ridiculous earthworm, sole agent of truth, sink of uncertainty and error, the glory and refuse of the universe!' Then we are forced, under pain of destroying ourselves, to justify consciousness by itself, to set it up in the heart of the contradiction so that it may resolve its terms. Greatness and meanness linked, there is no creation without a chaos which threatens it. 'Neither angel nor beast', and 'he who would act the angel acts the beast': in these phrases, common sense joins forces with the highest awareness of the self.

I was in a condition to receive these primary truths: common-places so often reiterated without understanding, but which suddenly reveal the essential. Pascal gave me no chance of escape, for he showed the naked workings of the escape mechanism. Through him, the fatality whose yoke I laboured under became unbearable. His proofs left nothing in shadow: they held authority not over the reason alone, but over the will. So true is it that consciousness, when it sees its whole fabric illuminated, is inseparable from the impulse towards the one Being. Moral indolence is the fruit of ignorance: for even when one thinks one knows oneself well, this knowledge is lacking in one element if the instinct for the absolute is not awakened. I fully realise that the impulse by itself is not sufficient safeguard against a moral collapse: but it keeps the demand for perfection always alert. I may abide by the law without ever grasping the essence of morality, and break that same law, but save myself through the painful repentance which consists in the contemplation of wounded human essence. I fall, but I rise again: I am a sinner, but I carry the germ of holiness. I never become fixed in my transgression: never once do I forget the something beyond myself, which is the basis of my presence in the universe.

True purpose does not consist in sticking to the letter of the law, but in that fierce hunger for perfection which may very well emerge in the midst of a life full of disorder and as such reprehended by the self-righteous. Baudelaire, whom I came to know rather late, is an example of moral heroism, fighting against an infinitely broad and complex nature, and one doomed to impotence by the very excess of its contradictory aspects. A religious mind grafted upon a poetic temperament, both equally strong, struggle for dominion over his being. There are few human dramas as terrible as that: one finds the incidence of it everywhere, even in a banal existence.

The hour had not yet struck when I should become aware of it: but my reading of Pascal (all unknown to me at the time) was already conducted on two planes of existence. I began to feel, like a splinter in my flesh, the contradiction of the double nature: I was commanded, I realised, by a bewildering logic, to resolve that contradiction by living it. It became a spiritual necessity to have a purpose in my life: there could be no more equivocation before the steady scrutiny of the mind: I must choose a rule of conduct and adhere to it in everyday life. But at the same time, the opposition of the double nature assumed the outline of a universal myth, taking on a dramatic character whose extent dwarfed my own conflict, so much so as to make me forget it. I welcomed the temptation familiar to the poet, of substituting an heroic *gesture* for the effort that a man like the rest must make step by step, of identifying himself with the mythical hero to the point of confusing the themes of the fable and those of personal salvation— I accepted it without being able to unmask it, and my embryonic metaphysic, had I known how to analyse it, would have shown me beneath its, as yet, clumsy reasonings, the secret ferment of a Manichean symbolism.

Pascal the Jansenist liberated me on the moral plane: he gave the presence of God its true significance, and reunited the impulse of the soul and of grace. On the plane of aesthetics—a domain still unknown to me—he laid in contradictory fashion the bases for Promethean enterprises: for, in order to change the whole sense of Pascal's thought, it is enough to deprive God of His royalty. The effect of grace is cancelled, but the will to raise one-self persists, being mistaken itself for an end: and man, para-doxically, pretends to draw the absolute from its depths, even while aggressively boasting that he is finite. He wants to be God of an indefinite metamorphosis, within the limits of his universe. The rest of the story we know, although very few have really lived it beyond the prologue. It is a tale that man has been telling himself since he became man: he thinks himself a demiurge, for want of being one in reality. Literature comes from the fact that his words outstrip his actions. But the strange thing is, that a

F   81

sorcerer's apprentice can find ammunition in the very man who denounced in the most irrefutable manner the meaninglessness of that pride which wills itself to be a creator.

*   *   *

At the end of the second year came the fever of competition and the crammed final weeks of study. I worked seventeen hours a day. But with what a prospect in view! If I passed, I should be setting out on a path which pleased me less and less: if I failed, I should have to continue for another year a mechanical grind the boredom of which made all my efforts futile. Very conveniently, I fell ill—from a mixture of overwork and disgust. Alone, on holiday, with a few books for company, I came to a decision: I would be a philosopher. It was quite simple. I would enter the University, and study for two degrees at once, in sciences and in philosophy. The attraction of a less confined sphere and studies more consistent with my tastes filled me with an insinuating eloquence: I flattered my uncle in his profession, and to soften the family's regrets at not seeing me in the cocked hat of the Polytechnic student, drew them a picture of myself in professorial gown. I triumphed, but not entirely: my uncle stripped me of the fine confidence that my school honours had sustained up till then. He remained convinced that I had given in before the obstacle, and had joined the respectable average of good pupils who stop too soon. He attached no value to university studies. He was shocked at the way they were carried out: there was not a shadow of discipline, it was a lazy man's way of working. I doubt whether he had the faintest conception of philosophy: he regarded books which dealt with it as mere idle talk. For that reason, he was scarcely capable of understanding my sudden switch-over. And as he really knew nothing about me, it would have been vain for me to try and outline my essential reasons. He advised me, however, to ask the opinion of one of my masters: what follows will show the unexpected consequences of this banal piece of wisdom. They were certainly the last my uncle would have thought of. The spiritual universe is full of portents: the one which now greeted me on the threshold was one of the major events of my life.

In one of my recent books may be seen the following dedication: *To my more-than-a father, the Abbé François Larue.* The man who was to become the friend of my most serious years inspired a sort of holy terror in me when I was his pupil. He taught mathematics in that faculty, and possessed a clarity verging on genius. With that, he had the most unflagging sense of irony imaginable, delicate, cruel, swift as a flash, and yet his goodness was such as to use the spur without wounding. It was not so much us he made mock of, but man in general; it amused him to seize upon his lack of intelligence or common sense, to show him blinded with light, filled with intuitions which he could not vindicate, and then, having let him stray at will down various sidetracks, to bring him back by a flick of the fingers to a path of such simple and obvious truth that his mind was filled with shame. To spend two hours 'on the mat' before such a judge was a test that few could withstand: with a mocking sympathy, he followed us in all our divagations, helping them along by suggesting variations, and pinning us down in our deductions. Then, when he thought the game had gone on long enough, he retraced, step by step, all our mistakes, with pedantic exactitude, yet full of a humour that made us shiver, ferocious and gentle at the same time, packed with unexpected sallies. Timidly, we adored him: but he avoided the slightest familiarity.

The presence of a great mind makes itself felt through a certain outward manner: the least subtle among us were sensible of the inner distinction of the Abbé Larue. We sensed, behind the teacher, a man of powerful intellect: he kept this secret, but his smile, the gleam in his eyes, the mobility of his features, all betrayed the eternal youth of knowledge. He was one of those of whom Valéry might have said, as he did of Doctor Coste, that they 'are able to exert their mind and develop its culture to the full, without any outside hope, nor any illusion other than that which resides in all thought'. He was an admirable Pyrrhonian, or at least so I for a long time believed, until the day came when he found the opportunity to rise to his true greatness, to abandon his role of spectator and take up the fight for freedom.

A spectator who bewitched his actors, knowing intimately their ways of thought yet always a step ahead of them—not by magic but by a genius for analysis—and possessed of so sure a judgement that, from the brief exchange of a few sentences, he grasped the entire structure of another mind—knowing this, I went to him expecting an oracle. He received me coolly enough, having no liking for forced intimacies. I stammered, almost weeping from timidity. There was a military bearing about him (he was an officer in the *chasseurs*), a severity of aspect, a clarity of language, a liking for rapid reflexes, all of which I knew well, but which, when I found myself alone with him, left me tongue-tied. He lived surrounded by beautiful and even precious things, all of which were new to me: I saw him in his proper setting, one peopled by noble figures, a Michelangelo slave, some details from the Parthenon. His room was flooded with light, a rare thing in a Lyons apartment. I felt as if in another world.

Suddenly I became voluble, hoping perhaps to be finished the sooner. I tried to retrace my first groping steps. I confessed that I knew nothing, but hankered after an intangible something which would give me a purpose in life. I wanted to arrive at the truth, at the end of a methodical pursuit. Mathematics were not opposed to this, but all mathematical proofs really showed was the conformity of the mind to its laws. The mind could not really overstep its boundaries, although it might appear to be dependent only on itself. What I wanted was to live, to burst beyond my frontiers, without losing any of the assurance that logical thought gave me. Is not philosophy, I asked the Abbé, the very science of existence itself, going straight to principles and striving to establish mind in the real world? Cannot that same mind, whose internal logic is infallible, raise itself to a knowledge of the world by a continuous chain of reasons? This was the substance of my speech. But while I posed a host of questions the Abbé Larue remained silent. My Cartesianism frayed out into clumsy repetitions: I made an effort to appear less of a novice in ideas than I really was.

As if changing the subject, the Abbé said abruptly: 'Listen to this'. Picking up from the desk where it was lying a superbly handwritten copy of *La Jeune Parque*, adorned with aquarelles by Barta, he read me the famous sequence which depicts the coming of spring:

> *Que si ma tendre odeur grise ta tête creuse*
> *O Mort! respire enfin cette esclave de roi! . . .*
> [*If my tender fragrance dazes your hollow head*
> *O death, breath deep at last this slave of a king . . .*]

He read perfectly and in the rhythm. Each word had its full form, its sonorous curve within the whole. There was no over-stressing of the vowels, and the melody was always ruled by the diction. For the *carmen* of poetry and its singular modulation have no other musical support than the judicious arrangement of rhythms and spoken sounds. A perfect poem never goes beyond the natural resources of the breath: a singing tone adds nothing but superfluous and even dangerous ornament, for it falsifies the pure quality of the art. The Abbé Larue could not have made a better choice than that fragment from *La Jeune Parque*. From '*Ecoute . . . N'attends plus . . .*' to the end ('*Un fleuve tendre, o mort, et caché sous les herbes?*'), it rises in a marvellous crescendo, in which the struggling upward thrust of the sap and the chromatic ascent of the words become indistinguishably blended. The symbols, linked by a law of internal development, create by their

85

very progression the vertical space of the forest. It is enough to attune one's breathing, to lift it from stage to stage by an easy play of nuances and half-tones, to restore to the fair form the energy from which the poet fashioned it.

I listened, my attention held not so much by the sense as by the rhythm: this unknown language flooded into me, breaking down the dykes of logic; for I did not attempt to understand, the better to feel its grasp. But a new logic, a vast, stirring procession of symbols, flowed through me like a river which carves itself out a bed in solid ground. In cold blood, I would have called this flood of light which bore me along irrational: accustomed as I was to the mathematical figure, whose abstract character guarantees its universality, I did not know that the universal may express itself in a particular form. Still fettered by the classic distinction between mind, heart and senses, I had never experienced until then this total harmony, this sensual and sensible reason, a principle of choice which depicts, in the work of art, one particular aspect or outline of universal energy: and which presents to the mind a certain mysterious reality, a certain moving substance, whose movement and contours ordinary rational analysis struggles in vain to grasp. I will explain myself more fully when the time comes: I want to prevent, as much as possible, *a posteriori* reflections falsifying the description of my progress towards art. For the Abbé Larue was the first person to bring me into contact with this *other* truth. I was neither deaf nor blind, but intoxicated by it: I was ready to accept this language, as one agrees to imagine a beyond, thereby leaving the imagination free play outside the constraints which the mind imposes on itself.

But this was not at all what the Abbé Larue intended. He saw in poetry, and in art generally, a mode of thought bound by its own laws, which are laws of reason. In his mentality there was a horror of vagueness, of the image for its own sake, and of that discontinuity in the beautiful which too many artists call freedom. While, speaking of logic, or rather of philosophy when it aspires to logic, he used to say: 'For all the proofs that so many minds have destroyed themselves in unearthing by processes of reasoning, I can imagine a contrary reasoning, which destroys those proofs in turn', when talking of poetry, he added: 'The manifest truth of *La Jeune Parque!* It is worthy of the most beautiful geometrical figures, of the most rigorous exercises in analysis'. In Plato, or Descartes, or Bergson, what he deemed irrefutable was not the ideas, but the style: splendid pages, redeemed by the perfection of language. To a greater extent than the philosophers, the poets seemed to him to invest reason with a body by the vigilant and concerted exercise of the potentialities of the senses: with the poets, the idea was born of the matter, and assumed shape within an indivisible totality, in the poem or the statue. And if one could always strip a work of art down to some logical framework, penetrate the harmony of the symbols by ordinary reason, and explain through a step-by-step analysis the simultaneous syntheses of the creative spirit, that was all the more a proof of the unity of thought, which at the highest level integrates its different modes. But to reveal the naked structure after the event is merely to rebuild an artificial skeleton. Without the flesh of symbols, the idea is merely a pile of bones. Art manifests its truth through the life of the form, and finds a breathing echo in those whom it has captivated.

Always mistrustful of the metaphysical ferment, lest that ferment should throw up fine monsters out of chaos, the Abbé Larue was for a long time in my eyes a pure aesthetician, even in the sphere of sciences. He had the most exacting, the most alert scientific mind that I have ever met. But science, in his opinion, which ascends from the exact relationships which it establishes between its symbols to the myth of its grandiose theories, and descends again to the former to imbue concrete experience with life, advances by the same movement as those arts which are apparently most remote from it. For a long time steeped in Valéry, whom his own inclination for irony made him cherish more than any other, he refused to postulate the absolute: and like the poet of *Charmes*, he even came to thinking that ' the universe is merely a flaw in the purity of non-being'; that consciousness is *a beautiful lie*, discovering its supreme delight in the strictness of its laws.

When I first made his acquaintance, he had reached a point in his life in which his aesthetic nature prevailed. And the aesthetic nature takes pleasure in impugning the absolute, even while it proclaims itself as the absolute. Born for action—that 'sister of dream'—he no doubt suffered for his own serenity and for that closed world which, however, he defended against any alien intrusion: he found freedom through meditation, but refused to be taken in—and then, was suddenly filled with uneasiness at being taken in by his own refusal! I saw later how he discovered a soul of another sort, when his *active* spirit found once more the human raw material of history, a material both everyday and mythical, in which it could work. But even in the days when thought seemed to him a splendid illusion, he believed in the beauty, if not in the truth of ideas. He would readily have maintained that the former makes a basis for the latter, and that language, 'the pride of man', touches on perfection each time that the mind becomes enamoured of its own austere function.

I wrote recently, on the subject of Paul Valéry: 'Valéry condemns himself—and with full awareness of what he is doing—to never envisaging that there may be, in the very idea of the Beautiful, a secret finality; that no creation is ever made legitimate except by a *why* which infinitely transcends it'. It was this anti-metaphysical bias which struck me in the Abbé Larue: the latter agreed, however, that metaphysics, transposed into the sphere of art, might serve as a pretext for symbols. The fundamental themes of philosophy, as he saw them, were merely myths grown cold. And as the myth remains eternal beneath its successive abstractions, a powerful imagination moves easily in the abstract, as long as it does not fall prey to it. He did not, therefore, dissuade me from making a voyage into the territory of the philosophers, but put me on my guard against the hopes which I seemed to him to entertain, of ever finding confirmation or certainty there. He claimed, at that period, that the question of being is both absurd and necessary: absurd for whoever tries to resolve it in the scientific or ethical sphere, yet necessary as a spur for whoever amuses himself by building, out of the contradictions it provokes, a universe of conflicting symbols.

Our conversation drifted more and more into a monologue, for my own still trammelled mind was unable to follow his more adventurous spirit. I sensed, in the Abbé Larue, some major drama of the intellect, but my lack of a critical sense prevented me from grasping it. And even had I been able to, I should have been fearful of discovering its nature, for I had—and still have—an almost panic shyness where someone else's secret is concerned. From our long interchange of views, I retained the impression that he regretted not being a creator: that he regarded metaphysics as ruinous when they are taken seriously; and that the concepts on which they are based, and which the metaphysical mind tries vainly to elucidate in a rational way, are in reality vast complexes of images, which the imagination may utilise at will, without fear of falling into error, since the mind is a law unto itself, and that it exists in the possible as much as, and more than, in the actual.

He added, however, that if anarchy can assume a seductive guise, and appear to some as the very emblem of their freedom, it soon causes monotony and fatigue. The incoherence of movement is transformed into inertia, the apparent ubiquity of the mind becomes pure discontinuity, and the bright fireworks of potentialities sink back into nothingness. Even if it were only with one's pleasure, with a certain quality of enjoyment, in view, it was better to preserve an exact control over the forces that the imagination brings into play: beauty, which is, perhaps, no more than an illusion, but the only permanent and effective one, has its principle in its tangible limits, the mind refuses to encroach upon the laws which make it coherent—which does not, however, prevent it from self-exploration, even into its native incoherence; but this must be done with that implacable attentiveness, the enemy of any loss of balance, which Nerval shows, for example, in *Aurélia*.

Once again, I found that my mind was still immature: I simplified these ideas down to its own scale. The insistence on form, the importance in art of consciousness alert to its own functioning, the existence of a logic of images whose essential truth cannot be discussed by reason, although it is impregnated with reason—I made of these notions, which found no echo in my own experience, so deep a mental record that one might have thought that a shadowy yet clear-sighted double went ahead of me in my thoughts. I had sought out the Abbé Larue, to hear him affirm, in a fresh sphere, the powers of logical language: I left him having discovered another language, another idol of reason—Beauty. It is true that I would have been quite incapable, never having up to that point experienced the awakening of an image in myself, of understanding the Beautiful in its double nature, symbolical and rational: for that, patient practice is needed, and the suffering of art.

I also dimly perceived that the most profound thought only endures when it is rent within itself, in the crucifying doubt of its own value. The aestheticism of the Abbé Larue concealed not so much a disappointment with metaphysics as a determination for immanence at all costs, even to a point where metaphysics are silent, powerless. He did guard-duty on the frontiers of the mind, both to prevent it from overstepping those frontiers, and to forestall it being forced, by the mystery of being, to bow to the unthinkable absolute. It was by no means an easy position: an absurd, yet heroic, wager—man and nothing but man, an integral individual entity, undefined yet altogether limited by its law. The Abbé Larue came later to understand that the notion of the great individual did not embrace the whole human range: his mind discovered the transcendent that his priestly heart had always acclaimed. It was the war which determined this revolution in his thought, the invention of a specific finality: I shall come to this later, but I mention it in advance, to show that the Abbé Larue was one of those people whose thinking does not proceed by a system, but develops within the universe as a mental organism. Of all the perspectives that meeting him opened up to me, this was perhaps the most fruitful, and he himself set me a marvellous example.

*   *   *

Soon, I shall have emerged from my past. Soon, I shall have conquered that freedom which for me is entirely new: to be at peace with what has been. But there is one last effort to be made, and I must remain lucid to the end. I remember—I was seventeen at the time—having birched a cousin of mine, whom, as he had neither father nor mother, my parents had taken charge of, entrusting him to the same aunt who brought me up. It was during the holidays. I took my vengeance for my uncle's domination by becoming myself an oppressor. My cousin was barely ten, and extremely limited in intelligence. To terrorize him was easy, and I arrogated to myself the right of punishing him. Drunk with my own degradation, I beat him, feeling nothing but scorn for the unfortunate child. And yet, however painful that picture is to me now, I have learned such lessons from it, and have meditated so often upon it in the depths of repentance, that my heart is at last reconciled with it.

It is easier to unburden oneself of one's sin than of the delights of melancholy. For the normal mind, abjection contains its own antidote. But those idols of memory, which regret bathes in a deceptive light, hold our gaze fixed upon the past, in a mortal complacence which is doubtless the greatest sin: it was her nostalgia for Sodom that transformed Lot's wife into a pillar of salt. I myself found that the tears I shed in memory encrusted me with a salty bitterness, and I took pleasure in a particular setback, a certain sadness, which gave me the feeling of being fatally marked out. Nothing undermines more the balance of sensibility than this Narcissism in suffering with which some adolescents aggravate their early disappointments in life.

A solitary temperament, repressed over a long period, and unacquainted with the real world, runs every risk of going more than half-way to meet the failure it dreads. Such a nature summons up its energies too soon, and struggles obstinately in a blind alley: isolated, it cultivates its unhappiness, thus finding itself interesting and enjoying the belief that it is exceptional, while taking its appetite for misfortune for an inverse desire of the absolute. At eighteen, one is too full of latent forces which have still to come to grips with the concrete world, so that this age, above all others, is one of anguish and semi-despair, one's being is filled with too many diverse needs, and the range of the possible is too limited, or the energy which wishes to embrace all things at once, without experience or study, too incoherent. The adolescent, who has barely begun to live, already has the impression of having lived too much—and this is because he is afraid of the void which is opening, and can only think of spreading himself. So sharp is this fear in some that they hurl themselves at a certainty, even when it is not at all one made for them.

Abruptly, I emerged into the fresh air. There were few lectures, plenty of leisure, and excellent excuses for escaping from the tutelage of the family. But my mental solitude was so great, and I felt such an urgent hunger for love, that I deliberately chose myself an idol: fine, ash-blonde hair, a slender figure in her mourning black, a youthfulness of features rather than beauty, a certain perfume, a smile—this was the first girl who had appeared on my horizon. Up till then, I had had nothing to do with girls, and knowing them only through my dreams was almost too naïve a prey for the illusions of feeling. But I was driven by a sense of urgency, a peculiar vanity. For it made me proud to be in love: I was gripped by a strange need to put the seal on my existence by an *irrevocable* engagement. Once before already, I had deluded myself in this way, when I hurled myself headlong into the absolute.

The paradox of poetic natures is that, no sooner have they imagined the absolute, than they want to possess it: they treat the eternal as an object, and instead of referring themselves to it, refer it to themselves. Hence the apparent identity of language between mystics and poets: the latter, however, remain turned inward on themselves, and their experience does not break the law of words. I experienced love, therefore, as a myth: it consecrated the role I should play in my destiny. Everything in me took its direction and was unified in one unceasing presence—my own, seen through the person I loved. I felt the exaltation of genius: I admired my love, and its music in my soul. No more need be said: my failure was a foregone conclusion.

The revelation was a self-willed one: and—who knows?—may very well have been provoked by a dim memory of those novels in the style of Delly that my aunt was so fond of, and used to let me read. It was bad literature, full of rosy clouds and flowering orchards. But from the romantic elegy to the inane popular song and the sentimental film, the mortgage on true feeling has only grown heavier. Love is no longer anything but an excuse for the selfish effusions of the ego. The charm of romance has over-shadowed the vital questions of destiny. To fall in love has become the easiest thing in the world, coming before any inner experience or any decisive encounter with life. Scarcely has the image of love emerged than it becomes fixed, and soon sets in a mould. Without a pause, the revelation of passion is followed by its avowal—a fresh triumph for literature!

Not a week had passed since I persuaded myself I was in love, when to remain silent became unbearable. I was sitting next to Her, in the philosophy library. We were working together, and her hair brushed my cheek when we spoke to each other. I declared my feelings as one takes a cold plunge. I had, of course, gone over that moment a hundred times mentally, but the effect far surpassed anything I had imagined. She gazed at me, terrified, and then burst into tears: and before I could pull myself together, she had fled. I followed her, running like a madman through the ridiculous labyrinth of corridors. I guessed she had hidden herself, in order to cry and untangle her own emotions. The building was vast, and full of odd corners, but I was in a mood to demolish it stone by stone. I found her at last, cowering in a dark alcove. She was like a fluttering, wounded bird. The same fear flashed across her face. I consoled her, and kept on asking her questions. She admitted that she loved someone else: he was far away, but he wrote to her sometimes. She also said that she was very fond of me, that she did not want me to suffer on her account, much more of the sort, and that she treasured my friendship. There were a thousand other feminine arguments, all liberally interspersed with tears: I too broke down and wept openly, which put the finishing touch to her confusion.

From all of which, I managed to acquire a certain, muddled intuition: my passion was far from finding her indifferent—she was plunged into confusion, but flattered. I had also acquired, I do not know why, a certain lustre in the eyes of my companions in the faculty: and curiously enough, in her eyes as well. She had not had the strength to give me a flat *no*, as she would to a simpleton. I was filled with a bizarre joy. *It was bound to happen,* I kept saying to myself: and at the same time, I hoped.

The idea of fate was necessary to me, in order to nourish the poetry of despair. This love had to be impossible, and pass entirely into dream; for then the dream presented itself as an ideal kingdom, in which the beloved image would be revealed in its essence, more beautiful, and richer in inner life, than she herself

94

realised. By becoming the eternal lover, I would make this woman an accomplice to my dream: another insistent reality would enter as a third factor between herself and her love. This reality would say to her: This is what you could be—and one day, perhaps: This is what you are. To lure the real woman by the imaginary form I carved out for her, and to stir up a conflict of fortunes between the tangible currency of her love and her reflection in the absolute of my dreams—such was my strategy, still unconscious yet full of guile, from the moment the irreparable had come between us.

I was the first to fall into the trap: it was the very thing that I wanted, besides. She, for her part, had a rather cold nature, brusquely disturbed by wild flashes of sensibility: she was, in general, lucid and reasonable, but liable to lose her head in an unexpected crisis. I never left her for an instant. Her sweetheart was doing his military service, and I thought I could detect by certain signs, her periods of sadness followed by exaggerated outbursts of joy, that she loved him more than he loved her. My imagination was entirely wrapped up in her caprices, and I wallowed in romantic unhappiness. But at the same time as I adored the impossible, and lyricism awoke within me, I kept my gaze fixed on the possible, and selfishly calculated the other's indifference.

Once again I was living on two planes. I willed and waited passionately for the other man to abandon her. I multiplied my presence, so that when she was abandoned and opened her eyes on her solitude she might see there a world instead of a desert, and a world she already inhabited without knowing it. My curiosity had increased tenfold: my mind showed me a thousand forms that, six months before, I should have encountered unseeingly. To this woman, whom I wanted always to be new, I presented each day a new being. I went ahead of her on the path of our common discovery. I read nothing, saw nothing, had no sensation in the world except for her: I steeped her in my own thought.

She stood me in stead of a soul. I did not grasp the workings of this projection, and thought I was making myself necessary: I began to be caught in the trap I had laid.

While we were pursuing this ambiguous relationship, and each one deriving something from it, I surrendered myself from time to time to the pleasures of despair; in the abyss of unrequited love, I listened to the crumbling of the world. These onslaughts of poetic vertigo exhausted me: I went for long walks by the river, drawn by the nightbound water, and rapidly drained of all thought but of the void. And suddenly, in this gulf of images, the arch of a bridge would loom up, magnified into a cathedral: or out of the mists of the Lyons evening would arise a spectral procession of lamp-posts. The city revealed itself to me like a transformed vessel: my steps rang on the deserted quays, down the echoing streets, and on the squares that rode like rafts at anchor. I loved the shadow of the churches: with heavy cope, it stifled my melancholy. People came and went, brushing against me as if against a stone. The icy flagstones, the tomb-like odour, isolated me in an eternal past. I broke free from it, to plunge into the maze of sordid little streets, the *traboules* as they are called, with their smell of saltpetre, sort of vaulted alleyways like catacombs, and communicating, from house to house, by courtyards like deep wells open to the sky.

In a landscape of ruins which my melancholy multiplied, I played at feeling myself alone and, as it were, exiled from ordinary time. I caught the sickness poets suffer from, of making fables of their feelings, of being unable to feel without creating a mental picture—a real plague. But it gave tone to my language, the eloquence of the simulator who depends on the innate sensibility of words. Caught in this sham, I soon reached a point where I could no longer distinguish the real emotion from the invented one: the real cause was obscured behind all the variations played upon it. The slightest sign (a solitary gull in the winter sky, the whistle of a train crossing the river), as long as it caught the note of my vast and vague nostalgia, could with its harmonics awaken the remote vistas of my solitude. I became drunk with the idea that I was carrying all the unhappiness of the world in my heart.

I had had this weakness for unreality since my earliest years. I was still out of contact with the world, having had nothing better to do than to interpose between us the veil of imaginary loves. My sensibility functioned in a void, having no grasp on its alleged object. I was still virgin, and singularly gauche in my relationships with women. I trembled to feel a woman's body near me, but knew it was forbidden to me. Thus were revived the prohibitions of my recent education: I was filled once more with a fear of the flesh, born of my obscure instinct. This fear drove me back into dream, estranging me more and more from the inaccessible living being whom only in dreams I could embrace. Thus my love (or my supposed love) was made up solely of the ragings of the spirit: a real passion would have saved me, in which mind and body are one. As it was, the vulgar romanticism of my passion only made a deeper division in me. My foreboding of failure drove me into the extravagances of dream, and the dream in turn only increased the chances of failure.

At last, the impossible happened, and dream and reality merged. She loved me. It was in the last days of May, and we had a month ahead of us, before separating for the holidays. We went through all the usual gestures of lovers—the kisses, the long silences side by side. This young, animal body yearned in every fibre for pleasure: my own body embarrassed me, and I was not simple enough to forget my lack of grace. I analysed my movements, and by a physical uneasy conscience, disturbed the spontaneous harmony of love. She was like wax, awaiting my impress: but my body was all the more formless for my mind being geared to act. My mental tension exhausted my vital energy and drove it from its natural tenement, which was left in a state of miserable abandonment. To tell the truth, I was mentally ashamed of my

G

body, and considered it incapable of achieving the slightest beauty: with my mind's eye, I looked down upon it, humiliating it in its very reflexes, turning it into something timid and idiotic.

Such a total hostility paralyses passion. Inexperienced as we were, and groping towards one another, only a great deal of tenderness between us, or some great shared impulse would have been enough to overcome our early awkwardness, and conquer the shyness that such blunders made more acute. My sweetheart, however, did not really love me: she *wanted* to love me. Her body harboured the memory of the other, to which mine was not attuned. She had, however, both physically and mentally, an underlying passivity, which would have made her plastic to my bodily impress, as she was to my mental powers. She was simply waiting; for, in the complex game of love, there are people who only give themselves after having received everything. Their clay needs the caresses of a Pygmalion to bring it to life: they surrender to whoever creates them. But Pygmalion was sure of himself. He conceived his statue in body and soul, not being himself divided. On the contrary, I had no love of myself: I was rather my worst enemy. My eroticism was two-sided: coming in part from a proud mind, in part from a shameful body. The shadow of transgression passed over me: my least gestures were ugly, not at all in themselves, but in the way they jarred with my dream—a fact which my mind took pleasure in unmasking.

When the holidays arrived, we separated. She was vaguely disappointed when I left her. One day, she had almost belonged to me: I had felt her melt into sweetness, that moment found her wholly offered to me, and I knew, I knew with a fatal certainty, that the mark of destiny was upon us. I was seized with panic at the thought of those terrible obstacles which bar the way to possession: clothes, false gestures, ridiculous details. . . . I was already my own onlooker, as I have not ceased to be since: and always with ill intent. To foresee too much is to balk oneself: we throw up imaginary obstacles, only to capitulate before them in advance. Our inhibitions all derive from the same mental mechanism. We are afraid of our freedom, of the risk it entails. We want to gamble only on certainties, and are never certain enough to gamble at all. Everything becomes an excuse to retreat, we can find a thousand reasons for doing so, including the famous notion that 'there's always tomorrow'. In many people, common sense is confined to the role of appeasing their uneasy conscience, and forging weapons for dishonesty.

On that particular day, of course, I had the notion that I was resisting the call of physical desire. But I only discovered this handsome scruple after the event, when shame masked my cowardliness. Most often, some renunciation on my part has merely been an act of cowardice which I affected not to see—or saw only too well! I wonder what use such pieces of self-denial are to God: will we not be judged, perhaps, by some crucial fault we have not committed, *from fear*? I myself remain convinced that, on that particular day, grace, for which this woman was the altar, was held out to me. I recognised it, but dared not make it mine. The moment of communion vanished: my love was not *shared*, and we each returned to our solitude. I re-entered the firmament (or rather the cloudland) of my dreams; for the real sky is a tree nourished by deep-delving roots, whereas my sky had no roots, and the wind of absence would easily sweep it clean. When I said good-bye to my sweetheart, I restrained myself from crying that fact in her ear.

Far from her, I wrote poems which brought her to life for an instant. My need to feel her near me imbued the words with their elemental magic. I surrounded myself with signs and substitutes, which became the sacred fetishes of her presence (her hair, a little of her perfume on my cuff). I mingled her with nature: tree, cloud, or spring revealed her in a thousand forms.

Up till then I had seen nothing more in symbols than a bold flight of imagination: an image was not a field of forces but an agreeable and fortuitous grouping of words, a mixture whose only innate characteristics were its hue and aspect, while its various elements (the vocables) remained unaltered in their sense. For a sensual imagination, which represents words concretely, such groupings are common enough. The partisans of automatic writing have claimed to systematise them, by postulating the total autonomy of each element of language, and raising verbal cannon-play to the status of an aesthetic. I knew nothing of such murderous sport: but I was still far from recognising the obscure biology of the mind. To create an image was, for me, to arrange an encounter of words conceived as exterior to one another, to underline a relationship between appearances in such a way that it was either invisible or visible, according to the illumination of thought.

But now I had stumbled upon a whole source of meta-morphoses. The curious Protean nature of love spread to the universe, the most remote appearances combined in indissoluble symbols, which, in turn, took their place in an organic syntax of the imagination. Admittedly, my lyricism of that period hardly went beyond the surface of being or the perceptible order of the universe. But the energy of feeling was already invading the sensual matter, correspondences were being established between the progression of images and the movements of sensibility. I felt the language of the soul awakening within me.

It may be that I abandoned myself too freely to this new exaltation, which did not go without an unconfessed anguish. My absent sweetheart wrote rarely, and I looked in vain for an echo of my love in her letters. Coldly, having given her word, she stuck to it; but had I been less blind, I would have known how to decipher her embarrassment, and understood that my victory was a delusion. I was cowardly enough to await an explanation. I clung to my dream as a shipwrecked man clings to a buoy. I returned to Lyons in the last days of September: my love vanished with the leaves—a final letter was waiting for me.

With what delight I lost my footing, and what a morbid deliverance I discovered in despair! It is true that I had cherished and, for no reason, cultivated despair in the very heart of love: I had continued to wish for it, drawn as I was like a magnet by suffering, just as, earlier, the recital of the religious fervour of the martyrs had filled me with enthusiasm. The hurts of passion are the orchids of aesthetics, and the poet often prefers them to the buttercups and daisies of a happiness which it rests entirely with him to take or leave. If he chooses masochism on his path to the absolute, it is because he must be unhappy to become a demiurge, at least while he is in the first stages of his art. His ready acquaintance with unhappiness guides him safely through its shadows, and he derives from it a sombre knowledge which touches on the universal. But the illusion of the romantic agony is to encompass the world within its own struggle. It never transcends certain limits of knowledge, while the true struggle with destiny is situated far beyond them. To pass from the reign of blind fatality to that of consciousness, one must leave the ivory tower of dream, and accept a common humanity. The sense of unhappiness is thereby deepened, both in its universal and particular aspects. But it loses its absolute sway, becoming merely one of the springs of the whole drama of mankind and of the individual, now bearing it along, now borne along by it. A poet was to teach me that fact, in the midst of the crisis I was in, and at the appropriate moment.

CHAPTER FIVE

That summer, as in the previous one, I had had an announcement inserted in *Le Patriote des Pyrénées:* 'Baccalauréat. October term. Private tuition in sciences, arts, by teacher with degree.' There was no lack of students who had failed before, nor of parents anxious about their progeny. I was sure that the manna would fall. My qualifications were open to doubt, but not my good intentions: I managed fairly well, without bringing shame on my pupils. I spent all the money I earned on books, mainly on history and philosophy. My reading was 'serious', poetry finding no place in it. I loved handling new books, feeling the paper's texture, sniffing the ink at the bend of the pages. I was grateful to them for belonging to me, and chose them, besides, just as people who hold friendship sacred choose their friends. But what I was really looking for was the substance: and of palpable appearances I registered only a few meagre characteristics and nothing of the subtler harmony of architecture in print. It is true that, on this score, French publishers do not exactly pamper us, and even less so ten years ago than to-day.

One day while I was ferreting about in my bookseller's, I dislodged a volume from the shelf. It was *Sueur de Sang* of Pierre Jean Jouve. They were poems, and I had vaguely heard of the author's name, but it conveyed nothing to me. On the point of putting the book back, mechanically I flipped over the pages. It was beautiful—airy as a temple. An architect's purpose reigned over every page. An indivisible totality, woven of complex harmonies between whites and blacks, the empty and the full, light and shadows, made the poem's presence felt long before the mind had grasped its spiritual framework.

Mallarmé, obsessed by the white page, tries to capture the inexpressible in a net in which words are the knots: he dreams that the white spaces are the substance of the poem, that the line which he draws out or breaks off is the asymptote of the void. The void is nothing by itself: the mind creates it out of its rupture with itself. A series of instantaneous stresses, broken at their extreme climax, gives the illusion of something beyond the words, of a stupendous electricity for which words ignite the spark. The delimited texture of the poem is posited as the diagram of a nervous phenomenon, and the words (even reduced to their essential abstraction) as a makeshift version of a purer language, which the mind exhausts itself trying to formulate. The aesthetics of *Un coup de dés* drive consciousness into an intolerable position. Such extreme vigilance is the threshold to anarchy: it heralds the immense disorder which must ensue, the divorce of the mind from the universe.

A page of Jouve, on the other hand, has a monumental appearance, built upon a sustained impulse: its breaks (for breaks it has) are intervals of silence, in which the proportions are composed. Nothing here is left to chance, however fertile chance might be in miracles. If the arch seems suspended, it is because its curve links with the sky: the stone has become music, without breaking off its movement. It is like seeing a church apparently in ruins, but whose remaining fragments have kept intact their airy architecture, and testify to a permanence whose only basis is the mind. In turning the pages of *Sueur de Sang* I sensed in advance that the typographical canons re-established and renewed by Jouve were only the material aspect of other, inner canons, of a complex hierarchy of symbolic laws, lightening from base to summit the edifice of the human psyche. My impression was obscure but strong: this book had a face, and levelled its gaze upon me. And in the same way that we are moved by glimpsing, in and behind the particular features, another and more secret truth, which the visible face both expresses and conceals, here, in and behind the severe beauty of the page, a still unuttered but active speech made its imperious claim on the attention, and gathered the mind into an exact state of suspense.

Of what long maturing process this form made tangible is the end, what spiritual rule it implies, what methodical ruthlessness in the choice and linking of symbols, and perhaps even more, what a plastic sense of the truth, what insistence on dignity in the act of writing just as in moral conduct, only those for whom art is a religion will understand. I mean to say: those who feel the slightest error, the least confusion in taste, as an insult to the harmony of the world. This unparalleled sensitivity is the sign of a painfully sharpened intuition. Let whoever does not understand regard this merely as an aesthete's whim, or the tyranny of a madman proud of his genius. Yet even in a conflict over a comma, a doubt over the placing and value of a space, I see a very high moral affirmation: it is certainly not just a question of taste, but of truth. When practised with such vigilance, art is a virtue which provides man with his laws. It becomes judge of our most intimate thoughts, and moral conscience is entirely at one with it.

But I am anticipating my acquaintance with Jouve: later experience colours my early memories. For so long now I have united the man and his work in the same admiration, that my memory superimposes successive impressions, like those artists who, in order to compose a single picture, paint ten rough sketches one upon the other, each of which is both an approximation and a whole. For, if our knowledge of a person is the integral sum of a series of meetings, each one of these contains them all, both future and past: we love only in the eternal, where within the field of simultaneous vision is projected a whole reach of time.

When I bought *Sueur de Sang*, merely for the sake of its handsome appearance, I did not suspect the importance it was to assume for me. Hence, I have only been able to determine retrospectively the early details of my dialogue with a poet whom

I read at first as a methodical and rational exercise. Up till then, I had only read Valéry, who had not convinced me of the necessity of poetic language. I found him useless and charming, and, despite his philosophy, not far removed from the Chénier of *La Jeune Tarentine*. In reality, I looked upon poetry merely as a poet's pastime: I quickly tired of reading it, and could not understand why it was placed so high among the arts. Nevertheless, the glitter of certain words, the deliberate absence of 'literature' that a glance at these pages sufficed to show, gave me a feeling that I had met with some great truth of language: I was to undertake a study which would determine what value I should give to poetry as a form of knowledge.

In my vague lyrical attempts, my only law had been the effect of charm. Even if I admitted that this charm could operate on others besides myself, I had also to recognise that it was easy, requiring only a little skill, a certain elegance of feeling. Among the thousand and one examples of poetry that we find in the average anthology, there are sometimes differences of degree, and of technical 'perfection': but rarely of nature. One of the most idiotic remarks I have ever heard (one of those that make you want to strangle someone), was lisped to me by an intellectual young woman the other day: 'We really have some very *nice* poets just now, haven't we?' And yet, that dreadful adjective *nice* might well be applied to almost the whole of poetry. Hearing it, one is almost ashamed to be a poet, for simply *to be nice* is a pitiable enough function in the world in which we live, the world of man with its eternal pains and perils.

But if there was one thing that had struck me about Jouve, even having read only a few lines, it was that one might call him by any epithet (including the most pejorative ones); but no one, not even the blue-stocking of my encounter, could dream of labelling his poems nice. It followed, thus, that this must be a very extraordinary man who could write in verse, while repudiating in such obvious fashion all I had thought to be poetry. He must

105

have felt a deep urgency, to use a language so different from any other, and so firmly guided by will. In a few pages of highly concentrated prose, illumined by a powerful insight, Pierre Jean Jouve introduced *Sueur de Sang*, at the same time justifying his existence as a poet. Or rather, he defined poetry as a fundamental operation of the mind, as a necessity of the spiritual life, without which certain essential aspects of knowledge would escape us.

Over and above the execution, the charm, the conventional graces, the magic, there is this curious mode of self-awareness, this *power*. It is not the power of words, but power over them and, before that, power over the human substance they express. Such power is a tamed energy, directed towards an end: it is a specific energy, peculiar to man, unable to take shape except in man, yet grafted on to the universal life-force, and thus in contact with all that moves, waxes and wanes in the world. What this energy may become remains open: the greater part of it still lacks form in the human mass, but it functions secretly, seeking an outlet into the future. There are privileged natures, functionally differentiated from others (not long ago, I called them artesian wells), which take over and assimilate this energy: their role is to project it, to demonstrate it in action, in the destiny of all and of each. It is the most difficult task of all, for it is one thing to tap this energy, and another to dominate it, and to invest it with a form in the balance between the known and unknown, all the more so as energy eludes definition. It never manifests itself openly, and its effects can always be ascribed to nearer causes: it conceals itself in the outward form, for the known hides the unknown, and most often denies its existence.

The paradox of energy is to be both actual and latent: and the corollary, the paradox of consciousness, to assume as known the groups of forces that the analysis of appearance reveals to it, and to admit, explicitly or not, that the totality from which it arbitrarily isolates them remains unknown. But there is always the threat of the unforeseeable, however close-meshed one imagines the net of relationships in which knowledge claims to ensnare energy. It sometimes happens that knowledge, illuminated by intuition or assailed by hazard, turns back to question its own structure. Then the moment has arrived once again for it to take the totality on trust, and to thrust energy forward in a symbolic form: to extrapolate the curve of the real, while remaining faithful to the latter.

This, which is true in the scientific sphere, is even more so in history and the progress of ethics: man has a need to base himself upon his future image, a virgin space yet one already full of him. The system of abstract relationships which constitutes the apparatus of knowledge ends up, like an iron corset, by imprisoning in too narrow a form that organism capable of indefinite expansion—consciousness invested with vital force, which grows restless and presses towards a higher degree of elucidation. And if the pressure of an accumulated force, mobilised in depth, is exerted against the barriers of a knowledge no longer strong enough to contain the flood of being, abruptly the whole of history seems to break asunder, and man loses his meaning, his reference to the universe. Then, if some bold myth (whether born of art, or of science, or of both at the same time) does not force him to regain his footing in the immediate present in terms of a future which gives scope to the energies of which man is no longer master—not in terms of an arbitrary future, but of a *projected* one in conformity with energy's laws of evolution—or if man lacks imagination at such a critical moment in his history, catastrophe strikes at the very marrow of his thought.

The function of the poet—and generally speaking, of the creator of values—is to disclose the fatal sickness of his epoch long before it declares itself openly, to unmask, beneath equivocal symptoms, the underlying corruption of energy, and to prevent the latter from flourishing blindly in the great body which no longer bears it along: to divert it from the seductive appeal of anarchy, and from that morbid exuberance which one sees in decaying organisms, which is only the disintegration of the vital force. And on the contrary, to bring it back to its centre, in man collected, reassured, reinvigorated by his limits.

The pulse of life conditions consciousness, by which it is in turn conditioned, and borne to its human level. But should this impulse lose consciousness or abdicate within it, and far from rediscovering its primitive spontaneity, it breaks down and flounders in the fetters of mental chaos—not of the original chaos, but that of the eleventh hour, irreparable as a crumbled universe. The breakdown of the life-urge sows confusion in that subtle and so fragile organism, the edifice of thought: if man relaxes from his vigil, the life within him is turned into death. The poet (the creator of values) stands at the very point where life is most threatened. He recognises the threat and wards it off. The spiritual life is a struggle which places man in jeopardy every moment.

To make energy run in the channel of life does not mean merely to divert it from that propensity for death which would make it proliferate like a canker: it is also to enclose it in an embryonic universe, in an evolving form which it will bear slowly to its fulfilment. The seed itself is nothing, but potentially contains all: it is the first, and the most concrete of symbols. In the same way, the verbal symbol is much more than the word or group of words which show its apparent contours: it contains an invisible area, attuned to others by obscure relationships, which consciousness will gradually unearth, by a progressive journey from darkness into light, from the symbolic image to the object.

That is at least what I read, or believe I read, in the preface to *Sueur de Sang*, which bears the striking title: *Inconscient, Spiritualité et Catastrophe*. I will not go so far as to say that I read all that in it right from the start, or that my present exegesis does not bear the traces of my most constant preoccupations. But this preface is couched in such a style that, hardly had I begun it, when it reverberated through my whole being. It is of no importance that

Jouve, in writing it, remembered about psychoanalysis: it transcends the latter as the great theory transcends the simple hypothesis, and would remain true irrespective of Freud. I realise, however, that it must be incomprehensible, and hence all I have said about it above, to anyone who restricts man to his immediate ends, refusing to admit a specific finality inscribed in the very nature of consciousness—a sort of auto-development of man in the heart of the universe, in a design which infinitely transcends the foreseeable designs of life, and encloses, with both anguish and hope, the possibility of a transcendence, an unthinkable transition, an assumption in absolute consciousness.

In the spiritual parabola of Jouve, *Sueur de Sang* occupies the lowest point. All original creation begins by a descent into the underworld and a confrontation with the powers of darkness: it is from the depths of the abyss that the spirit springs into the heights. *Le Paradis Perdu*, with the crashing of an avalanche, closes behind us the pass one may only traverse once: remote, and now unimaginable lies the innocent Eden of the old myths (and, symbolically, the peaceful country each one of us has had to leave, at the personal bidding of destiny). The only salvation is to advance, to plunge down into the vapour of darkness which clouds and conceals the abyss. *Noces*, the first poetic act of Jouve (*Le Paradis Perdu* is not so much a personal act as the integration of an original myth in modern consciousness), consumates the marriage of the lucid mind with the material night in which it is engulfed, guided no longer by ordinary reason, but by the sense of the symbolic life, a reason both more obscure and more pregnant.

Sueur de Sang is the second incarnation, in which the poet makes the world his very flesh. Since man entered the world, the world has been the womb of mankind: the universe is a visceral region, where, in suffering, a birth takes place which consciousness, turned inward upon things and having become organic knowledge, must keep in rhythm and lead to its end. In this way, history takes place in a double region, that of time external to itself, and that of duration pursuing its involution. From the first viewpoint, history is clear, even logical, resolving itself into a succession of events: from the second, it is chaotic, dense, traversed by inextricable movements. Even in the absence of consciousness, it plays out its course none the less: but in the confusion of its energies, it runs the risk of stifling the germ it carries. *Man is carried in the belly of chaos:* and consciousness, when it attempts to regulate this chaos from outside, only adds to its confusion, creating partial mechanisms which exert pressure on the unknown mass, drive it back within arbitrary limits, and make it all the more redoubtable. It is from the inside, by assimilating the organic thrust, and by balancing in a form the innumerable pressure of energies, that consciousness models simultaneously both man and the indissoluble universe of man. The more profound becomes this biological consciousness, equally present and identical in its action from the carnal materiality to the heights of the spirit, the greater will grow the chances of prevision for ordinary knowledge: hazard is merely a hiatus in consciousness, called to order by the great whole.

It is true that mechanical thinking (in both the arts and sciences) has reached a point where only an aspect is grasped, and the sense of totality has been lost, or lingers on only in dreams. We are, to-day, more helpless than in the first days of consciousness: but we have acquired the power to recognise what we lack, which is a first step towards a new and lucid integration. What we must now do is to take an inventory of chaos, at first by empirical methods, but which, being affirmed or eliminated by experience, will give way gradually to rules of thought.

Within this perspective I see *Sueur de Sang* as a maieutic of symbols. From the moment I started reading it, I had the impression of being plunged into matter—matter in which mind, flesh, and elements are one. This was no arbitrary return to the original chaos which intelligence believes it has left behind, but that chaos itself, as it persists in the heart of the human universe. And this chaos is uninhabitable, the most blunted consciousness finds it suffocating: but *it exists*. Without its permanent threat, consciousness would lose its purpose—to struggle and grow unceasingly at the expense of that which denies it. There is no leaning, in Jouve, towards the unconscious as such: consciousness 'influenced as much as possible by the unconscious' is primarily, and in very deliberate fashion, a descent *towards*, and then an ascent *from*; no matter how far it ventures, it always hugs to its centre.

This determination to uphold consciousness at all costs, however alluring the marvels of the unconscious may be, is shown in the shaping of the language, in its almost clogging cohesion—each image must be read as an inseparable part of the whole. Unlike the improbable bric-a-brac which only lately was hailed (and still is by some people) as the last word in aesthetics, Jouve's chaos is not a continuity of heteroclite objects, but a node of living forces, terribly dense and compressed, and which are only made more compact by their reciprocal hostility, each binding them all faster in its attempts to break free. I admired from the start the way in which Jouve was able to render the monstrous life of chaos. This life, vegetable, visceral, of a vast and confused plasticity, oozing light, devouring and digesting itself with ferocious leisureliness, made me think of the first, unmeasured ages of the earth. At the same time, it impressed itself upon me as a daily reality: I had some acquaintance with the back alleys of Lyons, with all that was damp, and slimy, and filthy, with the swarming of unmentionable desires. The symbols of this poetry exactly fitted my experience. I transposed the sordid reality, and concentrated it in the powerful images revealed by *Sueur de Sang*.

It is neither the range nor the volume of evil that teach us its true nature, but the sudden sensation of its density, its specific weight in the universe. *Sueur de Sang* justified its title, for in it

III

evil was suffered in its essence, and the world was the Golgotha of the spirit. While reading it, I remembered a passage from the *Mystère de Jésus*, which declares that 'Jesus suffers the pangs of death until the end of the world: one must not sleep during that time'. There is nothing blasphemous in this parallel, for does not the believer share in the suffering of Christ? *Turbare semet ipsum.* The man of truth, when he perceives the deep-rooted evil in man, receives grace and power. He is able to take over, in such measure as his spiritual and physical strength allows, the burden of the infernal world. He torments himself, and bleeds in 'his chains and physical servitude', to be freed from his spiritual servitude, from the evil which holds enslaved both his own and all other spirits. One cannot free oneself from evil except through the positive knowledge of evil. I had made no great progress in the life of the mind, but I knew from experience that evil recognised as such presents the mind with the question of its nature. From this, one cannot escape: one must either save oneself or damn oneself consciously.

I knew as well that there is another negative sort of knowledge, which plunges man into chaos to distract him from this choice. I admit that I had read Pascal as one analyses oneself. Yet I had never been able to believe that anarchy of the instincts was synonymous with freedom, and still less that its end was the superman. In the present crisis of values, some people pride themselves on following their contradictory tendencies to the bitter end. Such shameless spectators do not live, they watch themselves existing according to their instincts: they feel a vain pride in the apparent frenzy of the instincts, in the possibilities they discover, which others before them have drained to the dregs: there is a bitter disillusionment which comes sooner or later to punish this impotence towards life. There are misguided spiritual natures who make an ascetic rule of the completely dissolute life, as though man could both raise himself and destroy himself: as if one could reach the All by the deliberate disintegration of everything. Man is neither angel nor beast, and if many play the beast while wishing to play the angel, no one has ever played the angel while trying to play the beast.

Sueur de Sang was at the opposite pole from a delight in evil: first of all, because in it a personal consciousness suffered for others, bending its will to rise to the surface, and secondly, because the struggle to coordinate its movements, within the materiality pressing all round it, was waged with a spiritual knowledge both of the soul and of the abyss. The idea of salvation was constantly present, the book became less sombre from page to page, and the final *Pièta* heralded a resurrection. When evil peered through, it was in all its terrible ugliness, which the symbols unmasked instead of camouflaging: hence the reproach of bad taste levelled at it at that time by aesthetes incapable of conceiving the dynamism of beauty.

For this ugliness revealed a certain beauty, because man stood at the centre, and fought the dragon naked. Monsters are never beautiful except by contrast, and it is the function of art to concentrate their ugliness by the forceful abbreviation of symbols. Spiritual beauty is only complete when horror lies tamed at its feet. As for myself, being tired of the beautiful as I found it in Valéry or in Gide, which was a matter of constantly repeated artifice, I discovered that the word brings things to life, and that it may even sanctify whoever utters it: art, being a higher form of human consciousness, compels the artist to play out his own destiny in forms, colours or words. Each image is a gesture of the mind, ordained by a fixed end: a poem is a moral act.

The energy of *Sueur de Sang* inspired me, and multiplied tenfold the obscure forces of the world around me: through this book, I began to measure the real conflicts of the human universe. And as Jouve, in all consciousness, wrote his poetry within a great Christian tradition, the axis of which is the Cross of the Saviour, I recognised in it, transposed, one of the things I had meditated on most deeply. For, from the first, I had been gripped by the mystery of the Redemption. The mystery, in this case, was wholly in man: salvation was achieved through the sweat of human blood, by an exaltation, a sacrifice, an oblation of man to man. Admittedly, Christ remained at the centre, but only as an image: an absolute myth, but not a redeeming presence. Nevertheless, the transcendent sky opened into infinity over the world. Already the poet sensed, without being able yet to voice it in song, the painful contradiction, the marvellous reconciliation, which he was to sum up fifteen years later in these two lines:

> L'art qui parle de Dieu ne gémit que de l'homme
> Et l'art qui nomme l'homme ne languit que de Dieu.
> [Art which speaks of God cries only for man's fate
> And art which calls to man yearns only for his God.]

Already the dying Hart, Christ dying 'over all the country of my faults' called me to rediscover, by the paths of art, the trace of the lost God, whose gaze seemed to have been extinguished when I saw that all I cherished in it was my own image.

*　　　*　　　*

An influence can only be truly measured when it has been integrated and transcended. I do not claim to have judged at first glance a work of such vast perspectives. Even less was I capable of projecting my own design. Sueur de Sang was both obscure and necessary to me: I did not explain the text to myself, I lived it. Certain words stood out, as if charged with vigour: they seemed to determine all the others, and create the region in which the poem was built up. This region was dense, almost tangible, always active, moulded by moving forms. For the words were indeed material, and retained the weight, shape, odour, attributes of the thing named: at the same time, they signified desires, gestures, inner movements, which they voiced with a strange realism. The same word was thus indisputably the thing, and at times so concrete in the realm of the obscene or ugly that people *of good taste* were scandalised; but also the spiritual substance in the first degree of consciousness, grasped in its most confused workings, in its initial struggle to break free from the chaos of the unconscious.

It is easy to produce art, or at least a work which bears all the appearances of art, while leaving in shadow those energies of the soul which are most distressing and least admitted, yet which total art cannot ignore. Jouve made these energies his starting-point: the conversion of man to himself, the beginning and end of his art, would have been vitiated from the start, had he not taken as his poetic material this unstable and restless mixture of matter and spirit which constitutes the clay of being. The more terrible was the brutal nudity of the words, the stronger was the symbolic virtue of the universe of *Sueur de Sang*. Its sexuality was neither disguised nor indulged: it was not veiled in an air of complicity, but neither was it exhibited. It appeared in its own form, its ineluctable reality. Taken in its proper sense, no word struck Jouve as impermissible. He might have thought otherwise, had he judged the beautiful from the outside, by the texture and sound of the words: but the beautiful, in his mind, was clearly the expression of a certain knowledge; it would have been to destroy its essence to conceal what ought to be said.

But although the sexual aspect was important, it never became an obsession. If, in *Sueur de Sang*, it reappeared on almost every page, it was, after all, the primitive form of the anguish of man faced with himself, and as such the first which demanded elucidation. The eroticism of Jouve (as the preface clearly stated) could not be taken in any narrow sense: to seek in these images the diffused expression of sexuality alone, would have been a grave mistake. Now that this early book may be judged in relation to Jouve's work as a whole, it is easy to see that the *great Eros* whose divine action it sings, is universal creative energy, which consciousness has the role of integrating in extent and depth.

In the poems which came later, *Matière Céleste, Kyrie, Porche à la Nuit des Saints, Hymne,* the sexual themes were to be reduced and given their place in the ascent of the whole: without ceasing to be fundamental, they would henceforth be recalled only among others, for which the time had come to dominate the work.

These later themes had already begun in the sensual heat of the symbols—or rather, they were as if buried there, only able to break free by thrusting upwards the heavier matter. For the work of consciousness resembles that of an alembic: the spiritual quintessence is the last to be distilled, and the most subtle desire is only fulfilled when all the others have been subdued.

In *Les Noces,* which I read a little later, nothing seems yet to foreshadow this slow distillation of the world. The most diverse themes remain implicit in it, bathed in an equal light: these are poems full of space, in which mind and matter, mingled in the same innocence, remain free within their respective impulses. The poem which was to mean most to me was *Symphonie à Dieu,* which unfolded before me the epic of the earth before man. Mind has not yet become incarnate, a blank light reigns, and the delight which has no name: but the harmony is almost too infallible, its perfection is related to nothing, not even to itself—this is the unbearable beauty of a music at times so near to Mozart. But what a bursting of bonds there is at the end, what a rush to shatter the inhuman immanence, when in the last pages there arises the *True Body*, 'man of nerves and sufferings and seed', contradiction incarnate who comes to break the perfect cycle, and divide energy against itself: who comes to pursue and bring to light the unconscious secrets of life, to transform these secrets into creative purposes, and by degrees to raise life itself to absolute consciousness—as if God had chosen man to be Interpreter of his eternal work.

And in fact, when man appears, the scene changes: the drama leaps to its climax, and chaos steps in upon harmony. Energy from all its aspects reveals a cannibal ferocity: from mineral to plant, from plant to animal, and from animal to the obscure part of man, a cosmic coalition is formed against the undefined threat which consciousness introduces into the universe. Nature, that praying mantis, devours the spirit, her spouse: and if it escapes her, she devours herself. This is the first act, sombre and bloody, of the drama in which consciousness must triumph. The sign of contradiction has had its effect, for all things are ranged against each other. But when the extremity of division has been reached, and nothing can carry the worldwide civil war any further, the spirit arrives at the indivisible essence, and finds the common centre of its being and its universe: henceforward, all negation must merely be a repetition of some earlier negation. The struggle is now circumscribed, for the spirit has measured the resistance that energy can offer: and whatever further setbacks consciousness may still have to face, they will never be more than local ones. Conscious progress towards unity is the only path for expansion that universal force finds open. But this progress is strained as it nears its end. If consciousness relaxes for an instant, an abrupt regression throws into jeopardy the whole distance already covered.

Sueur de Sang is the first act of the drama, a jungle of forms with man alone at the centre. The light never penetrates through into it fully: but in it a thousand carnivorous presences prowl, and a thousand stifling tragedies are enacted. At times, as though to challenge fate, a marvellous bird flits briefly through the unknown, which only makes the dense mass thicker. Nevertheless, man with painful slowness makes a path for himself through the monstrous dream of chaos. That this chaos is in himself, every alert reader well knows. There is nothing gratuitous or merely descriptive in the images: an implacable severity is discernible even in their fascinating exuberance. The real being the analogue of the soul, the coherence and dynamism of things (or of the words used in their stead) reproduce the structure and rhythm of inner events:

a powerful imagination, serving as medium for the sensibility, projects into a drama of forms what psychological analysis is incapable of seeing. We invent nothing which is not in ourselves: in our personal ego, or in the specific self whence arise our most secret impulses.

From the frequency of certain symbolic images, the poet is able to deduce his personal constellation: the key-words, the guiding forces of his spiritual world. It is the same with the reader who, instinctively, chooses certain poets as his own. Behind all the palpable reasons for preferring them, what he finds in their verse is his own psychic substance. This prevails over all their art, down to its particular qualities. There is no nuance of style which is not a function of the inner inspiration. When the reader feels that one image is more active than others, it is because it expresses himself better than others: and he will single it out, even though he may appreciate the rest from an objective sense of the beautiful. In the universe of his poets, it is his own mental world that he defines. He recreates, according to his own energy, the forms offered to him. And when he puts himself entirely into a poem, when the symbolic relationships out of which it is woven seem to him absolute, what moves him is something more than its beauty—it is his own basic presence, which the subtlest examination of his soul would never be able fully to reveal.

What makes a work lasting is its faculty for integrating the greatest number of individual natures, without ever being exhausted by them. I do not think there is any need to reiterate that universal assent in an epoch is by no means a guarantee of its duration. On the contrary, true universality, the permanence of the complete man, has as its supports those same individual beings who may live far beyond their own epoch, for the simple reason that they return to the sources of energy. There is one type of beauty which is merely an accident of fashion, and thereby made attractive and celebrated: but the beauty whose essence is the true one appears only to minds imbued with truth. It plots out a region of the future, a harmonious field of play for energy. It is psychic knowledge, a theory of the soul if one likes. Precise in its general aspects, plastic in the detail of the symbols, it establishes a frame for meditation, a range to the impulse of the spirit, without hampering or diverting the impulse itself. Such was, and still is, for me the work of Jouve. Those who take the trouble to study my own work thoroughly will discover that the physical influence has been changed into an elective affinity, and that our paths and our methods are no longer the same, if indeed they ever were the same. Nevertheless, I cannot imagine what my work would have been without Jouve. Without him, should I even have chosen to express myself in poetry?

Sueur de Sang held for me just such an attraction as the virgin forest would for a child. Having lived in an enclosed world, I had great, repressed surges of imagination: and together beneath the flagstone of family Duty, we lived in company with the wood-lice. I say wood-lice and they are quite enough—not everyone can afford monsters! Yet I had a sneaking suspicion that the monsters were crouched in the tacit silence around us. Conan Doyle describes a strange region in the heart of South America, where still frolic armour-plated dragons of the tertiary period. And does not each one of us suspect similar survivals in himself? While they live on in us, it is a very perilous preventive measure to try and ignore their existence: my education had given me proof of this. Rather than be devoured from within, I preferred to exorcise these monsters by a frontal challenge. As I lacked inner experience, the symbolism of *Sueur de Sang* was of great help to me. Behind the aggressiveness of the images, a fundamental wickedness was astir, more concentrated, but the same by nature as that of the conventions and rites with which my social sphere bristled. The fear of living was unmasked, and I followed the work from the roots. And I saw that these roots plunged deeper in myself than I would have dreamed. But Jouve with his vigorous metamorphoses offered me a grasp on the elemental: several layers of existence were disclosed to me, as well as the means to attune myself to each, and to gauge my different rhythms, social, specific, cosmic, and finally, personal.

I acquired a taste for thinking in images, regarding them no longer as static, but as endowed with energy: my aversions, my revolts, my need of freedom served as a salutary motive power. I began to apprehend instinct and sensibility like movements of matter, and to give a plastic form to my inner conflicts. The abstract universe had existed, without my abandoning my faith in rational unity. But symbolic thought was opened up to me, moving and complex as nature, and demonstrating the same laws of evolution. I began to look on everyday spectacles as signs: the symbol was implied in the real.

This sympathy through which I found the inner world also brought me particularly near to the earth. I come from a fertile district, where the life of the soil is strong, and one can literally feel the grass growing under one's feet. Everywhere there is the secret chemistry of the rich earth, the plants drawing nourishment slowly through their roots, the organic upthrusts of life. I could not but be impressed by Jouve's art of depicting landscape. For the landscape continues to breathe through symbols, and its energy to flourish: and in it, with what seems to me a unique boldness, the poet blends together the opposing forces of matter, flesh and spirit. A landscape becomes a moral situation, arrested in movement. And as the imagery of *Sueur de Sang* is strongly sexual (heavy, stifling with odours, painful and sometimes exquisite) there emerges from it a wild sensuality which strengthens the atmosphere of the drama, for nothing in the symbol is mere decoration. I was more aware of this than anyone at that moment in my life. Love had woken my sense of metamorphosis: *Sueur de Sang* directed it towards secret and altogether more concrete ends than a purely descriptive lyricism.

If I was already familiar with the femininity of nature, still, up till then, I had seen in it merely an element of charm, a play of forms with which the artist amused himself at will. This was the impression I received from *La Jeune Parque*: a conventional eroticism, not very far removed from the pastoral scenes painted on trumeaux. But for that matter, my own upbringing had been the worst possible—teaching that love is an ideal abstraction, and regarding sex as taboo. Here, however, sexuality assumed the aspect of a sacred driving force: in the vast vision of an evolution that love raises by degrees to the spheres, the anguish inspired by sex is at the threshold of an infinite perspective.

With desire is born the fear of the abyss. The first operation of life, and without which there would be no life, seems fettered by formidable prohibitions. It is as if, from the outset, consciousness had to surmount its almost irreducible opposition to life. Hence arises the feeling of guilt that consciousness must drag along with it. For the person cowed by fear, all that aspires to life in him is guilty: for the person filled with life, all that is fearful in him is guilty. But this ambiguity is only apparent: it disappears as soon as the mind accepts the risk of knowledge. For the duality of consciousness and life, however strong it may seem, is not an article of the essential: it is, on the contrary, the condition of a superior identity, that of consciousness and Being—God must be won by a hard struggle, or rather the image of Him that humanity bears within itself. It is clear that fear before life is guilty: but risk is attended by fear. The higher consciousness is raised, the graver grows the possible fall. As the controls of the mind become more sensitive, the least error threatens to be fatal: knowledge is menaced by its own perfection. And so it happens that periodically a mass of fear is accumulated, the pressure of which threatens to drag knowledge down into chaos. We have an example of this to-day: fear is widespread throughout the world, and gives rise to the worst excesses. Panic is its loophole: war frees one from the fear of war, a flight into sex from the fear it inspires. We 'know everything in an atmosphere of storm', declares the *Récitative* in *Matière Céleste*. And when the storm breaks in ourselves, two

121

reflexes are merged into one—that of the ostrich who hides his head in the sand, and that of Simple Simon who jumps in the water from fear of the rain. The 'repressed' and the 'emancipated' suffer from one and the same disease: their vital force is thrown out of balance by the terror that consciousness has of itself.

In my family circle, the distress caused by sex was so great that no euphemism could conceal it enough: outside the family, however, sex was exhibited with morbid aggressiveness—although less so than to-day. Neither one of these two forms of terror could survive without the other: they acted on each other as irritants, and no one was more likely to surrender to the second than the person who had been cowed by the first. At nineteen, the age when storms first brew up, I was rent by these twin terrors: both localised sex until it became an obsession, and both severed it from the impulse towards universal order. Jouve, at one stroke, returned it to its place in that order. He shed light on the anguish of sex, showing in it the primitive vertigo of man faced with life, explained by what mechanisms it is determined, and the methods of breaking them. He made sex blossom out, grow various, transcend itself, so that it was no longer more than a stage to be passed (although of primary importance) on the path to unity. I was cleansed of my false modesty and of my lascivious fantasies. In *Sueur de Sang*, in *La Scène Capitale*, I recognised the tragic violence of a struggle in which the energy of the race is played out. To silence sex is to silence life: to surrender to it is to annihilate consciousness. In the first instance, consciousness, obstructed, germinates no longer, but is petrified by moral rites. In the second, its unifying function is denied, it turns in upon itself, and becomes a seething chaos: it exhausts itself inventing new experiences, and always falls back on to beaten paths. The spirit refuses to be incarnated in either, and to accept a destiny which commits it.

Sueur de Sang is a book which offers no loophole or retreat. It is part of the poet's destiny: and it compels the reader in his turn to enter the struggle. This integrating movement of certain forces in an upward leap which transcends their natural projection, this transition to a higher plane of existence which the psychoanalysts call sublimation (but which is no more, after all, than a piece of metamorphosis, such as the mind is able to produce at every instant), is achieved by starting out from sexual energy, seized in the efflorescence of its possibilities, and concentrated by a moral will. The sexual force is certainly dangerous, even explosive, and like a volcano of images, Pierre Jean Jouve provokes its eruption. But if he shows it everywhere as voracious, it is in order to know it better, and not to be seduced by it: to know is to measure, and to measure is to overcome. An unceasing vigilance is exercised throughout the book: it shows the moment of weakness, and how the mind regains control at the very instant of surrender. We are people of the abyss, 'of the abyss over which we sleep': the drama does not come to a head on the surface, but in the vegetative depths of the self.

This is why true morality scorns morality, and symbolic reason ordinary reason. The essential is to be lucid, and to grasp energy in its primitive images, in the stones and lava of the volcano: to make it evolve from symbol to symbol, by degrees or with abrupt breaks, according to the laws of a mental transformism. If we knew better these laws of symbolic filiation, they would doubtless show us elementary forms of a Protean nature, giving birth to symbolic species in an ever more complex hierarchy. Energy, through its double impulse, is first dispersed, then concentrated: it blossoms forth luxuriantly, filling space to saturation-point with such a dense press of forms that they begin to devour each other. But the movement of expansion is followed by the organic impulse: once the differential limit has been reached the drive towards unity emerges to save the mind from repetition.

What Jouve calls *the erotic self* is the perpetual and uncontrolled genesis of symbols: the nearer they are to the origin, the more sex prevails in them. A consciousness which applied itself solely to collecting symbols would end by going mad, or by imitating madness, which comes to the same thing: it would repeat itself in the void—as the sexual obsession clearly shows. But when consciousness, rejecting its pretended objectivity, becomes passion and will, when it selects, reduces, and disciplines its symbols, its own structural effort liberates it. Having a foothold on the common basis of mankind, it senses the biology of history, the knowledge of which may perhaps deliver man from time. By extrapolating the curve it traces, it conceives, beyond its relative transcendence, the existence of a transcendent absolute. Art, at the summit of consciousness, becomes morality and religion.

What else had I been seeking for so long? What had I hoped for earlier, when discussing with the Abbé Larue the question of truth? I could not imagine living without reason: my existence could be nothing else but a synthesising activity of the mind, which would give to my particular themes their universal orchestration. And now, chance had beckoned to me in the least ambiguous fashion: in this architectural book, in its concerted equilibrium of appearances, I had at a glance sensed a will towards essential harmony, a total demand for truth. This demand was inscribed in the visible form at the same time, and by the same creative movement, as in the invisible form—in being. Of course, had the symbols not been so immediately obvious so that they impressed themselves on me almost physically, and had I grasped them only by their exterior qualities, their plastic values, the geometry of their relationships, I should perhaps have admired them, but I would neither have experienced them in their substance nor mingled them with my universe. As it was, this book that I had approached *through reason*, and to give myself a chance of discovering poetic truth, carried me far from my earlier systems, from my abstract notions of beauty.

I was invaded by images, my whole being was trampled by them. I was both fascinated and submerged. I found my footing again in the elemental, and coordinated myself in this new world in which my old coordinates no longer made sense. I was converted, or in other words, underwent an internal transformation: at last I knew how to hail beauty, for these symbols were incarnate, made of my flesh, of my blood, of my tears. My enthusiasm was fired by each new work Jouve produced: and even now, I cannot read a page of his without a thrill of delight. The truth I had looked for outside myself, as a datum to be recognised by certain signs, was now within me, implicit but entire: it was *the language of being*, a language all the more universal for being highly singular. I had not yet acquired the gift of tongues: but, unsure as I was about myself, I nevertheless felt that I was born for this truth that poetry carries within it. Even were I to remain dumb, I should not be less of a poet: a man who takes each word in its plenitude, who puts his life into his words, and his words into his life.

CHAPTER SIX

WITHOUT design on my part, my meeting with Jouve takes its place as the keystone of this book. To reveal its significance more fully, I have considered it in the eternal, without interposing external episodes nor dealing with it in the fabric of everyday. All that I have said up to now, however, would be incomplete if I did not place this meeting in its context at a crucial point in my life. I read Jouve during those same holidays on which the fate of my love was to be decided. It was thus during a time of trial and distress, when my imagination, in order to combat the effect of absence, invested my memories with a heightened glow. The more the real world eluded me, the more I nourished myself with images. The poetry of *Sueur de Sang*, peopled with feminine symbols, became the vehicle for my dreams, so powerfully, so tragically did it celebrate in woman that *other world*, forbidden but necessary, home of the lost unity, garden of the unity to be.

In spite of de Vigny's line which I repeated to myself at that epoch :

Les deux sexes mourront chacun de leur côté
[*The two sexes will die alone and separate*]

I had built my life of the feelings upon a perhaps subtle distinction between desire and love: the former inclined to the unconscious, aspiring to lose itself in a torrential and nameless life, the latter wholly animated by consciousness, uniting two separate beings without violence to their particular natures—prefiguring that total Body in which each will be all, at once eternally himself and the Whole. Desire, in the way that I saw it, implicitly denied

126

the primitive separation, the wound on which consciousness was grafted. Love, however, based its very existence on this wound, and proclaimed it a blessing, for the distance keeping man and woman separate is the world, and to love is to know together, to prefigure the final unity and accomplish it in one of its innumerable modes, to pair two particular fates in a double and higher particular fate.

Voici que je m'entends vers vous tout seul un autre qui commence
A chanter avec la voix plurielle comme le violon que l'archet prend sur la double corde

[*Now I stretch towards you in single comprehension another who begins*
To sing with the plural voice of the violin that the bow strikes on two strings]

says Claudel in the *Magnificat*. That is certainly what love is: it contains desire, not as a blind instinct, but as a force which it directs to its end. My education, by making love disincarnate, or in other words by condemning desire, rendered desire dangerously autonomous. The order of feeling was thus severed from the order of instinct—I have already shown with what consequences.

Had my experience been different, my reading of *Sueur de Sang* would only have helped to integrate desire more fully in the bosom of love. But I had barely started on the book when there arose the rupture of which I have spoken. On this love I had staked my whole being: it had delivered me from bondage, and created me anew in a new world. When all the forces of the soul are concentrated upon one object, and when the existence of the latter conditions one's own existence, if that object should suddenly disappear, one's own life is robbed of meaning. Many people have been in love and broken it off, without the balance of their sensibility being endangered by the break: love, if it had complemented them, had not fundamentally recreated them, and wounded, they gather themselves together, finding themselves

127

again, hurt but still alive. But I without transition had passed from nothingness into being. Lacking experience both of myself and of life, I had launched myself into love in order to find a reason and a centre—which was an initial transgression against the real, an initial corruption of feeling even before its birth. Scarcely had I fallen in love, as I had wanted to be, than the object became something out of reach, and my love a myth of the soul. I lived full of the exaltation of the impossible, like a mystic finding the bitterest ecstasies in being separated from his God. My whole mind, never having been so regaled before, was in a state of tension: I was in love with love. Then, suddenly, the impossible became possible, imminent: but my hyperborean dream could no longer grasp it—or perhaps time had played me one of its tricks, by exiling me from the woman at the very moment when she would have given herself. I thought Paradise had opened, but I continued to stray through dreams, instead of seizing upon the real. When the whole thing was finished, I was like the mystic I have mentioned, but with all his faith gone: he wakes and laughs at himself, at that being he thought he was which disintegrates within him.

It was at this moment that I found Jouve salutary. In a few months, all the hidden springs within me had burst forth: and now I was ravaged by their overflow, and once more shut in upon myself, in an excess of vain forces that love had canalised before. Through *Sueur de Sang* I regained my footing in this disorder. I had constructed my love like a myth, and only a myth could save me from the corpse of my love. Admittedly, I now realise that such a therapeutic method only made worse my failure before the concrete. It is all too clear that I was fleeing from an actual situation, before having proved to myself that it was really untenable. I could not bear being alone. My throbbing sensibility had at all costs to find for itself a way out into the open. But it was not the sort of life I was then leading (and of which I will speak later) which could open up such a path. I had fallen into a circle even more mediocre if possible than that of my family. Wholly absorbed in my love, I had created no other atmosphere for myself, and I found myself now more isolated than ever. Was it cowardice on my part to plunge back into dreams? Or rather, had I still not discovered that the living world existed? I had no foothold anywhere: I had been given no preparation for life. I had rejected the conventions that would have allowed me to survive in a ready-made world, but I remained a prisoner of such a world. I had liberated myself only in my mind: I did not know where to discover reality, and waited until it should come to me. But reality is not external to us: it takes shape with us. And it may be that I was not sufficiently formed for the real to reveal itself to me. Or it may have been my inveterate habit of dreaming of some far-away beyond (vice of the child, and later of the lonely adolescent) that blinded me to the simple and necessary everyday. More than ever, I took the tragic view of my unhappiness. In the images of *Sueur de Sang* I found the echo of my own love, and the universal drama of love: I slipped from one into the other, and magnified out of all proportion my own adventure.

But it would be wrong to think I related my fantasies only to myself: as soon as I had lost all tangible hope, I effaced myself behind the symbols. To do otherwise would have been madness: but fortunately (or unfortunately, whichever way one looks at it) my mind has never ceased to control me. In reality, taking my unhappiness as a theme with numerous and lofty harmonics, I used it as a means to fresh knowledge. I both encouraged it and retreated from it, as it happens in certain dreams, when a person splits into two and carries on a strange debate with himself: until a point was reached when my unhappiness was merely one particular disposition of my mental being, which allowed me to grasp, at a much higher level than my own banal affair, one of the major forms of fatality.

It is said to be the fault of poetic natures always to escape from their coordinates: the immediate present does not exist for poets, since they lack will in the practice of the real. But if this vice (congenital or acquired) leads them into hyperboles of feeling, it also has another side to it—an acute sense of permanence. Being more singular, they are more absolute: condemned to take more safeguards than other men, they carry each situation to an extreme where, stripped of individual attributes, it links up again with the fate—or the dream—of humanity. Nevertheless, many poets remain suspended half-way between themselves and humanity: their personal ego and their universal *Self* contradict one another; and they fail to emerge from that state of adolescence in which their own, hypertrophied sensibility imagines itself the echo of all sensibility. Some reject the real, and translate in their poetry the vague nostalgia of their being: others, held in thrall by the concrete, assume it to be poetic material, and vainly inflate the immediate to the scale of the eternal present. These two opposed misinterpretations each find approval with an essentially apoetic public. The partisans of the first judge by what is agreeable, the partisans of the second, by what is useful. The former think that poetry should distract one from the real, the latter, that it should increase the hold of social conscience. The former exile themselves from outward form, the others exile themselves within it.

I was to learn, on the contrary, that poetic reflection only departs from the given in order to establish it more firmly. Once the general symbols have been attained, it makes a return to the visible forms, which it deciphers and justifies—since man *hic et nunc*, whose actual language is outward appearance, cannot understand himself except in terms of his total perspective, which coordinates his various behaviours. This explains why a great unhappiness, by the very disorder it brings with it, calls for a conversion of the spirit. When the latter plunges itself in tragedy, it may easily for a time disguise itself in its upheavals, and complacently imagine itself an exception, dreaming that its unhappiness is divine. But this flight into the sublime cannot last for long: the more we play-act our personality, the more we see its emptiness. If I maintained for a time a romantic attitude, it was because I lacked experience of ways of thought: but it was not long before I understood that behind my own unhappiness there was an absolute thing, *Unhappiness*, and that my distress would vanish, was vanishing already, but that knowledge was taking its place.

I had set out with the highly erroneous idea that spirit and flesh are separate, that the work of the flesh is wholly animal, while the gift of loving is entirely spiritual. In my relations with my beloved, this misunderstanding had only been aggravated: it was the cause of my failure. My early readings of Jouve's work confirmed me in my error. I read him in a state of crisis. As this woman was now forbidden to me, I transformed her into *Woman*, and adorned her with heavy sexual symbols. Both frightened and fascinated by the cosmic form of sex, I watched the gulf widen between feeling and the senses. My mind split more and more in two, its sensual prevailing over its moral aspect, even while remaining under the interdict. The more I probed at this contradiction, the greater it became in extent: the sexual symbols gave way to other symbols, and out of my now effaced personal drama arose *the* drama of man—that of the incarnate spirit.

This contradiction, however, has certainly not disappeared in its primitive form: the feeling, or the need, for spiritual union, repress desire which, if it hankers after satisfaction, must dispel, or prevent from forming, the *aura* of the heart. But however painful may be my state of isolation, whether I am outside that which I love or at the very centre of fulfilled desire, I remain convinced that my personal anguish cannot be resolved without the essential contradiction being resolved beforehand. I have taken the spirit of division to such an extreme that my thirst for unity seems as old as man: and before I can be reunited with myself, the eternal Adam must have found his salvation in me. When in spirit and in truth I know how to recognise man, his destiny, his terrestrial and transcendent end, and the working of the absolute within him, I shall in addition be reconciled with myself: I shall no longer have to despair 'of having performed the labour of incarnation'.

*   *   *

In the midst of the torments caused by my melancholy return from the holidays, I was to some extent distracted by a fresh situation, and one which, incidentally, I rapidly came to find hateful. To lighten the burden on my father, it was decided that, while continuing with my studies, I should take a teaching job. I do not think my father had much to do with this decision. But my uncle who, for two pins, when I abandoned the royal road of the Polytechnic, would have accused me of betraying my father and mother, had had his dreams so rudely shattered that from that time on he regarded me as barely above the mediocre. He was, moreover, permanently scandalised by all the leisure time I had on my hands. He strongly urged me, with a wealth of moral pretexts, to begin as quickly as possible earning my own living.

I was not put out by this notion, as I anticipated from it a freedom that, at nineteen, I had still not tasted. Thus I returned to the college where I had already spent six years of my life. The Director received me with just those marks of condescension that his kind know how to show to poor ex-pupils, when the latter come to them with some request. As it happened, there was a constant shortage of teachers at the Brothers' schools, and we soon came to an arrangement. I was to teach in the third class, and my subjects would be French, history, and geography, which I loathed. I should also have to take my turn as duty master, in the dormitory, in recreation, and on outings. For all of which I was to receive three thousand francs a year, spread over ten paydays, less the eighty-five francs a month that the cashier deducted for my board and lodging. Two hundred and fifteen francs a month clear—to me it was untold riches! Up to then I had never had more than twenty-five francs a month in my pocket. I would have a room all to myself, my own secrets, a small universe the key to which I held in my hand like a talisman for my new life.

But I had counted without the Brothers. I had been a pupil of nearly all of them: a good pupil, showing myself full of respect, even as I eluded their grasp. Having become their colleague, their next-door neighbour, their companion at table, I saw their lives from the wings: and although I had imagined it to be mediocre, it was far worse than anything I had dreamt of. Planted in their midst, I was to undergo my apprenticeship in abjection. Seeing me as an intruder, clearly not to be assimilated, they were torn between suspicion and curiosity. I was constantly being spied upon, by eyes that were nearly always full of ill-will. Whichever way I turned, I awakened morbid susceptibilities, for these wretched shrunken souls, so accustomed to hating one another, detected evil intentions in everything. To talk with them as man to man was like trying to walk a tightrope. And how was I to find some focus of interest that would hold them? All they had between them were petty rivalries, hypocritical persecutions, quarrels that had gone sour twenty years ago.

The Brothers despised the laics, poor devils, most of them over fifty. The latter returned their scorn, with a hint of envy: and in addition were jealous of each other. Some made a little extra by driving themselves to death with teaching: others, doomed to take the youngest classes, and stuck fast in unshakable indolence, grew old with only the poorhouse to look forward to. Whether they were of the first type or the second, nothing gave them keener pleasure than the trials of a colleague whose class had got out of hand. This consoled some for their own weakness, which by contrast acquired almost an air of authority: while others, the strong ones, who knew how to hand out canings and impositions, became all the more proud of their firm teaching methods. Nearly all of them looked on the pupil as a sort of wild animal, who must be tamed and brought to order. I thought otherwise, said so, and made it plain to all. This aroused their anger, all the more so since I succeeded without too much difficulty in a job which each of them had painted in the blackest colours.

I was liked by my pupils—which in itself was an unpardonable crime in the eyes of the masters, who suspected me of heaven knows what underhand intrigues. Yet nothing could have been simpler: I was young, I recalled my own school days, and how and why my teachers had disappointed me. I believed that each of these youngsters had his own personal need, and perhaps his own ideal of perfection: so I tried, no doubt in naïve fashion, to discover and develop it. I abandoned the routine methods of teaching, and ventured on various experiments, some of which succeeded. I managed to create a fine confusion, entirely incompatible with method. My own audacity got me into trouble: things came to a head, and I was given a dressing down by 'His Paternity' the Director, who at the same time took me in fatherly fashion to his bosom. He seized on the occasion to remark on my irregular attendance at divine service and to enquire into my moral well-being in terms which made me curl up like a hedgehog, bristling all over. I felt that I was a marked man: my colleagues' system of spying had now spread to my outside life. They knew all about me, in terms of grossest caricature. I was their prisoner now, as I had been my uncle's. It was only the prison that had changed.

My room was very tiny, but well lit. Its glass-panelled door opened upon the axis of a long corridor where the masters' rooms were situated. We had to keep our rooms clean ourselves; but in fact, many of my colleagues lived in a stench of old pipes and pure filth. There were two washbasins in the corridor for our morning ablutions: these had to do for twenty of us—and no one lingered long over the job. The Brothers washed at four o'clock, with loud commotion, before going to their devotions. They were back again in an hour, dragging their feet, coughing, spitting, talking in loud voices or moving the furniture about. The walls were so thin that every sound came through: my right-hand neighbour mumbled through his prayers, the left-hand one talked to himself without a break. There was a continual coming and going, a banging of doors, a crashing on the stairs, proofs of an amazing activity. Early to bed and early to rise, the Brothers carried on an undeclared war against those trying to sleep in the morning. After several furious attempts I was forced to abandon my slumbers. At eight o'clock in the evening the college gates were closed, and all the masters were expected to be in. If they wanted to stay late in the town, they had to take a servant into their confidence like youthful truants, or bribe the concierge, a fearful one-eyed creature with a cretinous husband. At nine-thirty, there was a compulsory lights-out. The teacher of the tenth class, who took the infants in sing-song fashion through the alphabet, also did night-duty. He would prowl around the corridors in slippers, and if he saw a gleam of light, called upon the offender to put it out at once.

For me, the night hours were the most tranquil and fruitful, and I took great pains to camouflage my infringements of the rule. I had stretched black paper over the frosted glass of the door, and stuffed rolls of paper into the cracks. But all in vain. The night-duty teacher, a horrible gnome, came hastening along the corridor. He was so small that he could see the rays of light beneath my door from a distance. I could hear the brisk chink of his keys as he mounted the stairs. On the landing, he muffled the sound, but in spite of his velvety movements I sensed him bearing down on my poor tranquillity. He rapped, and waited for me to put the light out: and the next day he put in his report. I used to put the lights on again, and he would return without any warning, sometimes two or three times running. His keys betrayed his impatience, jingling each time more furiously. He muttered heaven knows what imprecations. I had no worse enemy. Yet I was one of the major pleasures of his day, and his revenge against the universe.

One day, bent on regaining peace and quiet, I promised myself that I would give him a lesson. Dismantling all my camouflage, I purchased an enormous light bulb, of at least a hundred candle-power. I went down to the end of the corridor, to revel in the effect I had produced. There was a scandalous flood of radiance. I did not have to wait long. There was a jingling of keys on the stairs: then a brusque silence, full of stupefaction and menace; then the keys came crashing towards me, imperiously brandished. My enemy thundered with an avenging fist on the door. I made no move, lying doggo: he knocked again, still with no reply from me. He opened the door with his master-key. I was wearing the most innocent air in the world: I was naked. He stared at me, transfigured by a supernatural incomprehension. Then he fled, amid a frenetic jangle of keys, never to return. Doubtless, he did not want to see the devil twice.

In such small communities, where everyone relapses into his own nature, stupidity soon flourishes unashamed, and the ugliness which is inseparable from it. A few of my colleagues were clean about their person and surroundings: while they had their eccentricities, they were the easiest to bear with—although all were complete egoists. Two or three were not without character, and one was almost a saint, but lived in another world, and seemed only by chance to exist on earth. There was another, an Alsatian, with a square feldwebel's head, who had been my professor of German: he was severe and just, and I had been fond of him. When I met him again, he was the same as ever, with his rather gruff kindliness, full of thought for others. There was something surprising about his virile appearance among all these pale spectres, who feared him and seemed to avoid him.

The rest were a human menagerie. One would stand in the lavatory, urinating as he told his beads—he had certainly never read Luther. Another—my neighbour—talked in his sleep night after night. He had a female cat, and stole milk for her. When the time came for her to have kittens, he stayed up all night with her, murmuring tender words of affection: but as he had not taught her clean habits—it would have been a hard enough job—the atmosphere in the corridor suffered. Another kept birds, which he caught in order to sell to hypothetical bird-fanciers. He never opened his windows, for fear the poor wretches would escape, and in order to get in and out, opened the door barely a few inches. One day, I saw an owl in his room, which he had attached to his desk by one claw: it was a great loss to him when the owl died. Next door lived his mortal enemy, who complained of the smell from this aviary, and lost no chance of playing a trick on the bird-man. As for the smell, he was really in no position to complain: his own room was like a rubbish tip, and he made his bed once a year, at the same time as he changed his sheets, for he was too lazy to get a fresh pair every month from the linen-room. This squalid individual did little jobs on the side, buying old head-phones from the second-hand dealers, rigging up odd-looking crystal sets, which he resold very profitably to the pupils. The latter could thus lull themselves to sleep with the latest song-hits under the pillow.

But the most picturesque beast of all was the professor of Italian, still young, completely crazy, and a poet and tragedian in his spare time. He had got something published in Milan, and would launch out on interminable tirades in his sonorous language to all and sundry. I do not know whether he was French by origin: he must have been French in fact, since he added to his income by a singular activity. He was the Lyons sponsor of an embryonic group known as the Socialist National Party, or something like that. In the course of the year, he travelled all over France, from by-election to by-election: standing as a primary candidate, he gathered together a few votes, which he would sell to the highest bidder, if by chance there was a second ballot. His room was directly above the Director's apartment, for whom he nurtured a violent hatred. He used to practise with dumb-bells, which he would let fall on the floor, to trouble his employer's dreams. One evening he drew me into his room, and offered me some wine, which he was drinking from the bottle. I was sitting between him and the door, which was adorned with a large target. All of a sudden, he pulled out a jack-knife and sent it flying over my head straight into the bull's-eye. I admired his skill, stammered out my compliments, and leapt for the door, pursued by the drunkard's cries, inviting me to come and have another drink.

Such were the teachers to whom 'our families' entrusted us: at times I could no longer cope with their disorderliness—while as for their conversation! Fortunately, I had two friends: one a student like myself, staying there for the same reason, a kind-hearted youth, a philosopher, and full of zest; the other a little noviciate Brother, baby-faced and shy, but who had a soul, and a great need to express it. The fact that I did not die of melancholy—and, on certain days, of disgust—I owe to them. The little Brother brought reproaches on his head through his attachment to us: it was pointed out to him that he was endangering his vocation by associating with us. But with his pure heart, which we would not have shocked for anything in the world, he could not understand such remonstrances, and suffered as much on our behalf as for himself.

Not being able to draw him away from us, the Director imagined he was playing the part of a spy: and the little Brother was made acquainted with shame by the very person who pretended to be protecting him from it. I saw him pale with rage, even while he remained submissive; but he was very near to tears. It may be mentioned in passing that every religious college has its network of spies, the bases of which never vary. Some time later I was teaching in an Institute, where, for that matter, I was well treated. I had as a friend a young priest, who had just come out of the seminary, and was a teacher like myself. The Superior took us separately aside, and with a host of circumlocutions and euphemisms, suggested we should keep an eye on one another. We laughed a great deal over it together, and turned it into a sort of game. It is true that the good Superior, who was not lacking in virtue but who all his life had remained warped by his seminary training, had other sources of information. Pupils who were to enter the seminary, who were thus poor, and whom he held firmly in hand, carried our least words back to him. It was not hard to detect the unfortunate wretches, they had such a sheepish air.

In an atmosphere of formal piety, all the laws of thought become deformed. The normal man is an anomaly, and the singular one a transgressor. On the walls of my room I had a few reproductions of Maillol and Rodin. The little Brother saw them: and I sensed that these nudes filled him with a vague feeling of shame. The truth of art meant nothing to him: the nude remained the sign of the flesh, he was fearful of temptations and lowered his eyes as he would have done before a pornographic picture. I tried to make him see the specific purity of beauty, and to unravel the tangled relationships between morality and art. He understood, but his sensibility remained warped: young as he was, he was already fixed in a mould. The older ones, on the other hand, did not understand anything beyond the fact that I had naked women on my walls.

One of my pupils who was considered a dunce, gave proof in his French exercises of rather outstanding gifts: his work was crammed with mistakes, but had a perceptible quality, even a certain maturity, which would have startled more blasé teachers than myself. I discovered that he painted. In his drawings and paintings he let himself go entirely: he already knew a thousand and one things, and knew how to discuss them with fervour. I saw him often, and showed him books on art, reproductions of sculpture and painting. This gave my colleagues a fine excuse for gossip! It may well be imagined what they thought. The boy had the worst possible reputation among the masters: he was fair, rather feminine, and the dark rings under his eyes were attributed to vice. His home background was only discussed by hints and insinuations. No one dreamed that he might be unhappy, and thirsting for light; yet his exercises showed it clearly enough, and his need to liberate himself came from the depths of his soul. But, in short, we were suspected of having a relationship whose image must obsess those boarders-in-perpetuity, the masters of colleges. With the most offensive hypocrisy, I was warned against showing too much indulgence towards this good-for-nothing, while his own life was made harder as a counterweight to my favours.

These few strokes will serve to convey the atmosphere. The student and I ended by walling ourselves up in an aggressive unity of front. This was not merely a question of morale. At the masters' table where we ate, we were given convicts' fare. The Director took his meals on a dais, the Abbé Larue on his right. He dined off very different dishes from ours. If by chance, however, he was absent, a servant came and shamelessly removed the plates from the Abbé, who was thus reduced to the common lot. The Abbé, who rarely came to meals, found food for his irony at least. My friend and I noisily rejected the ordinary food, and taking it upon ourselves to stir up discontent, we bought provisions from a nearby shop, and distributed them with ostentation, hoping to offend the Director. But the Director had seen worse things than that: and our colleagues never dared to do more than murmur. When the moment came for action, they beat a retreat. We were left with our provisions on our hands: thenceforth we had to share them alone.

In the end, life became impossible there. Through a multitude of minor aversions, I was daily growing thinner. I made up my mind to fall ill in earnest: I had only to let myself go, and all power of further resistance left me. In March, I left the college, and set out for my own part of the country, where I was to spend nearly two years, reading, reflecting, and leading a semi-vegetative life, which was doubtless the deciding factor for my writing. Later, I came across my student friend again: he is a captain to-day, but still a student at heart. As for the little Brother, he has become an important person, Head of a Division at the college: he still has the same babyish air, but now he no longer submits to discipline, but imposes it instead. But what has become of my young artist? He seemed to be born as a target for misfortune.

*   *   *

With the massive door of the college behind me, how sweet the fresh air was! At the University, I had only five hours of lectures. The rest of the time I was free, and I spent long hours strolling about the streets. Lyons has few resources to offer. There are several superb vistas from the top of the hills or along the quays, a good museum, whose inner courtyard is an island inviting reverie, a host of churches and chapels, and an ancient but admirably appointed library On Saint-Barthélémy rise there is still a chapel dedicated to Philomena, patroness of lovers: the saint, an elegant waxen doll, is half turned in her shrine—just as a reclining beauty, to catch a confidence better, leans on one elbow on her bed. On the walls, there were innumerable ex-votos, mostly long letters in which lovers related their misfortunes. The chapel seems to have been tidied up since. I passed by there two years ago, to find the letters gone, and the marble washed clean of its graffiti. But the garden of the Palais Saint-Pierre is still the same, and the parvis of Saint-Jean, and the gulls over the river.

I saw once more the small room where Jean Wahl gave lessons to senior students. I remember a paper I read as a student in his presence, on time and eternity in Spinoza's philosophy. I had covered the subject thoroughly, amassed piles of notes, but pretended to be improvising. The paper was only supposed to last an hour, being followed by a commentary from the teacher and a discussion. I was horribly intimidated by Jean Wahl, and plunged into my exposition like a drowning man. It seemed as if I would never get to the end: the hour had long since passed. There was something tense and threatening in Wahl's very impassiveness. He could stop me, I thought, by a simple 'Ye-e-s', one of those 'yeses' only he knew how to say, which really meant 'no', and which he uttered with drawn-out emphasis on the 'ye-e-', as if he hesitated to admit the obvious, or as if he were holding back to increase the murderous hiss of the final sibilant. In the end, he stopped me with an 'Is there much more of it?' more eloquent than any commentary.

That was nearly twelve years ago: our relationship has never really recovered from it. Quite recently, at the College of Philosophy which he created outside the walls of the Sorbonne, I spoke at his request on contemporary English poetry, and he himself presided, sitting next to me. The old image arose, and was superimposed on the new one. I had been speaking for half an hour on the forerunners, Hopkins and Hardy, when I became aware of the time, of Wahl seated on my right, and had a painful sensation of *this has all happened before*. I was overwhelmed by a sort of dizziness. I plunged in among the contemporary poets, losing them, telescoping several, and becoming so anxious to finish that I mixed their names up, confusing Dylan Thomas with Sydney Keyes, and the latter with Alun Lewis. Wahl followed in my wake, picking up the names I had dropped, and whispering the right ones to me when I made a mistake: all of which only increased my confusion. It is true that I had dreaded this occasion, from the moment it had been suggested to me. But it is a great pity to have studied under one of the finest minds of our time, and to have often met him since, without ever striking the right note in our conversation!

Nevertheless, like all his pupils, I had a passionate admiration for Jean Wahl. Without him, we would have remained ignorant of philosophy in evolution. Not that he spoke much of this in his actual teaching. I have retained only a hazy memory of his explanations of Malebranche or Hume, and, to be honest, these subjects left me indifferent. It was his particular sphere alone which attracted me, from the glimpses one gained of it from a page of his on Hegel, or an article in *Recherches Philosophiques*. Jean Wahl was also a poet—in fact he cherished the title. The best of his verse was gnomic—a deft and rapid probe, a flash of insight, not so much a universe of symbols as an aphoristic side to his philosophy. For me, he was, more than any other, *the* philosopher, a witness to the pangs of the spirit, to the dialectical contradiction: he was the man with the scalpel, taking division to extremes, so that the drama of being and its resolution might both be total. But I never dared to approach him. He had besides a certain aloofness, largely despite himself, and which doubtless made him suffer. I merely sensed where some of his deeper interests lay, and among the books I read during that period there were many that I connected more or less rightly with him.

Like so many other disciplines of the mind, philosophy was undergoing a language crisis: it was attempting to become more supple without losing its exactitude, reconciling movement and permanence. In the analysis of experience it abandoned the fiction of an objective universe: the particular subject, with his harmonics in the object, and his own individual manner of colouring existence, now seemed to be the nerve centre, the theme of a symphony of which the world was the score. Parallel with pseudo-scientific psychology there was developing a metaphysical psychology of the existent within his own destiny. Situations now replaced categories: and just as each situation, when the mind reflects upon it, reveals to the existent his unknown harmonics, in the same way, in his particular behaviour, each living being is merely a nuance of mankind, one of the possible harmonics of a vaster sensibility. Thus, philosophical enquiry into any complex state of the soul (for example, anger or desire) proceeds by a double movement, towards the particular centre and towards the universal foundation of the species. My personal knowledge, my experience of the concrete, form the warp of a mental fabric of which all human sensibility is the woof. The transition from the particular to the general is replaced by osmosis between the singular and the universal. In this way the reciprocal exile of subject and object is brought to an end: a mutual metamorphosis unites them in a single becoming.

I do not know whether Jean Wahl would subscribe to such a definition of philosophy, which relates it to the poetic act (although the latter starts with the symbol, the former with the factual situation). But it is worthy of note that certain philosophers have taken the trouble to pursue their analysis in novels, and that Wahl himself has tried, in his poems in which the *Self* plays such a large part, to grasp the philosophical *instinct* in its spontaneous operation. Gabriel Marcel, whose *Journal* I was finding such delightful reading at that time, seemed to me an example of that *universal singular* which arrives at the universe by the paths of interior analysis: here, introspection and prospection are one. The fact that the author of the *Journal Métaphysique* was also a musician and playwright, seemed to me to correspond to certain necessities of language which our time is beginning to perceive, in the impasse into which the modern confusion of tongues has led us.

These are not just so many different forms of expression, isolated one from another, which the profoundest intellects summon up in turn. These forms, having lost their original flexibility, have become the objective categories of art, conventional aspects of man. Each one has killed its context. By dividing it against itself, they have ruined creative thought. To shatter their false autonomy is to rediscover the unity of language, and to give them back the freedom of expression, the diversity of means, which they have lost through inner poverty, through fear. For a form only flourishes by integrating all the others: these last are

144

spontaneous, while the first is deliberate, and certainly modifies substance, but without arresting its movement or its capacity for metamorphosis. The emotion which grips man in the presence of the essential is the same in all the arts: the secret of true art, therefore, is at one and the same time, and by analogy, to unify the diverse, and to diversify the One.

Nothing could be further from that cocktail of gratuitous forms which claims to be a rediscovery of the naïve invention and eternal humour of art, but which is in reality a mere parody of appearances, a hash of disintegrated elements. It is only the aesthetes of discontinuity who amuse themselves with this glittering spray, this empty froth of the imagination. True imagination is something else: it is the human substance in movement, apprehended and directed by consciousness. A Cocteau can take every liberty, because he commits himself to nothing: he is a fashion house, changing the fashion every six months—he has a fairy touch and a supreme ease of manner! But in the universe of the absurd, thought is replaced by the *gag*. Everything leads on to something else, but everything is sterile: an uninterrupted succession does duty for truth and duration. There is nothing easier than to change a pumpkin into a coach, and a coach into a fieldmouse. Whoever thinks that everything lies in appearances can play with appearances at will. But he is a prisoner of his very virtuosity: if he stops to think for a moment, everything falls back into nothingness, and the public into its apathy. That which endures, makes itself felt, and demands reflection, is tedious. Art is surrendered to the surprise stunt, which is never certain to come off, since the faster the metamorphoses operate, the greater becomes the danger of boredom: until at last the fairy wand is shattered, from belabouring the flanks of the unreal. Babel is a fairground of images: everything is sold there, from false beards to false mysteries, from puns to weighty paradoxes.

Perhaps as a result of too serious an education I have retained a taste for the austere, and the need to justify my thought. I hate the absurd, not in itself, but when it is set up as a maxim for art. In true comedy there is a gravity and a terrible uncertainty which make me seek it out and prefer it to other expressions of the beautiful. Nevertheless, I have little patience with intellectual fantasy, which confuses humour and disorder: and, what is more, methodically cultivates disorder, to give it the appearance of an absurd order, a challenge to the laws of the intellect. I believe that I am made for the absolute, although no more nor less than everyone else: admittedly, I was fortunate enough to encounter minds, or books, which gave me the highest conception of our power over the absolute, and the feeling that the substantial word, without ceasing to reveal the possible, holds the universe in place. The innumerable unity of the diverse has never done injury to the reason. My faith in language is complete. But I find tedious this world in which 'all these speakers of words have created insubstantial monsters for themselves from the surplus of their adjectives', as Claudel, who knows what he is talking about, remarks.

Nevertheless, this world has its time and place in history. The extreme division in which we are now plunged has inverted our nostalgia for the One, which, from being negative and concentrated on the earlier Golden Age of history, has become positive and guides us towards the future which we must occupy. For present-day thinkers, however divergent they may be, inward man can reach no understanding of himself outside the history from which he proceeds, whether he masters it or is enslaved by it. To diagnose the malady of language is already to recognise the finality of human speech, a finality situated in history, and the instrument of which is the communion of men. Any forthcoming metaphysic is inseparably part of the historic vision, of an immanent religion which will be the springboard for the ultimate spring towards the One. The drama of language to-day is the drama of religious consciousness: has man a meaning or not? A

Christian perceives this more clearly than others, for the temporal aim of Christianity is the fulfilment of history. But perhaps it causes even greater anguish among non-Christians; for, whether they affirm or deny, they are threatened by absolute doubt, and at any moment, their dialectic may turn against itself.

*   *   *

The chaplain of my college at that period was the Abbé Monchanin. He is now beginning to be recognised as one of our pure contemplatives. Beneath the black soutane, he had a frail, almost non-existent body, and his face was emaciated, extremely mobile, with a glance that flashed out like fire rather than light. His lips were like rapid wings, not pausing to embroider words, but swift bearers of thought. He had fine, transparent hands, which were lifted instinctively by the gesture of oblation towards the sky. In his barely furnished cell, he looked like a captive eagle, grown thin with nostalgia, a little huddled up, and worn by a long exile, but still living in spirit upon the heights.

He had a universal attitude in all things, and was a pioneer of knowledge. There was no sphere that he had not surveyed, no mode of thought whose evolution he did not know. His was not a simple hunger for knowledge for its own sake, but rather, prescience of the unity of the human world, and of the integral nature of all thought, even the furthest straying. A powerful genius for theology, revitalising the School structures, led him to elevate all history in an ascensional movement. The mystic in him was confirmed by the man of thought. His ascent was inscribed within the future curve of humanity: and from the summits thus attained he threw down a rope ladder, each joint of which seemed to him a symbolic stage, visible from above, and foreseeable from below for whoever knew how to interpret the conflicts and convergences of history.

But unlike the Abbé Larue, who looked on the operation of

history merely as a syncretism of immanent myths, a manifestation and no more, of the unknown *psyche* of our species, the Abbé Monchanin centred it round the Word incarnate, and based the historicity of history, taken as universal destiny, upon that narrow temporal shore on which the living God set his feet. *Et Verbum caro factum est:* for both of them, that was the gist of the matter. But Larue the historian reasoned only within pure immanence: the transcendental justification of man was not to be mixed with his immanent explanation and the science of human actuality. He thought that history has its own existence, and that the Word must be understood as a progressive revelation of man in the universe. For Monchanin, on the contrary, the Word had been made flesh only once, and all history was centred upon that unique instant: *et habitavit in nobis.*

Through and for all men, Christ had consummated the historical drama of the separated consciousness and reunited it with Being. Without him, history would have been merely a Heraclitean flux, born of night and immediately engulfed by it again: through him, every man became contemporary with the eternal, and his life a microcosm of history. Every man, whether he knew it or wished it or not, was related to Christ. And not only from the divine entry into this world, but from Adam to the last man, all reconciliation was brought about through him. To be contemporary with the eternal means that every man is contemporary with every other, and communicates even without being aware of it between one point and another in the destiny of humanity. History, as seen by the universal mind, is both a successive explanation and a simultaneous revelation. Christ, the absolute contemporary, triumphs over irreversible time, and constitutes the source of a communion which brings me into touch, not only with some being yet to be born, but with some being who perhaps lived and died long ago. What we call immortality is not only our state after death, but our individual presence in every man, a presence of which we suspect neither the intensity nor the extent.

Our name before God is the particular form which it behoves only us to give to human destiny: not only is no fate unimportant, but our least thoughts and our least acts model the destiny of all.

Doubtless, an immanent vision of man (the Communist one, for example) may include, as a vast image, a unity extended in time; but it cannot conceive it as reversible, for reason is univocal, and the causal procession never reverses duration. When the Abbé Larue talked to me about history, I was left vaguely unsatisfied, although I did not dare to say so to him. A phrase of Léon Bloy, which I understood badly then, has remained in my head since: 'As time does not exist for God, it was possible for the inexplicable victory of the Marne to have been decided by the very humble prayer of a little girl who will not be born for another two centuries.' The words of a madman? Rather, the words of a poet. For eternity, not time, is the true conductor of the orchestra of history. Is it more logical to say 'the past is big with the future' than the reverse? When Monchanin spoke to me of the Mystic Body, history was shot with innumerable simultaneous insights. The objective present was merely a vectorial figure in an infinitely actual field of forces. In living *here* and *now*, we were acting *everywhere* and *always*: in truth, each one of our gestures shook the very substance of the absolute, and awoke repercussions in the universal destiny. As if the absolute had become incarnate so that man might be totally responsible for man, and that he might be so in a visible way, that he might read suffering or joy in the features of the Man-God.

The philosophers taught me to conceive a transcendent Presence, and a morality based on this Presence: I could imagine, through this presence, the reciprocal repercussion of innumerable destinies separated by the centuries. For the idea of God cannot be an individual one, and whoever conforms to it has communion in eternity. But thought can only postulate the transcendent as a necessary beyond: to conform to the transcendent Idea is not really an act of adoration. This negative knowledge does not go beyond immanence, and the moral order which it determines leaves man to the solitude of time. Thus, every religion is founded on a man-to-man relationship with God: and in this need for God to take shape, one must know how to hail a major truth. There was the old peasant who used to stand every day at the back of the church at Ars, making no gesture but gazing steadily towards the altar: and when the curé of Ars asked him, 'What are you doing there?' he replied, 'I look at him, and he looks at me.' All those who have prayed will understand: for this man, God was his absolute neighbour and friend. But if God had not put on flesh, nothing would have warranted such an ineffable closeness, or that certainty that simple people have that man is of the stature of God. However vast may be our intellect, we cannot cross a certain limit, and burst through into the transcendent. Consciousness, whose nature is to believe itself capable of the absolute, demands that the absolute justify it for the faith it has in itself: and that the absolute, in revealing itself, should justify itself as well.

The Incarnation is only shocking to the mind which denies its own end. Our reason must certainly be constricted, not to admit the possibility. In India, it is true, Incarnation is regarded as perfectly natural: the shocking thing is that Christians can think God only became incarnate once. But India has the sense of the divine, and not of God. There, consciousness aspires to non-being, and not to the total Being: it annihilates history, refusing to be a destiny, and to give a specific form to unity. Many times I attempted to grapple with Hindu religious thought. The Abbé Monchanin, for whom India was to become a sphere of apostolic activity, encouraged me in this. But I was never able to overcome my uneasiness faced with a world in which man counts for so little. In the ways of thought of India, everything happens as if *here* and *now*, those two fundamental coordinates for every man entering this world, were not coordinated with anything: man hasno real place, he appears, and falls back again into the inchoate.

Such a negation of history eliminates man: it resolves the drama of consciousness by calling it an illusion.

But the 'drama' of consciousness is nothing other than consciousness itself, in its essential reality. No negation can serve as starting-point to the awareness of being to itself. There is no other solution to the tragedy of consciousness but to assume consciousness to the end: and it is this solution that Christianity has chosen, without evading its contradictory character. For consciousness is at one and the same time an obstacle to the absolute and the path to the absolute: history is both immanent progress and transcendent Revelation. The absolute is both the asymptote of this progress and the centre of this Revelation. History will not make me abandon the mystique, nor the mystique make me abandon history: for these two approaches to reality converge in the person of Christ, which is unique because it is total. To be the Alpha and Omega, to take upon oneself the whole drama in a body which suffers *in extremis* for all flesh, to endure absolute laceration to save man absolutely, and to pledge the very essence of man, as God alone knows it—such an absolute act cannot be performed twice. God made himself flesh *once*, maintains Christian thought: and if only faith can confirm the Incarnation, at least reason cannot conceive it in a plural form, for God, if he wishes to save man, had no need to set about it twice.

*   *   *

But what does saving man mean? The notion of sin has no place in metaphysics: it remains a mystery for me, but a living mystery. In my education, the idea of sin was constantly present, but it was a sin only remotely concerned with the essential fault. If I had, like many others, accepted the idea of sin as my teacher, inculcated it, life would soon have rid me of it: it is pitiful to see so many Christians devoid of spiritual life making use of the tables of the law like a raft to get to the opposite shore. If they could only sink to the bottom for once, then perhaps they would find the strength, kicking off from the floor of the abyss, to rise in one upward thrust towards the God whom the very excess of evil would reveal to them! It is not necessary to commit *great* sins in order to be a great sinner: the stark fault is the act of consciousness against itself. Pierre Jean Jouve had made me feel this through symbols. Through the Abbé Monchanin, I learned of the Mystic Body: he made me appreciate the scope of this act, the importance of inner lucidity, and the dreadful responsibility of the mind.

A great sinner is one who *knows* that he is doing evil every moment, because it is impossible for him to be always and everywhere aware of himself. This anguish caused by our limitations is the state of sin that only the certainty of mercy can alleviate. There is thus joy mixed with this anguish, and which grows stronger by it, for the consciousness of our limitations brings forth the necessity for the absolute: and the absolute ordains that every moral being should exert, and take stock of, himself, and reach the utmost awareness that lies in his power, beneath the gaze of God.

I have always thought, since the awakening of my spiritual conscience, that the most lucid mystics of evil are very near to the greatest saints. They also live beneath the gaze of the absolute: but they wound the absolute mortally and deliberately. The least fault committed with the direct intention of striking at the heart of the infinite Presence becomes *the* sin against the spirit, a veritable demoniac challenge, at the moment when grace, wholly apprehended, is wholly refused. For every man there comes a moment, not when he succumbs to temptation, but when he commits the initial fault, the original fault in its proper sense, which seals his revolt against God. It is on this initial fault we will all be judged. I have seen God watching me, and because he was watching me, I perpetrated my sin before his Face. That I may long since have forgotten that moment makes no difference! It is present in each of my actions, in the habits I have acquired, which perpetuate a challenge the very notion of which I no longer retain. But the great mystics of evil never do anything which is not a conscious revolt: and whether it is against God, against life, or against man, is all the same. The old priest was perfectly right when he said to his flock, the humdrum sinners of the midday mass: One needs a great deal of courage to be a real sinner. Courage, certainly—and greatness as well. As for myself, I have neither that courage nor that greatness; but I realise more and more that transgression is an act of knowledge not merely diverted, but inverted: a *contrary* knowledge, a wilful destruction of the idea of me that God carries within himself, and which I glimpse through a shattering intuition, the ecstasy of which is the spur to my sin. I make of God and my eternal soul the shameful spectators of my abjection.

If these things were reflected upon, people might cease reiterating so glibly that it is easy to be a Christian. Is there a single other morality in the world which attributes more weight to our everyday actions? They make me smile, those people who think one is a Christian through a need to be consoled: and others, even more petty-minded, who regard faith as an insurance policy on the next world! It is a terrible thing to be a Christian, and the agony of the greatest saints has come from thinking that they have still not reached that state, and perhaps never will. As for myself, penetrated by my powerlessness to achieve it, since the moment I understood what Christian faith meant I have deferred my acceptance of it. But if I vegetate in its shadow, it is not because I do not recognise the true greatness it proffers. I am a negative Christian, a Christian without the grace of being one. I have knowledge and faith in the Christian interpretation of the world, and the certitude that Christianity is eternal (or in other words, that despite those who relegate it to the junk pile, its historic function will last as long as history, and even a little longer): all I lack is *patience*. Patience to wait for whom? He who is to come, and has perhaps already passed by? No: to wait, to be ready, for some unforeseen divine eruption—to be wholly open to the infinite Presence.

This does not mean that my negative knowledge does not orientate my whole life: the drama of consciousness is all the clearer and more tragic for it. When I do evil, I know the implications of my act: I go against myself, and disfigure my own unity. I do not pretend merely to be making a mistake, that fuller knowledge would help me to avoid. I have no delusions about the nature of evil: when I read that man is naturally good, I know all too well that the statement is meaningless. Evil in man is a power as fundamental as consciousness: it is one of the possible ways that consciousness can work upon itself. It is in my power to injure the dignity and integrity of another person, while knowing they are my own. I have the power to divide consciousness against itself, to destroy myself and the world with me (not by banal suicide, but by that hyperconscious form of suicide which corrupts thought fibre by fibre). I have the power to deny myself or to exalt myself illimitably, or to reject all relationship with other men or with the universe. I have the power to kill God. My freedom to do evil is not limited by the transcendent itself.

For those who do not believe in God, what I am going to say now will mean nothing—but before they were born, other men had killed God in their still-to-be-born souls. But there are some men who live with the dead body of their God: a heavy corpse to carry, and one which stinks. Such men see what a gulf the contradiction makes: and, in my eyes, their determination to bridge it by solely human efforts is all the more pathetic as their impotence, for all their stupendous efforts, appears as complete. The more clear-sighted end up by thinking that Nature, in fashioning man, overstepped her creative power and produced from her bosom a being she could not satisfy, having made him capable of an infinite which does not exist: which comes to the same thing as concluding that consciousness is an absurdity, or, reciprocally, that nature confronted by mind is absurd.

But everything within me rebels at such an absurdity. A tree, a beautiful prospect, a river meandering through the meadows, fill me with the quiver of being, as, even more, does one of those songs that man has created from his unhappiness. Whether this song has come from the anonymous crowd, or from the greatest poet imaginable (and here the extremes are the same), I feel myself filled with an absolute truth, which speaks to me in the singular as it speaks to every man. I know that I can destroy this truth within myself, but I cannot destroy its essence. I can kill God in my soul, but not in the absolute. But this essential truth by which I am sometimes dazzled does not exclude another one—that of universal suffering: and suffering itself is merely the effect of that appetite for destruction which seems to be inherent in life, and which consciousness multiplies unendingly. It appears to me that if life cannot create without destroying, consciousness, for its part, may take pure destruction as its aim. It is not simply pity which moves me, but knowledge of that evil of which man is both master and slave. Life only destroys through aiming at higher forms. But man destroys in the face of life. The absurdity is in him, and not in nature. The drama of consciousness is to be able to carry equally either destruction or creation through to the end. But I will not label this ineffable contradiction an absurdity: it is the basis of our freedom. What we lack is the power to pursue to the end these two contradictory terms, without losing sight of either. The moment we pretend to have achieved unity by eliminating one of the two poles, we are no longer free: yet when we think of one or the other, or of one within the other, we are gripped by an infinite anguish.

How is one to escape from this torment? It is clear that nothing can deliver us from doubt, unless it be some absolute term of reference. But all appeals to the transcendental go unanswered, and the most religious mind, precisely because it is such, gains no satisfaction from metaphysic reasonings, none of which justify the absolute for having exiled itself. The historians of myths will say that it was through a sublime piece of audacity that the Man-God was invented. I thought so myself for a long time, and only slowly did the figure of Christ emerge from its mythical ambiguity, which I had allowed to cloak the divine reality. When I came to know the Abbé Monchanin, I was some way from Christianity—and yet sufficiently near—to accept the idea that man had imagined the incarnation of God in human form, so that the absolute *as such* might suffer for the human contradiction; for it seemed, and still seems to me, that the essence of Christianity lay in the fact that the absolute thereby justifies itself for having created a free conscience, at the same time as it justifies conscience for employing that freedom. To save man means to give him trust in God and in himself. Only God may give himself absolutely. It rests therefore with God to make the saving gesture, a tangible gesture which establishes beyond refutation his Presence among us.

But the Incarnation is no more sufficient to save man than it is to justify God. It is necessary for God to suffer the extremity of human suffering, and he must feel in his flesh and spirit all the blows that consciousness unleashed against itself may deal. Christ is the sign of absolute contradiction, the unbearable Image of what we are and do not wish to be: the total truth lies within our grasp, awaiting our pleasure, so that it may not be said we were refused this freedom—of challenging the existence of God. He knows to what extremes men will fly, but he must bear to the end with the fury of negation which is in their nature: and be denied piecemeal before being finally abandoned. His sacrifice must be complete, leaving no part of him that is not broken and rent, for the crime is aimed at his very essence, and it is in his essence that he must triumph over death. The Redemption completes the Incarnation: without the former, Christ would have offered us only a moral, although certainly a divine one, and built solely upon love. But in order that this love should become the first duty of mankind, God had to be as capable of being man as man of being God. Christ, in dying by man, makes himself capable of the crime of man: his suffering comprehends all that man may suffer. He suffers not only the Cross, but every one of the tortures that man has ever been able, or ever will be able, to invent against man. For through him, the torments of all the earth reverberate in the absolute. This body, every bone of which was counted, and this spirit forsaken and despairing (let the profundity of the *Eli, lamma sabacthani* be recalled, when God feels himself forsaken by God) make up the sum of sin of all men: they are man reduced by man to nothingness. And however great the creative consciousness of myths may be, I do not think it could of its own accord have invented so total a myth.

After the Cross comes the Resurrection. Man has killed himself, and with him God. It is God in man who resurrects man. The contradiction of consciousness is overcome by carrying its effects to an extreme. The proof of man's indestructibility is established, because God loves him not only in spirit but in the least atoms of the flesh. No one does hurt to man without also hurting God: the death of Christ is something we all share, relating us individually to the absolute, and through it, to every man whose essence is tormented by man. And in the same way, Christ rising again lifts each of us with him from the tomb. There is no crime so enormous that it does not leave intact in its author that part of the absolute upon which the Kingdom of God is built. Hence the life of Christ becomes not simply the symbol of our own life lacerated and made whole again, but its reality, which it is up to us to grasp *hic et nunc*, without which our understanding of ourselves and of man remains forever threatened by illusion. For if Christianity were a myth, it would be the last and most desperate myth of all: one could go no further in the vision of an imaginary salvation, a personal and general justification of the spirit. For man cannot compromise God more than once. Abandoning myth for belief we would say: God cannot become incarnate more than once. This alternative appears clear to me, although I cannot decide between faith or despair.

*   *   *

Such indecision is nothing new. On the question of faith, I have remained as I was at twenty. A host of reasons have made me put off adopting a clear-cut attitude in the permanent conflict which occupies my mind. I do not deny the value of Pascal's wager.* But it stimulates one to choose only in terms of a beyond. Pascal is careful in his use of it for lack of a more convincing argument. His strongest religious arguments only serve to increase the opposition in our nature: they force us to examine the question of being, which is not beyond but within ourselves. I read Pascal formerly with a quasi-theological aim: he confirmed me in the notion that religion is *knowledge*. The religious mind is not one

*'If there is a God, He is infinitely incomprehensible, since, having neither parts nor limits, He has no affinity to us. We are then incapable of knowing either what He is or if He is. This being so, who will dare to undertake the decision of the question? Not we, who have no affinity to Him . . .

'Let us then examine this point, and say, "God is, or He is not." But to which side shall we incline? Reason can decide nothing here. There is an infinite chaos which separated us. A game is being played at the extremity of this infinite distance where heads or tails will turn up. What will you wager? According to reason, you can do neither the one thing nor the other; according to reason, you can defend neither of the propositions . . .

'Yes; but you must wager. It is not optional. You are embarked. . . . But your happiness? Let us weigh the gain and the loss in wagering that God is. Let us estimate these two chances. If you gain, you gain all; if you lose, you lose nothing. Wager, then, without hesitation that He is . . .'

The above brief passages taken from Pascal's *Pensées* may give some idea of the famous wager, and also of Pascal's method of argument. (Translator's note.)

which dreams solely of Paradise and of union with God after death: it is above all that which can only be satisfied by an absolute explanation of consciousness and its avatars—an explanation which may or may not be crowned by the paradisical vision. If it be admitted that we have no other hold on the transcendental than that which this vision may grant us, then the religious mind is not necessarily benefited by the gift, nor visited by grace. If God is really the total consciousness upon which all other consciousness is grafted—and he *should* be, otherwise the mind would be merely an absurd epiphenomenon—he may at will take possession of a soul, even if it is ill-prepared to receive him. But he may also leave it a prey to uneasiness, which is a condition favourable to all that estranges us from him.

But such a hypothesis on the relationship between God and man is, one feels clearly, no more than a human approach to the divine, a rational piece of induction which enters into religious symbolism without, however, reaching the ineffable truth of the symbols. The psychologists of faith will doubtless tell me that the religious spirit is not always free from a demoniac element, and that its gravest temptation is to conquer through reason the *ultima ratio* of reason. I have too great a tendency to speculate in terms of knowledge, thinking thus to add to illumination, and to desire the explanation to be perfect before I am struck by the divine lightning. I have no claim to the title of Christian with which I am usually credited. I live within Christian thought, without obeying its laws. Only in spirit do I stand in the shadow of the Cross, which is little enough when one measures the gap between intellectual truth and the truth made flesh. Admittedly, Christianity is my spiritual system, and Christ the only surety I have for myself and for the world; but I still have the possibility of making a clean sweep of everything, and returning to the void whence perhaps I have not emerged. It may be easily seen that I am far from believing: and however great may be my desire for truth, I wish to do nothing to court an illusion which, in any case, my analysing mind would immediately destroy. For I wish to understand, and often what others would denounce as irrational opens up to me vast perspectives of reason. But the more developed my vision becomes, the more contradictions abound.

No one can believe in isolation without accepting a Church, for to believe is to live in communion. Yet there is no greater obstacle to my acceptance of the Church than the Church itself, as I seem to see it. For more than ten years I have been seeking the Church. I know that it is the Body of Christ. And the theology of the bread and the wine, of consecration and communion, is more for me than mere symbolism. The 'This is my body, this is my blood: this do in remembrance of me' is not just the magic formula perpetuating the act of the Last Supper, but the very act itself, both historical and eternal. My conception of the Church takes its origin from the bread and the wine, which are the body and the blood of Christ, his real and tangible Presence. The central act of the Last Supper confirms the permanence of the divine sacrifice and the divine gift. Through the bread and wine, all men have communion in Christ: the oecumenical fellowship is a need as profound as that of eating and drinking. But Judas is always standing by, to accept the proffered bread of Jesus and to eat it: he is present behind Pilate, behind Caiaphas, behind the hangmen, behind every one of us.

Within the mystery of the Last Supper, the three great mysteries of Incarnation, Redemption and Resurrection are unfolded. In it, the union of all men is made manifest equally in crime and in salvation. It seems to me that the whole of the Church is defined in chapters 13 to 17 of the gospel according to Saint John. But where, in fact, is the Church now? In the immense Catholic edifice that the imagination of centuries has built, I see strange structures which conceal the main outlines. I confess that I do not understand the inextricable profusion of accessory symbols which diminish the symbolic force of the centre, and dissipate the pure religious impulse in minor devotions. In Catholicism, heresy lurks at every step: no one can be sure of not going contrary to dogma. It is true that in the formative centuries, in the age of the Fathers, a desperate fight had to be waged against heresies of substance which imperilled the very essence of the faith. Besides, the Church, like any organism, develops its potentialities within time. But one begins to wonder whether the Church, in defending itself against heresy, has not amassed definitions at the expense of organic vitality, and whether dogma, which should be a protection of religious form, has not become a strait-jacket preventing it from coming to fulfilment.

I think also that in consolidating its position and becoming a power, the Church has created for itself administrative rites so complex that many of its adherents lose sight of its function: it alleges that these rites are valid in the eternal, whereas they verge on simple superstition. Finally, its admirable liturgy no longer produces the massive effect which gave the Christian crowd the feeling of participating in the essential salutary act: it needs to be renewed, and to rediscover the sources of communication. Relieved of many modern overlays, stripped of the gaudy operatic trappings with which it is often invested by a music alien to its truth, with its development made clear and becoming an exercise for the soul, it would rediscover its true purpose, which is to teach people how to pray. In a living liturgy, prayer and knowledge go together, and mutually support each other. Although born in the Catholic faith, and long faithful to its laws, I never knew how to pray in the faith that was mine. Had I only known (or had I been taught), knowledge would have come to me as well: whereas now, I grow weary pursuing a knowledge devoid of faith's vivifying touch.

Even before I reached my twentieth year I began searching for some place where I could pray with others. I do not know what instinct for a long time inclined me towards Protestantism. In Béarn, where I come from, the Calvinists are both numerous and fervent, and it was in their chapel at Pau that I discovered the joy in common prayer that the routine religious exercises had been unable to give me at college. Even while taking into account the taste for novelty which may flatter the curiosity of the soul, I am forced to recognise that a more imperious reason attracted me to the Protestant creed. Its severe sobriety was more in keeping with my idea of religion; but even in this the reader is at liberty to see merely a temporary iconoclasm—and doubtless he will not be far wrong.

What Protestantism revealed to me—and what a precious revelation!—was the Voice of God. That very word, Voice, is the most beautiful I know, and I can never utter it without emotion. The minister opened the Bible—of which we Catholics knew nothing—and the strong voice was raised with the authority of the ages. I knew only the Sunday Gospel, which had become a sort of popular broadsheet for our religion, and had been disfigured, besides, by innumerable commentaries, the poverty and naïve lack of respect of which the manuals of sermons prepared for priests gave evidence. But I knew nothing of the Old Testament, of the Epistles, nor of the Apocalypse. Now, however, I saw that these texts made up the single indivisible fabric of the very words of Christ. Between the Old and the New Testaments, which was the warp of the other? The Gospel to come was unfolded in a verse from the Psalms or from Isaiah, and a verse from that Gospel resounded back in the dim past of man.

If the poetry of the Bible, on which all had been said, was bound to fascinate me, the vision of history which the Book revealed to me plunged me into a sort of exaltation. It was through the Bible that I understood the synoptic character of history. It may be read both as a series of events and as a simultaneous drama. The Protestants, in their sermons and prayers, take it all in with one glance and centre it upon Christ. In this way the Word is seen as the Spirit of History. The Word is the promise of God, never invalid, but always present and ready to materialise in each person; but it is also a breach coming from man, the coexistence of a transcendent continuity and of a discontinuity which disintegrates in time. Among the nations which have been influenced by the Bible, the sense of history and the inner sense are mingled: at a certain depth, the individual drama is united with the drama of the species. The same struggle between eternity and time takes place in the whole race and in the deep ego. And just as this is true of nations (like England and Germany), so is it true of mythical natures, and for the same reasons. Bossuet and Pascal, Spinoza and Hegel, Tolstoy and Bloy, were all nourished on the Bible. Their meditations, however different their aims may be, all end by struggling with the mystery of time: they attempt to integrate the two contradictory aspects of time—succession and revelation. Between the interior conflict which sets the discontinuity of successive moments against the permanence of the mind, and the universal drama which reveals, in the anarchic web of events, the thread of a design sensed without being known, there is no substantial difference, not even if it is taken to an extreme. The history of man begins afresh in each one of us. The Bible, as the Protestants read it, makes them contemporary with a history that Catholics have made the mistake of embalming. The Word which strikes Saul is addressed to me as well, and creates between Saul and myself a mysterious identity.

It is the Word, the spirit of language, which reconciles the eternal and ordinary duration. Every metaphysic of history, when its aim is to justify man, is founded upon the Word, of which for some he is the creator, for others the vessel and the witness. What struck me about the Bible was that in it, man was both these things at once: he was given authority to create. In this manner, the two contrasting aspects of history are reconciled: man receives the Word as a vocation, and in such measure as he remains faithful to it, he is the creator of God's designs, and weaves time within eternity. If he rejects this delegation of

163

authority, either because he feels it to be too onerous, or because he cannot bear to be an instrument, even a free one, he becomes no more than a mere plaything of chaos. The Bible denounces those who despise history, armed with the feeling that whatever they do and whatever happens they are the chosen of God. It also denounces those who proclaim themselves masters of history, and mistake their ambition for its end: and, finally, those who regard history as a school, and limit it to the resolving of certain immanent themes. This denunciation is aimed also at two mortal errors of language: that which, depriving history of the Word, or giving ascendancy to one particular word, walls up speech in a closed system of symbols; and that which, surrendering the Word to history, strips it of its essential mystery, and reduces its role to that of describing a successive chain of events. The hermetic philosophy of the Gnostics, and of the initiated of all types, whether they claim to be the chosen of God, or whether they base their superiority upon themselves, is just as culpable and false as the narrow realism of those who deny inner experience of being, and the radical upheaval produced by the vision of the absolute.

Of all the lessons I learned from the Bible, the loftiest seems to me to reside in the nature of human speech. I learned to respect in words, not the mere aspect of things but the very substance of man. I left behind me the province of charm, in which the manner of utterance outweighs the value of the thing uttered: hidden intentions to which I alone should have possessed the key seemed to me empty and futile, for they are mere deceits to hide the poverty of knowledge. At the same time, however, I went further than the external logic of things. The sequence of cause and effect, however strict it might seem, was confined to narrow limits. And even had the whole universe been rationally explained, that would not have been sufficient to appease the dissatisfaction of personal consciousness which is shocked by its own singularity. But the language of the Bible is centred upon this very singularity, which it raises to the universal while keeping it in its place.

The Word of God is addressed to all, but to each according to his own harmonics: nevertheless, it needs a favourable ground, a disposition of the being, an anticipation at several levels. If the divine Word is devoid of pride, by what right is there pride in human utterance? Hermetic speech is pure idolatry. But if the divine Word demands preparation, and germinates only in hearts stirred to their depths, is human speech, which is sanctified by the Word, to be so little self-respecting as to spread like a weed only on the surface of things?

The language of the Bible, made up of powerful symbols, strongly rooted in the concrete but aspiring to absolute heights, teaches us that the simplest words are inseparably part of the whole experience of man. It teaches us to contemplate them within the unity of various meanings that such experience on several planes extracts from their ordinary meaning. The mystery of language and the symbolic life of words lie in their marvellous irradiation and in their spiritual interdependence, analogous to the communion of men among themselves, and which, among men whose essence is the Word, reproduce faithfully the fabric of the moral world. Those who have read the Bible will understand how, through it, I came to feel the truth of aesthetics: the search for the Beautiful, which the artist makes his purpose, is inseparable from the word which every man has received as a vocation; and thus inseparable from mental communion, which true Beauty shows in all its vast extent.

Looking back after ten years, I now see convergences between intellectual explorations which seemed to me independent at the time. While reading the Bible, I was also reading the German Romantics. I did not exactly stumble on them by accident. My first acquaintance with a world from which I was to derive some of my own original themes I owe to Albert Béguin's great work, *L'Ame Romantique et le Rêve*. It is to him that I owe my first voyage beyond the frontiers of the French mind, a country of such rare perfection, where the forms of reason are arranged so harmoniously that one is in danger of forgetting the anguish of destiny beneath the mask of logical proof. Even after the events which have made Germany a disgrace among the nations, I feel no inclination to turn away from the universal drama of this people, a drama both historical and transcendental. Perhaps the unhappy genius of Germany presents the most striking example of a desperate undertaking, the temptation which no race and no individual escape—that of unifying, within pure immanence, the sequence of history and its revelation. Of these two terms, the second is transcendental, and can only be appropriated by man through a demiurgic act, which almost seems to be in the German's nature. Having accepted that notion, one might set out a collective psychology for this people, which everything impels towards failure, starting with its neighbours and its soil.

At the same time as Germany, I began to be interested in Israel. I was nearly twenty when I grasped the significance of Israel in history. Up to then, I had scarcely had the faintest idea of what the word Jew meant. Then, when I saw the fate of modern Germany growing clearer, I understood that this people, like Israel, had swallowed the Bible the wrong way. Israel, guardian of the Promise, had laid sole claim to it: Germany wanted to be the Promise itself. Both were exclusive, claiming to be the sole bearers of the Revelation. Both were opposed to the Christian axis of history. Israel was so proud of its dialogue with God that it denounced as the worst scandal of all the God who became incarnate for all. Germany went even further, for its whole people, posing as the redeemer, wanted to be the triumphant Christ, the Christ of armed might and the sword—and became in fact Antichrist. Or, to use other terms, Israel exiled itself from history, and considered itself transcendent, like the God who had chosen it: Germany arrogated to itself immanent force, and put itself forward as creator of the universal spirit. This explains the savage hatred between them, as there must be between the extremes of a divided consciousness. Identical in their pride, they both rejected the Incarnation: and not merely the incarnation of Christ, but the very fact of incarnation, the drama of consciousness in a body.

Israel, exalting itself above other peoples, in its pride of being the absolutely chosen, becomes the butt of history, in which it gropes without making progress: Germany, dominating other peoples, in the pride of its absolute force, hurls history into chaos in its haste to prove to itself the immensity of its might. Both anti-historic, both bearers of the anguish of history, and the victims, one of transcendence, the other of absolute immanence, these two peoples are both open to the same condemnation, for the challenge they make to history leads them both to usurp the eternal, and to dethrone God for their idea of God. The metaphysic of peoples is not easy to discover, and I may be mistaken in advancing my present argument. Nevertheless, it seems to me that between the Jewish God, who reigns over his people of Israel as over a rock built from their historic illusion, and the German *Gott mit uns*, a deified instinct which is portrayed in the will to power, there is a significant opposition. Israel and Germany both regard themselves as privileged by being the sole chosen race; but one proclaims itself as chosen *beyond* history, and the other insists it has been chosen *by* history or by the universal Destiny. But the total abandonment of history, or its total rejection, both suppress one of the opposed terms of the spirit. Lacking any counterbalance, these two attitudes often become reversed. A transcendental and mystical Germany may quite easily arise from the Germany of yesterday, and the famous Jewish realism, the appetite for abstract properties, may become effortlessly reconciled with the idea of a transcendent choice. But it is the transcendence of Mammon instead of that of God.* These two fates are in reality one—the fate of consciousness thinking to escape contradiction by embracing one of its terms.

*Thus, modern Zionism must be regarded as a veritable conversion to history. Nothing is more admirable than the struggle of the Jewish people for a national idea and a national soil.

The Bible has always denounced just these two extreme errors. From the Babel of Genesis to the Babylon of the Apocalypse, the nations which lay claim to universal empire and an exclusive rule over men are severely punished: for God has reserved for himself the task of bringing men together. In the same way punishment is meted out to the Pharisees of the Gospel, those whom Isaiah hears saying: 'Stand by thyself, come not near to me; for I am holier than thou'—for God has reserved to himself the task of sanctifying men. As the builders of Babel, who erect a fortress against God, are sacrilegious, so are the Pharisees and priests who erect a fortress around God. But as the sin of nations in no way differs from that of individuals—it merely projects upon the screen of history, in enlarged characters, the tribulations and contradictions, the errors and setbacks arising from a common basis on which our particular difference feeds—the lesson of the Bible confirms our personal union in evil and, in the specimen fates of these peoples, teaches us to understand our own undertakings, bound up with theirs through that specific coherence which history, in a tangible manner, is beginning to reveal to us in all its force.

*   *   *

There is little comfort, admittedly, in going through life tormented by antinomies. But in adolescence, when without experiencing them as yet one can perceive them, the mind becomes exalted at watching them struggle within it with the brand-new weapons of intelligence. And if one discovers, by being timely wounded in the affections, that one's sufferings may justify their struggle, passion excites one's ideas, and the philosopher of twenty adopts the stance of a mythical hero, exalting his grief into a universal theme, and resorting to the extreme attitude most fitting to his pride—until the moment comes when he realises that the antinomies of consciousness are not a spiritual game on the trapeze, but the eternal, and quotidien, condition of man, and that he must experience them in everyday existence before resolving or aggravating them by words.

I had to wait a long time, receive and give blows, and see my thoughtlessness punished by the suffering of others—with what ensuing muddle of sentiments, what lies, whose weight is still heavy upon me!—in order to recognise the terrible attributes and responsibilities of the mind incarnate. And to recognise as well the greatness implicit in those very limits: not even an angel is more beautiful than a perfect man, for the struggle to be a man is a marvel of consciousness in a universal matter, every fibre of which quivers, every force of which is set in motion, by our least gesture. But at twenty I was questing after mirages, roaming through deserts of abstraction. Again and again I reviewed the two terms of my intimate antinomy: personal solitude—communion with mankind. I went from one to the other, assuming attitudes, exploring contrasts, trifling with the abyss through the torments of my mind. I was, in short, ridiculous, as one always is at twenty, when one puts more trust in one's ideas than one's life.

For all that, these two terms were real, and their antagonism tragic in the real world. After all, it is a common enough thing— I say it to justify myself for a piece of folly which lay not in my ideas but only in the vanity I derived from them—to see know-ledge precede experience in many an adolescent. A powerful imagination, applying itself to the most abstract notions, makes them ignite like touchwood: and in the *commedia dell'arte* that the adolescent plays for his own benefit, many entirely spontaneous flashes of passion have the same accent, the same painful edge, as if he had drawn them from life. We experience nothing, besides, but what we have already thought of beforehand. I became enthusiastic over ideas which bore me now, when I re-read their didactic presentation in those books where I first found them. But I have certainly not forgotten them, rather the opposite: they have become flesh and blood, symbols and dreams, daily fears and desires. I first accepted them because latent forces within me had chosen them as a support, such ideas being the framework of forms that my forces were to conjure up.

At that period in my, rather skeletonic, mental development, I read avidly and almost without method, for the pattern of my reading was always escaping from the lines I had mentally laid down. I was impelled along all sorts of paths by my pure need to justify myself. One day I heard Philip on the subject of *Christianity and Revolution*. André Philip was young then, and had great authority with the young. In the turbulent language of feeling, he affirmed that the Christian faith is the very instinct of revolution, a revolution that man undertakes over himself, the necessity for which is perpetually present. This revolution carries history forward, and the progress of mankind, even in its economic laws, becomes part of the plan of God. Permanent inner revolution and successive historical revolutions are not at all opposed, but intermingled: it is the former which determines the latter, when the inertia of accumulated matter, and the sclerosis of old structures resist the expansion of a consciousness whose mental sphere is the future.

I became enthusiastic over these ideas, which linked up with my reflections on history. But I was even more struck by the man who so ardently proclaimed them. As Philip was one of his followers, I was led to read Karl Barth. I went back to the sources of Protestant theology, to Luther, whom I already knew, and above all to Calvin. Some pages of *In vino veritas*, their Socratic quality and the astonishing sensuality of the language, mingled with the bleak gleam of their thought, drew me to Kierkegaard: the abstract force of the *Christian Institution* and the Dane's admirable poetry filled me alike with sensual delight. But if a certain aestheticism entered into my religious reflections of that period— if I looked for the fascination of irreparable contradictions, either to surrender to it or to pit my strength against it—it is also a fact that the essential truths were thus taking possession of me, even while I thought I was master and could arrange them and even trifle with them, as spiritual myths.

Without noticing it, I was aggravating the painful schism in myself between the rule of mind and common sensibility, kept outside frontiers and threatened by famine or abrupt furies. My intellectual pride was laying the ground for protracted sufferings, which, being born of my mistaken attitude to myself, were to become the negative testimony to a truth which was my own error stripped bare and transcended by profound knowledge. For once one has fallen into error (nearly always before even having recognised it), it is not by denying it that one can rectify it, but by coordinating it with the whole of human nature. Life undertakes to show us not only the consequences but the purpose of our errors. Painfully, it incises the wounds that we inflict on our own nature; but it is the better to graft upon them the buds which are to bear our final fruits.

It is a long time since I read Kierkegaard. I did not want to let myself be influenced by a recent reading of him which would doubtless have given my thoughts a different inflexion from memory. As I have a poor memory for actual texts—I can read the same book several times, without really coming to know it, the successive impressions mounting up and arranging themselves without conscious order—I shall speak of Kierkegaard only through the themes he suggested to me: I do not claim that his devotees will recognise them for their own. A natural propensity, aided by an unfortunate love affair, led me to proclaim my solitude. My taste for mental dissection, in depriving me of the spontaneity so necessary in love, forces me *to wish* to exist, instead of simply existing. My first inclination is towards analytical reflection, and the unity that I reconstruct from scattered elements rarely answers to the unity that I was unable to grasp in the first instance. I indulge myself too much in self-explanation, and carry this too far into the future. The habit of analysis has led me to develop in myself the mechanisms of fatal attraction: it amuses me to trifle with them, but almost immediately I grow tired of them. For the object never serves me as more than a pretext, the vanity of which strikes me as soon as it offers no further resistance.

When I read the *Diary of a Seducer,** I had made little progress in knowing what love was about. But I had a tendency to watch the action of my emotions on others and myself, rather than simply experiencing them. The *Diary* made an impression on me, the importance of which I only appreciated much later, when I read *Les Liaisons Dangereuses*. These two extraordinary books constitute the breviary of the sin against the spirit—or, in other words, against the deepest and most inalienable privacy of being, which, however, is the most vulnerable when its defences, even unconsciously, have become weakened. God holds the right of dominion over souls, and our greatest temptation is to supplant him in this role, either because we desire to be loved in his place or because we wish to measure, upon such sensitive material, the whole scope of our powers. I have not always been able to resist this game, which is frightening in its caustic sensibility. But if it leaves only bitterness in its trail, at least it furnishes the strange pleasure of doing evil in full awareness, and with all the refinements of consummate aesthetics and consummate hypocrisy. It is true that one cannot undertake such diversions with impunity, and that nothing causes greater havoc than the appetite to destroy others. This, if any, is the moral to be drawn from the *Liaisons:* and so strongly does it emerge from these pages, that I am terrified now to read them. In the *Diary of a Seducer*, the shameless spectator is scrutinised in his turn, and by the most inflexible of scrutinies, that of God, which becomes his own.

The mind which rejects love, borrowing only its language with a view to sacrilegious possession, ends always by jamming its own carefully constructed mechanisms: in which lies either its perdition or its salvation. For the scope of its design brings entire self-

*This is contained in Volume I of Kierkegaard's *Either/Or: a Fragment of Life*. (Translator's note.)

revelation, and henceforth it is face to face with God, with no possibility of withdrawal: the alternatives are suicide or an impulse from the heart. A solitary nature, even among the emptiest of pleasures, is never distracted from itself: given to calculation, it arranges its means, frequently to multiple ends. It keeps a close control over its characters, watchful over their entrances, and above all careful not to confuse their roles. By this, it arrives at self-knowledge, not of its unity, but of the incessant diversity of its possibilities. But should such a nature become suddenly aware of its inner void—a risk which grows greater, the livelier its capacity for reflection—and its activity grows frenzied, its very lucidity a dizzy hovering over nothingness: that is, unless the immense responsibility of its allegedly gratuitous actions (which the mind knows very well are not gratuitous, but which up to now it has not openly confessed to) drives it back into the tragic impasse where freedom begins.

If the reverse side of solitude is the torment of the mind which cannot love or fails to find its object, its bright side and royal image is this full and precious freedom. It is only through being alone before evil, and powerfully invested by conscience, that one can understand what dignity lies in us. When, from one piece of weakness or carelessness to another, we slip without noticing it towards the basic error, our soul is a veritable slave of time, which mounts up like a cancer within us. We are in a state of perpetual sin, neither truly unworthy nor truly worthy. This incomplete awareness, this sudden slackening of a consciousness which submits to more than it wills—these make up our daily lives. The theologians tell us we are contributories to the original sin committed by Adam at the dawn of mankind, the historic burden of which is aggravated by accidental determinations in each individual, without our will being fully committed. The psychologists might say that consciousness, by becoming infinitely diversified, becomes more and more fragmented in its actions, which increases the dangers of its acting through omission, and forewarns it to summon up all its concentration for essential decisions.

This does not matter, for even if our experience of sin were, to a large extent, the wholly psychological one of an imperceptible drifting into evil, I refuse to see in this specific habit of transgression the essential component of my own particular sin. When I read *The Concept of Dread** I was already strongly influenced by the Protestant atmosphere, if not by Protestant theology. But I did not accept predestination, and looked for an absolute solution to the problem of freedom. Kierkegaard showed me that the absolute choice is offered to every man, at least once in his life. Each one of us commits the sin of our origin, and makes the *qualifying leap* in evil—and not merely impelled by the gathering weight of anguish, but after a pause in the eternal, when the eternal stands still, when total consciousness recognises itself, and when God reveals his Face. However impelling may be in each individual the fatality of mankind, the moment arrives when the general attraction of sin gives way to personal commitment: consciousness reins in duration, and dams up the determinations which we thought of as irreparable, and however urgent may be the mass behind it, deems itself capable of supporting it at that precise point where it is seized by the dizziness of abandonment. The faults I had committed up till then were in a certain way external to myself. But now, on the contrary, I suddenly find myself before the pure possibility of my sin: I recognise its nature clearly, and know that, in committing it, I take it upon myself before God, and against God. Or, to use the language of the psychologists, I have the choice—a perfectly free choice—between killing my personal dignity or consecrating it by a moral act. I know, furthermore, that my dignity contains the dignity of every man, and that it is the whole of man that I commit with myself. A moment ago, fate had driven me back upon the abyss, now it is

*Kierkegaard's *The Concept of Dread* has been translated with an introduction and notes by Walter Lowrie. Oxford University Press, 1944. (Translator's note.)

174

I who drive fate back upon my own will. If I do evil at this moment, it will not be through simple cowardice but through a deliberate concentration of my whole being, with a tragic solemnity, and in the light of a religious challenge which illuminates me in my most secret depths.

I do not, of course, claim that such absolute moments are the rule in the spiritual life, even if the practice of inner vigilance predisposes the mind to them. Even revolt against God may become a habit, and the demoniac become frozen in his grimace. Besides, we are all acquainted with instants of imperfect lucidity, which are, so to speak, a degraded version of such moments: we catch the echo of our profound freedom and of our entire responsibility, but covered or veiled by the beating of the blood in our temples, or by that half-sleep of the soul which makes of our transgression a waking dream. 'God wills it that thou be hot or cold!' the Apocalypse tells us. It is true that we are, nearly always, lukewarm, and not strenuously bent on sin, but powerless to dominate the accidents that lead us to sin, to discern the very instant when we are about to accept it. Nevertheless, we do not merely drag along with us the after-effects of our fathers' evil-doing, for if that were so, being flung into life by an arbitrary decree, we would be entirely abandoned to the contingency of a nature whose freedom would grow progressively weaker from the awakening of consciousness on. We are no more the slaves of evil than of grace: we are born to our particular destiny by an unequivocal affirmation of our free will. And if we choose sin, it is because our freedom, absolute in a finite being, drives us to deny our finiteness.

But our freedom is only absolute by being established on the absolute: we can only graft ourselves upon it, or hurl ourselves into the abyss. Man, in choosing sin, thinks he is his own demi-urge, while he really shuts himself up in the finite. From that moment on, the false demiurge, if it is a conscious and voluntary one, will try to multiply appearances and distend its finiteness to infinity: if it fails, it will turn upon the obstacle, preferring to destroy it and itself at the same time, rather than recognise its limits, and salute the transcendent beyond. Or else, with slackened will, and consciousness half blurred, it will submit without more ado to the gathering speed of transgression; but for it to be really responsible, even in the disintegrating state it has accepted, it must have understood at least once, and in the clearest manner, that it was master of this acceleration. There would be no personal morality if my consciousness, in the full exercise of its powers, were incapable of choosing, of confirming in itself the transcendent, or driving it into exile. Just as, in the intellectual sphere, a Descartes can wipe the slate clean, so, in the spiritual, each of us can act as though fate did not exist, and determine himself absolutely by an act which commits his moral life, just as birth does his organic existence. In his animal nature, he is not the master of his existence, but he is in his spiritual nature: he may live either in God or in death.

What Kierkegaard taught me was the lesson of our solitude. It may be that it impresses me more vividly than others, for solitude was for a long time my only true experience. When one is alone, one lives face to face with oneself, and face to face with the God who gives a countenance to our dignity. He himself is wounded by everything that acts against it: and the shame that results is so great that he who feels it no longer dares to look at his brothers. One has to live in solitude in order to understand how deep is our communion with others. For solitude only becomes isolation with sin, when I cut myself off from that inner man who is myself in all others: when I commune with myself, I feel the bonds that unite me with my neighbour, and with the totality of the living, vibrate through my whole singular being. If the mystic experience is a plunge into absolute solitude, a continuous lightening of appearances, a stripping away of the accidental in our relationships with everything and the All, then, after the long calcination of the objects which retain us, all that survive are those ineffable relationships which are the fabric of the living species, of the world, and perhaps of God. I can conceive an inverted mystic experience, where precisely those relationships would be destroyed: a mystique of absolute evil, the terrible isolation of the destructive instinct which eats into essence like an acid. The naked spirit and consciousness at its supreme point of self-awareness sometimes arrive at the crossroads of these two mystiques—or rather, even in the most positive mystique, the danger of a mystique of destruction persists and increases.

When a man has reached the point of recognising that the least of his actions or thoughts may illuminate or mortally wound the eternal human figure, according to whether his own freedom is fed on humility or inflamed with pride, he may, under the very eye of God, and by an unlimited procuration, either carry being into a beyond or annihilate it first. Extreme solitude is thus not at all incompatible with historic compassion: it is, on the contrary, given full and infinite significance by Christ suffering that same compassion and misery on the Cross. This explains why, with Christian mystics, the end of the spiritual struggle is identification with the Crucified One, and through him with universal suffering and hope. I do not know whether Kierkegaard ever achieved this end, nor whether he accepted history as a factor in contemplation. His disdain for 'historico-mundane' values rightly makes him suspicious of all religious Hegelianism. But a radical denunciation of historical immanence ends in a feeling of damnation *hic et nunc*, and of the absurdity of history, entirely given over to sin. The terrible Protestant doctrine of predestination might well be merely a fresh version of the exile of Israel amongst the gentiles. Instead of surrendering to the Hegelian temptation, which deduces the universal spirit from the operation of history alone, the solitary might plunge back into the pure transcendence of faith.

In my moments of abstract exaltation I revelled in that exile, and made it my boast. But we have all travelled through an historical epoch in which spiritual union imprinted itself so deeply in our flesh, that I will never again be able to adopt, before this world of men, the attitude of he who washes his hands of it. Very much to the contrary, for this same, fatal history has shown me that inner truth, fruit of that freedom which strives to understand and to will, acts directly on the historic mass, and bends and canalises it in the ways of salvation. It is possible that the reality brought to light by the instinct of truth may be an intermediate thing in relation to the event; but the event is affected by it, and the worst horrors are qualified in terms of this reality, as well as the highest values. Thus, in the solitude of the heart, we are able to commune with our brothers in history, and to participate concretely in duration. It is enough to reflect on the bread, with its central significance in the Church: this bread for which men struggle, the daily bread the need for which so often becomes tragic—an aspect that the hermetic philosophers of history fail to see—is also, in the spiritual heights, the Presence of the living God.

CHAPTER SEVEN

CERTAIN poets are born thus: their sensitive nature inclines them to images, and they instinctively express their emotion in verse. Such natures are often diffuse, and susceptible to the slightest nuances—simple echoes, perhaps, but rich in singular overtones. Their activity is not at all original. Open to any stimulus, they allow themselves to be determined by it, but the initial agitation spreads through their whole being, without meeting the resistance of their contemplative faculty. This results in complex chemical changes, so free and diverse in appearance, so supple in the possibilities they bring into play, that they give the impression of some higher activity: yet these are merely the reflexes of a powerful sensibility. Innate lyricism, and the faculty of vibrating in response, arise from the constitution of the soul, not from the mind; they help to refine sensitive natures, by developing their instrumental powers, but add nothing to their thought. Great poets have lived on pure sensation and emotion, without feeling a need of ideas, and without dreaming of justifying either themselves or their poetry in the sphere of knowledge.

Perhaps I am mistaken. But however great the charm of their verse, and however imperceptibly this followed the movements of the heart, I have always given it less credit than thought striving to reach itself. I know from experience that spontaneous lyricism springs from the vegetative part of our being. It fills us with a transitory euphoria, makes us seem agreeable or pitiful to ourselves, and attaches us to our own ego. How many poets— even among the best—write only in order to console themselves or to feed on their own images! The narcissism of adolescence, born of an excessive sensibility unstabilised or canalised by anything, turns up again, intact and precarious, among those great maladjusted beings, the pure lyric poets. The blows of fate which, among others, would coarsen the feelings or be dominated by the mind, maintain an indulgent sadness in these eternal adolescents who cannot make up their minds to adopt a stable attitude in life. The incurable weakness of the romantic is his obsession with the undefined and the unbounded: his is a latent and passive angelicism, which weeps for the Golden Age of the ancient myths, and the art of transforming into a harmonious plaint, a consoling lamentation, his own flight from essential conflicts. The English, to designate this evasive attitude with its vain melancholy, have a particularly expressive word: they call it *escapism*, a clever term with ironic overtones to castigate the runaways in the name of those who remain.

Certainly it is necessary that we should always retain a feeling of our insecurity, and that a panic sensation faced with life should always be possible, for consciousness only conquers its equilibrium by struggling against an indefinitely renewed vertigo. The country of man is movement, but an autonomous movement pursued through the tempests, the tidal waves, the flat calms of history and the universe. It is a movement *going counter to* the natural movement, sometimes taking advantage of the latter, sometimes piling up a force which shatters it. Not that consciousness is not natural; but it derives from the nature of man, and not of the universe which besieges him. He who can only bemoan his fate is swept away by the wave. He may find a certain sensual pleasure in feeling the brutal force he has been unable to master, in mingling with it while it is shattering him, and even in imagining he has become that force incarnate, even as it crushes him to the marrow. He may take such pleasure in being scattered in the spray of the waves, while he preserves the illusion that this scintillating disintegration testifies to the sovereign agility of the mind. But no matter with what fine words he adorns his own impotence at living, the outcome of his flight is destruction.

We cannot escape from our human condition. Once we have understood this very simple truth we have stepped over the threshold which separates the adolescent and the adult. It is only at the cost of many chimerical freedoms that we win our meagre and harsh freedom. But there is nothing grander than this voluntary poverty, which gives us a grasp on life, and establishes the language of men. From the moment that we accept our limitations, and make them as much our own as our body, words in turn become contracted to their true meanings: we cannot make them express more than they wish to, but they say what they do fully, and we are united with them in spirit. Our language becomes pregnant with experience, and is simplified in becoming richer. Instead of inciting us to escape, it retains us in our being, through the need for truth which it bears within it. This limitation is an impoverishment only in appearance, for the commonest words show themselves to be the most essential, and we grasp the infinite in the very centre of our finiteness. Our consciousness, with its inexhaustible harmonics, amplifies to the summit of the soul the tangible reality of common sense.

It is, it seems to me, within this moral perspective that poetry, like all art, must place its aim. Adult poetry is a poetry that weighs its words with the weight of suffering, of joy, of reality which they should have for every man. Every word is determined by a contemplation of that which it incarnates or depicts. Those who know the value of words know well that words, like men, enter into reciprocal relationships, in a close interdependence, which reproduce the fabric of universal union. Words are only free in that total life which infinitely transcends all of them, but which each animates in a singular manner. Each word has a history: and each is part of history, and of the times in which we live. Ill-pronounced, in a context which cuts them off from their real and active meaning, they are merely caricatures or blasphemies. One can no more trifle with impunity with the soul of words than one can with the soul of a man. And as, in truth, we have no other purpose but to elucidate ourselves within time and the eternal, the function of the speaker of words is inseparable from that of every man, *hic et nunc*, in the historic confusion of which the present anarchy of language is for some a symptom, for others, more far-sighted, a cause.

If there are a few men, amidst the excesses of modern verbalism, who are ready to assume full responsibility in their words—and that sums up the whole writer's morality—it is not merely language but the integrity of man himself which they will succeed in preserving. To enter into everyday experience and take it to the extreme in its errors and its truth; not to look upon modern man as a spectacle, but to be modern man, to suffer for him and overcome his contradictions; not to rail at barbarism, but to envisage it as possible, and victory over it as also possible; to hope without illusions and to go on hoping, since the power of the word is in man, and its failure depends on man alone; to be conscious of the real powers of the lucid mind, and at the same time of its possible abdication; never to admit that barbarism may be final, but to say rather that barbarism can only endure for a while, whereas in the spiritual sphere nothing is lost—such seem to me to be the moral conditions without which language is the worst of vanities.

If man is really finished, what attraction can still persist in words which are related to nothing? Why allow literature to swarm upon a corpse? Only the immense irony of the mind, and its immense stubborn silence, should hover over these charnel-houses conjured up by the appetite for catastrophe. It is all very well for journalists, on the look-out for sensation, to demonstrate in letters a foot high the decadence of language, to demonetize the gravest expressions, and to forget that words are forces which bring to life the thing invoked, whether it be crime, war, or fear. But an artist, even if he has an unconscious bent towards death— and in some part of our being we all have—is surely unable, in the full consciousness of his art, and out of respect for his daily activity, to deny in the heart of words that very thing which justifies them in his eyes, I mean the creative Word? On the contrary, our responsibility before words is identified with our freedom in history, and the effort of reflection which raises art to its final heights is inseparable from the will to salvation: it is a knowledge of man in the permanent form of his present destiny, a prescience of the abysses into which a misinterpretation of his nature might drag him, a mobilisation of those inner energies which will divert him from the threat by which he is fascinated.

Whatever activity the mind chooses for itself according to its own vocation, it can be no less than total to-day: there is no branch of science so remote, no sphere of art so privileged, that the question of the future of man does not enter into it in a primary and functional way. This is the price to be paid for the right to think. And I fully realise that the future begins at once, and not in some mythical distance which ideal speculation holds in reserve to justify itself for its failure in the concrete.

What we need are works which embrace a whole life, and with it the world: works constructed and planned, which reject as a weakness or a blemish the discontinuity of lyrical impressions, however vividly these may be summoned up. A day will come perhaps, when fate is taking a rest, when these fugitive impressions will have their function again, and give to life once more its sorrowful or charming diversity. To-day, the main thing is to learn to live, and to stand fast in a world in which all the laws of equilibrium are once more being challenged, to bring to light the granite of history, and to build upon it as a rational architecture the mental structure of man. What we need are simple outlines, which enter boldly into combination, but according to clear principles. In fact, we need space; and the less our range of vision is encumbered with objects, the more chances we will have of defining the true constant factors of being. Similarly, to think powerfully without being seduced by appearances presupposes a sustained effort which is part of the creative vocation: it is of small account if this effort lacks the glitter of fashion, as long as it has the efficacy of truth.

*   *   *

I was not a born poet. As far as I can still judge my youthful ways of thought, they were ready, it seems to me, to develop within the sphere of logic. Experience of poetic language came to me only after reflection on that language itself: it did no more than graft itself upon my need for knowledge, on to my quest for an answer to the various *whys* that the mind invokes by its own movement. But reflection on the language of symbols does not necessarily lead one to use that language. What I needed was some necessity of other than an intellectual order, to decide me to express myself through images. Meanwhile, as I have remarked earlier, I was held captive by my understanding: entirely pre-occupied with understanding, without beginning to live. The vital impulse of adolescence had aggravated the separation between the intelligible and the living: and sometimes enclosed in one, sometimes abandoning myself to the other, I experienced that sickness of first youth, whose ideas are divorced from existence, and whose existence, falling short of ideas, is merely a turmoil of confused desires.

My sensibility remained uncultivated. It was only later that I discovered that it consisted in a conjugal union between the life force and the mind. The adolescent Narcissus remained outside this union which poetry was to bring about, but which was not achieved without upheavals: and, unconsciously, he suffered for it, isolating himself in his pride of thought, then, a moment later, forgetting himself in the whirl of chaotic impulses. This double postulate was the cause of many a disaster, including the failure of my first love: and this failure, in turn, accentuated the sad divorce between mind and heart.

In the period of happiness which preceded this misfortune, I nevertheless wrote many poems, which, though bad, were

184

luminous and sensual. These were strings of images only loosely connected and in which woman served as the principle of metamorphosis. That was the period at which, without understanding either, I was reading the *Song of Songs* and Eluard. Although I thought my verses sensual, they were poor, naïve things: without experience of pleasure, and without insight into deep love, I made stereotyped comparisons, the very boldness of which was both perverse and chaste. My dreams were couched in flowers and trees, and even more than in real things, in the words which stood me in their stead. I employed words without knowing them, to soothe the vague yearnings of my heart. And if a few flashes of passion occasionally sear these sentimental elegies, that was because, in spite of the flowers and trees and fountains, in truth I felt alone, and was suddenly afraid.

I have kept none of these poems, and detest the memory of them. Their vocabulary was the conventional, worn and obligatory one of superficial amorous lyricism. One needs the genius of Eluard, and his 'long loving reflection', in order to release the inexhaustible symbolism of simple, everyday love. The tenderest feelings of love, the dreams, the pleasures of imagination or the flesh, are so utterly bare, so entirely reticent, that expression either coarsens or tarnishes them. One must have studied love at length, and thought and lived by it, in order for 'all to be miracles'. One thinks one is imitating the miracle, and one sets down mere commonplaces. How many young poets imitate Eluard because they are, or were, or would like to be, in love! They sink into the flattest jargon of surrealist preciosity— which might, perhaps, be forgiven them, if they did not pepper their writings with stupefying theories!

Being a provincial, I knew nothing of the latter: novelties only reach the provinces when their vogue is over. One has only to go ten miles out of Paris in order to perceive the vanity of the literary event. They are still symbolists in Lausanne, and surrealists in Landerneau. All things considered, a young man who is seeking a language has more chances of fashioning one all his own when he is alone, far from the clans and the cliques, and the centre of that sterile agitation in which art struggles, forgotten in the turmoil of ideologies. If he imitates those whom he likes, it will always be spontaneously: their doctrines, which would be a tyranny for others, will neither falsify nor stifle his expression. His critical instinct will be more natural, and nearer to common sense: being less paradoxical, it will be more solid and more human. His loss will be slight, if he is unacquainted with the art of talking for the sake of talking, which is the basis of present-day criticism. At least, he runs no risk of plunging irremediably into an impasse, like those writers 'full of promise' who keep their masters, customers or friends on a lead.

What gave my writing its strength was above all my own ignorance. I became enamoured only of that which said something to me. Belonging to no school, I was unprejudiced about any encounter. No *a priori* notion about language distracted my reflection. Eluard's accent was not mine: I was mistaken about myself, and my borrowed, and false, language was a part of my error. Our language develops with us, and he who has not yet defined himself can only imitate and learn to speak with another's language as go-between. When, abruptly, we are summoned back to our own life, which continues on ahead of us, we realise the linguistic gulf between borrowed and true experience. But without this form of borrowing, we would remain invisible to ourselves. It is by stages that we differentiate ourselves, that our life becomes utterance, and our utterance, life.

My feeble pastiches of Eluard were unable to withstand the despair I felt at the dwindling of all my dreams. I found myself mediocre, not only in the language of pure feeling but in feeling itself. Spontaneous as I may appear to be, that is merely a façade where love is concerned. My lightning strokes are deliberately planned. I throw myself into dreams at first, and when the reality arrives, my critical spirit takes the upper hand, and paints my folly in vivid colours: hence my doubt, and fear of the ridiculous, at letting myself be duped by my dreams, and the bitter defence of laughter, which cuts me off from myself. It is as if I could only conquer the universe of feeling, which I desire with such passionate determination, at the end of a long dialogue, at times disjointed, always dramatic, between mind and inclinations. Both the former and the latter soliloquize exorbitantly : I express myself only to keep them in contact, to make them intimate and perhaps inseparable, to arrive at that higher unity, that well-being of total man that some possess naturally.

But when laughter takes possession of me, it is a wild horse that drags me off tied to its mane : it lacerates me on all the rough flints of the roadway, and the taste of blood makes me drunk with my own humiliation. Such terrible moments are becoming more and more rare : it was around the age of twenty that I knew their full frenzy. When I relapsed into isolation and sickness, I frightened those who loved me.

I have always been loved by a few, with a singular depth of affection. No more than elsewhere is this the place to speak of her, who was to become my wife, and who was able to save me from my demons. She deserves that silence of the heart where tenderness is ineffable, like the air and our daily bread. However wretched and friendless I may one day become, I am sure that there is one creature at least who will have compassion on me, and that is a sublime assurance, a faith whose significance I know. There are moments in our life when we exist only through those who love us : she, who never despaired of resurrecting me from my many deaths, alone knows the price she paid for that miracle.

It may be that she was helped in this by a friend whom I later parted from with futile words, and whom I still miss. This was Robert Levesque, of whom Gide speaks with so much affection in his *Journal*, and who was my fellow-student at Lyons. To

Robert, I owe the fact of having opened my eyes on the world, not the world of ideas or passions—that, I haunted all too much, my eyes fastened on my dreams—but the simple and charming universe of every day. There was no one like Robert for making a thing of delight out of the smallest object : he regarded everything as a discovery, from the taste of a *croissant* to the design of a column. To go for a walk with him was to meet one surprise after another: he spent his life playing truant, and no doubt continues to do so. Had I been less surly, less closely shut in upon myself, the friendship of a man like Robert Levesque would have taught me what I only now begin to glimpse: the necessity for relaxation of the soul. But I did not know how to abandon myself to the tranquil simplicity of small pleasures. There was something about Robert's enthusiasms, which he doubtless derived from Gide, which got on my nerves. They seemed to me excessive, perhaps literary. He, too, kept a diary, and I could imagine him scrupulously noting down his sensations. There was an old quality about his youth: it was the youth of another generation, even less adapted than my own to the destiny which was already beginning to loom before us.

Men like Robert Levesque, with their luminous Epicureanism through which a man may attain to rare virtues, are somehow able to survive through catastrophes. But kindness, respect for others and for things, the instinct for freedom which makes the mind supple and enquiring, are qualities less and less fitted to understand the tragic times in which we live. They think they hold the truth, and are pained to see men drifting away from it. The great danger, for them, is egoism, which preserves them from the harsh blows of history, but limits their sensibility to the superficial delights of the moment. They will survive, but more and more restricted in their very pleasures, and will seem anachronisms to those young people to whom they believe themselves still near, but whose confusion demands other remedies than theirs. As for myself, I found Robert a temporary distraction, but without his in the least helping to develop my sensibility. He was armed, for all that, with a teacher's finest gifts—those that go unperceived. He was fond of me: and I am infinitely grateful to him for his affection, at a time when I was anything but amiable. His solicitude, his gentle anxiety for me, prevented me from slipping into the trap illness had laid. I do not know what plotting went on between him and my dear love, but one fine day I found myself on a train which carried me off towards the Pyrenees.

★   ★   ★

I left Lyons for six months—just enough time to get back my strength. As the train pulled out of the station, I gazed once more on the Rhône with its subtle curve between the quays, the University bridge, the gulls. The iron-grey day with its clear outlines quickened the austerity of the town, with the sage and reasonable air lent it by its rivers, the amphitheatre of its hills, its justly proportioned arrangement. It was beautiful in the declining afternoon, to which approaching night gave a keen edge. In its refusal to yield itself, I recognised all it stood for. In a moment, the shadows would swoop down upon it, bringing with them that anguish, those dense terrors that dog the heels of the rare passers in streets too broad for them. Throughout the long season of mists, anguish scarcely leaves the city, and the city strives to conquer it with cold, with the severe dominion of the wind. The north wind has a clean bite at least, and the mind responds to its brutal stimulus: it animates the life of the stones, flings its challenge in people's faces, assails them with unexpected space, and some-times, as if to reward the worthiest, strangely softens the sky.

For this Jansenist race can only live under the whip. The mist plunges it into depression, and certain days of winter isolate it so utterly from the world that it is no more than a huge derelict in the treacherous cotton-wool of the unknown. These people are reasonable but without resilience, through an over-stressed resoluteness which, in the majority, is confined and organised in massive prejudices. Possessed by fear, against which their prejudices provide only a negative defence, since they crush in them that spirit of invention which replies to the challenge of life by the values of life, they are extreme in their choices, now assuming the iron yoke, now covertly prostituting themselves. Lyons resists all giddy impulses by immobilising itself. But when such impulses do overcome it, it hurls itself into them chained: its passion is always culpable, and the clank of chains follows it everywhere. Even on fine days it does not know how to relax. Lyons has no tenderness: it is a perfect-breasted city which refuses to be feminine. In the sunlight, it has the air of a young widow from Ainay, not garbed in black, it is true, but severe in its hesitant grey, which is neither the bluish grey of the sky nor the mourning grey of the stones. And when the hot days come, it stifles, in long sleeves and high-buttoned bodice.

Few strangers can boast of knowing the city. The Lyonnais have no great reputation for hospitality. They fear the intruder, who lives by other rules, which are bad because different from theirs. For they are, in the depths of their being, so unsure of their own laws that they prefer to make themselves impenetrable and turn their lives inward, rather than risk the challenge of some breath, or appeal, or question from without, and to reply to which they would deem almost a self-betrayal. Polite, but sparing of their courtesy, they have little gift for conversation, not knowing how to yield themselves in words. They live under a perpetual siege, both from within and without. The lower classes are more open, and more mixed, having come from Savoie, from the Dauphiné and the Ardèche: but they quickly change, and the second generation closes in on itself. It soon becomes petty bourgeois, and shares that uniform character extending from the aristocrats of the peninsula to the suburban dwellers of Montchat.

If the Lyonnais do not share their virtues, neither do they share their vices, which, with them, are very secret, deep-buried, and rotted with shame. They enjoy no freedom in evil. They are in fact terrorised by it, but its fascination makes them practise all sorts of turbid pleasures. There is nothing—not even their notion of good—which is not contaminated by it. Even while they do good, they feel a nostalgia for evil. They possess the thoroughly Jansenist art of abasing the body in its simplest delights. The pleasures of the table are the only ones which do not fill them with remorse. In a climate so inclement to life, the majority become withered very young. They are egoists, with the constricted virtues of egoism, the family instinct, a tendency towards thrift, and, among the rich, a façade of proud simplicity, which makes them feel they are poor in spirit, while in reality they lack that ease which consists in enjoying beauty in display, and not display in beauty. They are frightened to handle their wealth, which is all in abstract investments and is thereby more powerful. They never waste a thing, but keep a budget of their pleasures, and whatever expense they then incur, however large it may sometimes be, is always accompanied by sordid calculations. Handsome gestures are not their strong point. They have their vices, certainly, but even these they skimp. They are poor at playing with the devil, who cuts their sensual pleasures short, and prolongs their boredom in remorse.

Nevertheless, there are certain powerful natures for whom Lyons is the natural setting: mystagogues, friends of the mist, who devote themselves to hermetic speculations, *initiates* of the second degree in this town which only accepts you after a long and painful novitiate. These latter are sons of the mist, and their knowledge ends in themselves, but not without having, by its diffuse emanations, weighed down the already confined air one breathes in Lyons. Others, through hatred of the mist, rush to the other extreme of reason. These fanatics of intelligence are moved by fear of the night, as the initiates are by terror of the light. And they remain for ever puritans, even when they become the expounders of some absolute form of freedom: they are locked up in their lucid ideas more securely than in any prison. Lastly, a few accomplished minds manage to wed mystery and light, the essence of hidden things and the clarity of appearances. These really intelligent people are uncommunicative, for the town offers them little encouragement. And some of them never manage to get rid of a subtle egoism of intellect, the fault of which lies rather with Lyons than themselves. But their sturdy intelligence is also diffused through the town, and gives it its spiritual virtue, its cold intensity, perceptible to few people, but to the best. I know no other town in France where the spiritual life is more concentrated than in Lyons: and at the same time, so constricted, so mistrustful of the marvels of language, that it only achieves expression with great difficulty, by overcoming a protracted aridity—I might almost say a protracted impotence, so largely is terror mingled with this reticence in speech.

The town that I was now leaving for six months I never saw again except in passing, and always with an uneasy feeling. But could I have guessed, throwing a last and almost tender glance at it, that it was expelling me for good? For ten years I had lived at its heart, but henceforth I would be a stranger to it. It kept my adolescence as a hostage, as though to make sure of my resentment: there are some parents who do all they can to make their children hate them, and never feel better than when they are cursing the ungrateful son. This righteousness, which dismisses the same thing in anyone else, lies at the root of family life and education in Lyons: it is merely, I admit, the righteousness of provincial life everywhere—but nowhere so ferocious and militant as in Lyons. I was glad to escape from it for a time, and to be at last that which it most detested in me—myself. Now, I would no longer be watched. The shadow of my uncle would no longer follow in my wake. I would no longer read, on shuttered faces, the servitude of the children or the inexorable mastery of the fathers. For my part, I had had enough of the austere mask of the Law: I sensed already that it was dead, and that I was about to bury my past.

All the same, I had often cheated that very Law, by a thousand ruses which bound me all the more to the town, or at least to that part of the town where the Law held no sway. They bound me, not in simple complicity, but by an almost sensual affection, rendered guilty by the prohibitions I had defied in order to explore it. What reprimands I would have endured without a murmur, to be able to saunter just once more down those black streets, or stroll around the booths of the *vogues*,* or inhale the darkness of the churches, or watch the rivers flowing beneath the bridges! But to be even a quarter of an hour late was to have to face a whole battery of suspicions: and behind every suspicion was a host of unvoiced thoughts, many of which wounded me and made me feel unclean. Yet my love of the town was the greater for being thwarted. I only felt alone and free of my bonds within it: it nourished me with an experience which my family upbringing denied me. Sometimes I felt free and anonymous, sometimes furtive and clandestine. Now I was lost in the flood of faces, now spied out by each one of them. Here, I was exalted in prayer, there, I brushed with a shudder against evil. Being not so much a spectator as a visionary, little susceptible to details of places, but almost too much so to their power of suggestion, I mingled my soul with the town, the latter changing to the caprice of my heart. If my heart was light and gay, the town opened itself to me entirely; but if it was gripped by anguish, the town became peopled with threats and inquisitorial spectres.

Dedicated to the Virgin, this town was haunted by prostitutes. It had its low quarters, and its elegant one, the former labyrinthine, cramped and sombre, the latter raised in the light, full of a spacious and peaceful air. In order to climb up to it, one had to escape from the sinister network of streets; but first, one lost

*A name given to travelling fairs in the Lyons region. (Translator's note.)

oneself in the obscurity of the *traboules*, where thoughts of murder lurked in the gloom. One got one's breath back at the foot of the hills, and calmed one's racing heart, still oppressed by the infamies it had patiently spied out. Then one began to mount Jacob's ladder, rearing up with giddy abruptness like a calvary. These flights of steps, on a winter night, were terrible defiles, which seemed to invite the sky to fall in. When rain and mist descended, they became glaucous and slippery, and I waded in the blood of Golgotha. And the town lapped up to my feet, its heavy, murky rumour ebbing and flowing in my heart. After that came a garden, with rich and crumbling earth, without any corrugations to provide a firm foothold: it was a steep but yielding rise, worn out with supporting the enormous edifice, the absurd monster which bent its back, for the convenience of Sainte-Marie Perrin. At last one reached the plateau, and felt the benediction of the wind over the town, and heard the muffled, sustained growling of the barely subdued beast.

I did not enter the preposterous basilica, conceived by some contractor with a fixation on public lavatories or Turkish baths, but went into the little chapel which stood next to it, marine and hollow as a shell, with an immemorial quality of silence, a castaway in the dense wastes of time. In this grotto where, among the candles, gleamed a miraculous Madonna with a far-away smile, the smell of incense evoked a haze of long-shed tears. Many must have wept in that place, from grief and joy mingled: it was a sanctuary of universal compassion, one of those rare places on earth where one feels both alone and filled with all things, the sufferings, the joys, the destinies of all men. Despite myself, I could not help comparing the secret retreat of the prostitutes and this luminous grotto: between the infamous and the ineffable prostitution flowed and was purified the world's eternal distress. Prayer down there, that despairing blasphemy against the burden of our condition, was hinged to prayer up here, and formed a part of communion in the Mystic Body.

One had to desire everything in order to understand everything, make the effort to love oneself in the depths of abjection, and remember that the Face of God awaits only a glance of love in order to shine on the face of man—of any man, even the most abject of criminals, or the most loathsome prostitute.

Fresh from traversing the back alleys of the town, I had wilfully charged myself with all the putrescence of evil: with my curiosities, my desires, my smug morality, my fear of the father, my powerlessness to pursue my revolt to the end, I was more defiled than the filthiest prostitute whose smile I had just avoided. She, at least, perhaps knew peace of mind, and had never delved into questionings of herself and her vice (and what is a vice, except the soul being arrested before evil, and in full awareness, doing evil). She was healthy, while I was sick in spirit, bearer of my own destruction and hers.

Because other creatures existed like myself, who spied out the evil in themselves, the quantitative sum of evil, which makes man reel under the yoke, was no longer an incomprehensible fatality vainly restrained by moral bands: it was a precise and personal burden, so heavy as to lead to despair, a living mass feeding on the animal being, and making one with it, viscera, heart, and mind. I wondered, and still wonder: are such beings necessary? Would it not be better for man to blame his evil on the powers of fate, or heaven knows what defective dispensation, which one day he may alter? Would it not be better for him to have some finite hope, instead of hoping against all hope? But the myths of progress have led to nothing, and if need be—I do not say in order to rid man of evil, but to combat evil effectively in man— one must have the courage to replace the mortal sickness of being at the heart of being: to propose, not an adaptation of the moral organism to bad conditions, which will become reabsorbed with time, either by a slow reform or by an abrupt mutation, but an integration of evil in the human substance itself, a challenge both personal and universal of man to man. For the law of history shows us, that at those periods when man thinks he is banishing evil from himself, there appears the tragic imminence of an inner seismic split, against which he has no weapons.

There is nothing which strengthens consciousness more than to know itself threatened from within. Then, the failures and fresh starts of history are incapable of harming this dramatic serenity, which is a virtue not of indifference, but of clear-sightedness, and which is able to act upon history with long-range remedies. With the city around me and within me, I felt that its life depended on my own, and that my salvation was its own. I learned that it has significance for the whole earth if a single individual finds peace of mind, without abandoning the drama which he lives through in common with the earth. The only joy we are promised comes at the end of infinite compassion: and any other is merely a happy accident, which we must know how to integrate in the universal passion.

It is not a theory of perpetual flagellation that I am proposing here. Moments of absolute happiness are a part of our patrimony, and we have the right to seek happiness in spiritual communion with all, for no true happiness is separate from the total destiny of man. Certain forms of happiness are even exemplary, and radiate charity. We are not commanded to go round everywhere with mournful countenance, as if this were the only monstrance worthy of the living God, but to be as much as possible like others, to be their neighbour. Such I was formerly, through a strangely impassioned quest, taking their evil from them with mingled shame and delight: there was a certain truth, but much perverse anguish, in this amorous hatred of evil. But this anguish was potentially mine, a part of my nature, and of my sin. Lyons brought it to consciousness: it was up to me to exorcise it, and to rid it of all ambiguity.

The denser my experience has become, the less have I been lured by the aesthetic of evil. I am a simpler person than I was ten years ago, less occupied with spiritual emotions, with shameful or angelic suavities. Evil is commonplace, when all is said and done: and all the refinements with which it is decked out are proof that we do not accept it as it is, that we ask of it more than it gives, the subtlety of a demon or an artist, or else absolute degradation. Of this I was still unaware in Lyons, where the seduction of evil prevented me from seeing it in itself. The bad Angel was beautiful, with a feminine and feline beauty. I liked the perturbation he caused in my heart, and blended religion with that perturbation. My way of the cross that I trod to Fourvière was made up of aesthetic stations, but, prevented from entering the real world by the constraints which I have mentioned, I lived, and could only live, in dreams. The chaos of my feelings grasped at, and arranged itself in, symbols, for which the atmosphere of the town favoured the creation. And as they were stronger than I was (my intuition going ahead of my experience), I conformed to these symbols and, without proper knowledge of myself, projected myself in a giant world.

But with all that, I had no other access to several major truths except through this releasing of enormous images, by which, like all good explorers of dreams, I imagined myself only half taken in, but which in reality I lived by: later, when reality had invested the whole sphere of dream, these images which I had thought of as poetic went through the same purification as myself. Divested of the accident of their origin, of the complex of transitory emotions which had engendered them, and which surcharged them with verbal sensuality, for the sole and perishable delectation of memory, they slowly assumed their proportion, founded me within their intelligence, and became the universal forms of my thought. I only grasped the meaning of the Communion of Saints, for example, after a series of approximations in images, in which truth, which is the aim of art, struggled with sensuality, which is its ordinary temptation: and not only with sensuality, but with demiurgic pride, the temptation to create an imaginary beyond for the true.

This symbolic approach to being, by a twin movement of encirclement and infiltration, is a process of thought whose laws we find strange. Enslaved as we are by analytical methods, in abandoning them we quake to lose the virtue of intellect. But when it has once become clear that unitary or symbolic thought has no intention of demonetizing understanding, but of integrating analysis itself in a vaster logical effort, nothing will be able to prevent a promotion of the symbolic faculty to reason, and a cessation of that secular disfavour which condemns it to go begging, in the tawdry finery of hermetism, the indulgence of dreamers alone. Poets feel such things: they often have a clear enough intellect, but they lack a language which would reconcile concepts and symbols. And perhaps man's crisis of substance will have to grow still worse, before unitary thought emerges fully armed from necessity.

What I do know from experience is that thinking in images sets at stake, both physically and mentally, the whole hierarchy of being: it is not detached from the object, but committed in concrete existence, and step by step includes the universe. And thereby, man *thinks in concord* with the world which surrounds him, he is both part and whole. I was the friend of a great city, inseparable from it, and borne along by its secret rhythm: it taught me to think within an evolving experience, without either deforming or interrupting it. All symbolic thought resides in that. There is not one of my works of poetry in which the city does not play a part: whether it be mother, mistress, whore, the image of the modern Gehenna, or the crucible of an obscure communion; whether it be the city I traversed as a youth, pursuing happiness but with misfortune at my heels, or the Babel of our present solitude, which fortifies itself vainly against nature and the Eternal; or the Church to come, the new moral edifice for which the cities of to-day, so tragically hostile to man, awake in us a painful need.

CHAPTER EIGHT

THERE passed two years of illness, but of tranquil rest, of an almost vegetative indolence, but intense mental activity, of idle walks and much reading. I felt a tumultuous need of poetry, stimulated by those whom I most admired, and which made the verses rush from my pen. These were two years of happiness and complete freedom, and what can I say of them? Each moment was so full and happy that I have kept no memory of it. All the poems of that period I have destroyed. They derived their whole vocabulary from Jouve, with whom I was in regular correspondence.

In October, 1937, leaving for Cherbourg, where I was to teach in a college, I paid a visit to the poet, and was bold enough to show him my first attempts. First attempts? It was more like a life work, the hundreds of specimens in a loose bundle which I gave to him. Jouve was living, at that time, in a severe and stately apartment at number 8 in the Rue de Tournon. It was not an apartment which let in much daylight, but rather a sort of haunt of the spirit, in which one only felt at ease with the lights on. Jouve had planned it himself, rather as an architect than a decorator. The furnishings were bare and staid, and there were panelled walls and tapestried hangings. The objects were few, but all justly balanced, and set up within a perspective rather than imprisoned by a fixed space. The pictures opened upon empty space, made to deepen the wall, and suggesting a ruined ogive, a motionless sky, earth burned by the spirit, as if the eye were only directed towards the outside in order to apprehend essences. They bore the signature of Sima, a great painter who regards the

199

earth as at the dawn of myth, in noble masses of matter and daylight.

The apartment bore the stamp of its master. I recognised, in Jouve's house, the same proportions as in his poetry. The man had a severe distinction, intimidating, but without arrogance. He had made it a rule always to be identical to himself, in his behaviour, his setting, and his thought. Everything in him was deliberate, arranged in concert with the whole of his characteristics. For his character was so powerfully though narrowly determined, that an object displaced by a millimetre, or the importunate rustle of a leaf, gave him an impression of strangeness, and was enough to make him suffer. He was composed in manner, but without calculation. He suffered the tyranny of objects which he had endowed with too profound a life: was enslaved, therefore, and found that his sole freedom lay in the perilous balance, perpetually jeopardised, which he was able by the force of his art to maintain between his innumerable creatures. Out of a grain of dust on the table, he made a spiritual obstacle. He staked the whole of beauty on the disposition of a word in the universe of the blank page. Doubtless he was even afraid of his own writing, for he had compressed and controlled it until, in its rhythm and spacing, it was analogous to printed characters. This analogy existed in the mind, but not in the letters: as if Jouve, caught between two extreme fascinations, that of confusion and that of exactitude, had only, by surrendering to the latter, increased the danger of the former, and was thus the victim of that implacable order which forbade him all spontaneity. For he made the least movements of being ever more sensitive, ever more anguished.

The monacal rule Jouve had adopted, far from freeing him, had become a torment to him. He worked within this rule, never finding it sufficiently severe, to such a point that writing became an atrocious ordeal, and the stubborn silence of words almost insurmountable. But it may be that he was only great by virtue of these terrible inhibitions. Guilty of desiring the essential, he sought it out in all things, thereby annoying the superficial and the foolish, who accused him of indulging a mania, but compelling the respect of serious natures, to whom his presence was a lesson in the severe dignity of beauty. I recognised him at once: he lived within the landscape of his own poem, *Hélène*, made, like it, of daylight and obdurate rock. I already loved him: and meeting him filled me with a certainty, a faith in the uprightness of the man, which have never been belied. I was prepared to learn from him the fate my poems deserved, and I bowed to it in advance.

He told me directly that this was mere raw material, moved by instinct perhaps, but giving no hint of beauty to come. He enumerated my influences, analysed their mechanism, and made me see their fortuitous character. Utterance is only truly necessary, he told me, when inner experience informs each word from within: words are not the mere legal tender of the idea, but the idea itself, experienced in the singular, and bearer of a wholly personal energy, of a *qualitative universal*, I should say, neither repetition nor parody, but a pure creation or crystallisation of values. The only true poet is he whose experience becomes a language. My language was borrowed, my experience nil, at least when voiced through others' words. There was nothing less certain than that I might be a potential poet. Destroy the whole lot, Jouve advised me, or else, if you haven't the strength, then tuck these papers away in a drawer. Force yourself to be silent. Don't try to hasten the maturing of your thoughts: and don't mistake for them these ideas and images that attract you in other people, which they have gradually built up in a whole which is their own. Wait until the need to write is invincible, and even then, utter no word before you have tested it in its substance. Practise writing, and regard nothing as achieved at the beginning, for one has to break a lot of tools before finding one's own instrument of knowledge.

He spoke to me of his own protracted mistake, of his unanimist work, which he had all rejected. And indeed, one needs a rare form of courage to admit to having been mistaken when one has passed thirty, for poets, in general, begin young. But Jouve himself did not think so. He thought that the work of a poet only starts with maturity. The true song of innocence was a song of experience. It was not without some pangs that I saw myself severed from a past which I thought I had won. But there was so much forcefulness, modesty and kindliness in the master's authority that I accepted as some rare token of affection his direct and unequivocal words. Remembering this example, I have never disguised my thoughts when a young poet who seems to me worthy of the truth has asked my opinion. Certain harsh words that one forces oneself to utter are the finest testimony to confidence and communion.

*　　　　*　　　　*

For six months I remained silent, without even attempting the exercises Jouve had suggested to me. After all he had said to me, the old words seemed to have a hollow ring, and I had no others. I felt unhappy and without an aim. In this state of abandonment I lost my taste for food, and the least bit of reading irritated me. Before even having proved to myself that I had something to say, I knew that I was born to create: my life would be an act of creation from start to finish, or nothing. Nevertheless, I was filled with self-doubts, having as yet done nothing, and accused myself of impotence or cowardliness. In this state of antagonised inertia, interrupted by brusque frenzies, my tendency to melancholy became more acute. I allowed myself to slip into an inner dumb silence, much closer sealed than that which circumstance imposes on us, for it is like a mark of secret damnation. There are some creative temperaments which become petrified by their inhibitions: I know of no solitude more pitiful than theirs. They will never gain any pleasure from the world created by others, for they live shrivelled up upon themselves, and exhausting themselves in trying to revive the foetus of their dead world.

But the day came at last when once more I faced the blank page. I was as if outside myself, almost an automaton: the words which came into my mind had no connection with those I had used formerly. In this way I wrote a long poem, the first that I have preserved, called *Christ au Tombeau*. When I re-read it next morning, I was shocked at being unable to understand it, a notion which had not occurred to me while I was writing it. The same necessity which had led me to write it, and which I had felt from one line to the next as a salutary and sustained impulse, imposed itself now in monolithic form on my defenceless critical spirit. This thing—this monster perhaps—was there: nothing could prevent this impenetrable object, this proof of a new order, *being*, with no other qualification for the moment than its mere existence. The poem (or whatever other name one likes to give it) *was*. I rid myself of it by sending it to Jouve, feeling certain that the latter would judge and classify it coolly and calmly. If bad, it would end up in the waste-paper basket; if good, it would present a problem, but one whose meaning still entirely escaped me.

Could it be that creative power only appeared after a fundamental split between the obscure part of being, called for lack of a better term, the unconscious, and its higher balancing functions, understanding and will? To this I replied in advance that such a cleavage, accepted as an absolute fact, was no more nor less than suicide. I refused to throw into the balance my unity of mind. That 'inspiration' should be the pioneer of intelligence, I could conceive: its way of approach might be different, but not its end. But to keep in opposition two aspects, or rather two closed spheres of knowledge, would end in civil war, hence in madness and death. Doubtless this divorce arose from the primacy that a certain language had acquired at the expense of another, relegated to the catacombs of the inner space: in this manner was created the fiction of a universe of light, in which thought was elucidated, a focus of communion and exchange, a positive hierarchy of relationships, and of a chaos doomed to the shades, relic of primitive syncretisms, peopled with opposing symbols, taboos, frustrated energies and dreams. In the universe of lucid thought, indefinite analysis presented itself as the essential factor of integration: for logic, sustaining it in its progress towards the elementary, postulated an implicit synthesis, a series of rational hypotheses or stages at which thought marshalled itself before pursuing its enquiry. In the chaos of the unconscious, integration became voracious, and all fell into frightful confusion: the conquests of the lucid mind, and the order strictly imposed on appearances, found themselves condemned in their very principle, in the name of spontaneous nature, of the first uprush of energy. Here, ecstasy replaced consciousness, and the arcana replaced explanation.

Deeply as were instilled in me all the arguments of logic, I was not able entirely to relegate symbolic consciousness to the shades. I perceived that logic is always frustrated in its need for unity, as the symbol is in its need for clarity. Might it not be the case that both are wilfully shut in by their reciprocal hostility? I was not so sure of living solely in the full light of day, in an objective universe. I admit that I appreciated at their full value the certainties this universe gave me, and the freedom of action I gained from the very fact that it was foreseeable. But I could also clearly recognise what a dangerous price I had had to pay for these advantages, and I suffered from an abstraction which arose from the very functioning of my mind. Nevertheless, I did not live solely on the social plane, within a system of stable relationships, or such as tended to become so. My external equilibrium was only one in appearance, a restraining one certainly, but sustained by the apparatus of reason and will. And there was one grave fact that my experience of the town had led me to understand—I was able to lead two existences at once which had no knowledge of each other: one being regulated but empty, the other, confused but full. And meanwhile, I had need both of the orderliness of the former and the plenitude of the latter. In one, I was free but uprooted; in the other, bound, but nourished, through the channel of these bonds, by a life both multiple and one, in which the distances of space and duration were effaced, and where men and things interpenetrated in an incessant Protean activity, generator of powerful images, difficult for the mind to penetrate, but in which the sensibility increased and became differentiated like an organic whole, not without strengthening and differentiating those images in their turn, through the very movement which made the sensibility blossom out.

These images and symbols expressed after a fashion my dependence in respect to the real: a much narrower and more complex dependence than might have been supposed from the relationships with exteriority which made up my mental system. They lived on me, and at the same time I lived on them: I advanced through them in thought, not aimlessly, but in obedience to the laws of a certain *consciousness,* vital rather than intellectual, a consciousness working upon itself, like an organism which creates, restores and reproduces itself. Nevertheless, I realised that such consciousness is vegetative: it reintegrates us within the whole, but only to absorb us within it to the extreme limit; and to abandon oneself absolutely is to renounce one's own unity and personal integrity. Through two opposed movements of consciousness, man thereby finally consummates his destruction—either because, being all mind, his abstraction becomes unbearable, or because, with mind slowly atrophied, the alluring boa of dreams swallows its prey to digest it at leisure. I did not see the necessity of choosing one or the other end. I am a whole, yet part of a greater whole: if I abstract myself from this whole, I condemn myself, but if I abandon myself to it, it devours me.

Hence what is needed is the setting up between us of an organic law of equilibrium, a vital osmosis. I must integrate while being integrated: my mind, guardian of my essential singularity, must penetrate more and more, without however fettering it, into that obscure consciousness which plunges its roots and feelers into the whole. Finally, the telluric forces, the collective energies, all those unknown masses which exert pressure on mankind generally or the inner being, must be educated and nourished by intelligence, by a method to which modern technique, whether it treats with matter or the psyche, is merely an imperfect and often caricatural approximation. Holding it to be true that a major image is not an accident of the imagination, but the mental form of a situation too complex, too fluctuating and doubtless distressing, to submit to analysis at the start, I allow it to grow and thrust out branches, adapting myself to its rhythm, borne along by it, but not swept away, while observing its articulations and metamorphoses, and the constellation of symbols for which from one aspect it serves as focus.

This *observation* of the autonomous genesis of images is only the first stage towards the unification of the mind: it demands a greater perspicacity than simple logical clarity, since it must be wary of not disrupting the procession of images, even while identifying the weaknesses and deviations of the movement. Thus, it is always menaced, either by naïveté or by disruption. It must be provided with references, constants, analogies within the flux: it must forge, in a shifting material, an instrument of thought which does not exist. But one may trust in the mind, as long as it recognises its limitations, yet nevertheless refuses to adopt a falsely antagonistic attitude to that which seems strange to it. It was in such a frame of mind that I faced the challenge levelled at me by my own poem, provided it was a true poem, or in other words, evoked, in a mind with control over symbols, deep-rooted responses.

*   *   *

Jouve sent me a reply immediately, with such expressions of admiration that his letter threw me into confusion. Not only did *this thing* exist, but Jouve found it powerful and beautiful: I caught myself looking it over with complacence, without understanding it any better for all that. On the same impulse I wrote another poem, called *Rédemption*, which begins with these two lines:

> *Mon sang est remonté si loin dans l'éternel*
> *Que mes membres des tiens se distinguent à peine . . .*
>
> [*My blood has climbed so far into the eternal*
> *That my limbs are almost fused with yours . . .*]

These two lines, which already contained the whole of the poem which was to follow, helped me to understand, or at least to sense, a symbolic progress the motivating energy for which was already stored up, although its developments were still unforeseeable.

In its two parts, *Christ au Tombeau* turned out to be the beginning and the end. In the first part, he lay between Good Friday and Easter Sunday suffering in a state of extreme anguish, as if he found it equally impossible to be either living or dead: in the second, his wounds began to bleed, and he made his blood and spirit cry out beyond the tomb. Yet his resurrection was not completed, but must be repeated indefinitely: ever vainer, ever more difficult, yet more necessary, as the burden of blood increased. Such was the intelligible theme of this poem, or rather its outline of intelligibility, for it was to be enriched and clarified by experience. The second poem, *Rédemption*, was almost simple in outline: I myself (but here the notion of the personal *I* seemed to be integrated within a vaster *I* whose relationship with the ego remained obscure), I myself was the suffering Christ, and at the same time the instrument of his suffering—the Crucified and the Cross in a single act of salvation and sin.

The reader will not be surprised to discover, concentrated symbolically and to an almost excessive degree in these two poems, several of the great religious themes which I dealt with earlier, speaking of the dogma of the Redemption. Theologically, I was at that time under the influence of Barth; but theology does not explain emotion, rather the opposite. Emotion governs both the symbol and the idea. The idea was at a dead end: I belonged to no creed, and in everyday life the Redemption did not interest me. But this was only apparently a desertion, and the need for reintegration, in its archaic form which so shocks people to-day, made itself felt by the abrupt upsurge of the images: I thought I was merely the medium for some obscure truth, and did not tarry to discover what this truth had to say to me personally.

I understood only later, when the explanation came to me of my role in *Christ au Tombeau*, that the individual experiences in the singular the drama of mankind, and that the same fundamental situation, crystallised by symbol at the due moment, is repeated at different levels of consciousness in each individual of the species, while the species experiences it in its unconscious totality. After years spent in understanding myself, through unifying symbol and analytical synthesis—after years in which I have lived through much, unburdening myself of certain youthful obsessions, and thenceforth retaining only the essential from past experience—the symbolism of *Christ au Tombeau* seems to me to-day without obscurity, if not without mystery. Whatever other interpretations there may be (the psychoanalytical, for example) I wish to retain none which does not conform to my general design, as I believe I can discern it in my work.

Christ au Tombeau was first of all myself, in the sepulchre in which my adolescence still held me prisoner. It was a sepulchre built by my teachers, my parents, my own fears. It opened upon depths into which I had ventured, thinking to find there untrammelled space. But in those caverns of dream, those imaginary loves, always, at the end of great strivings, I came face to face with my own solitude. The whole city, with its churches and its prostitutes, its tutelary shadow and its narrow alleys, was no more than a grotto of innumerable echoes, in which reigned the barren anguish of my footsteps. I had been sealed off from the world, and in order to ensure my complete suffocation, I myself had created a whole region, peopled with the visages I had engendered, but enclosed, without reference to reality. I had alienated my vital energy, thinking to free myself by this renunciation. And admittedly, in rare moments of abandonment, I had felt the warmth of a sheltering breast envelop and pervade me (it must be remembered that I never knew my mother); but from this sort of prenatal peace in which the anguish of living drove me to take refuge, the anguish of dying, of not living, swiftly and pitilessly expelled me. With one hand I fumbled for outlets, with the other I walled them up. Upon the flagstone which shut me out from life weighed that terrible paternal power, the Law. The only freedom I had was to explore my underworld, to conjure up its metamorphoses, but always between the two poles of pleasure and remorse. This was a morbid form of enjoyment: a negative mystique of the imagination, which takes only itself as an end, whether it has God or evil as pretext. I was in a state of perpetual sin, of non-life. My steps only recalled me to myself in order to hasten my flight, or else to immobilise me, inert, in my fear and hatred of myself. I ended up by taking this rigid anguish for ataraxia: what I called inner life was my cowardly, grub-like existence within the images which protected it. But the inner life is open, and is nourished by the exterior as it nourishes it in turn: it is communion in solitude. I took pride in being inadapted—and inertia thinks it can save itself by pride. Yet there is nothing so ridiculous as the false courage of the dreamer, who dreams his life because he can do nothing else, and takes pride in it as a triumph over the banal existence all around him. True greatness is in fact banal, because it is rooted in everyday life. For a long time I had no notion of what everyday existence meant—the daily bread, the daily duty, the spirituality and the joy of every day.

But at last, having reached twenty-two, I had had more than enough of dreams. The world was beating violently at the door of the tomb. *My strength made me cry out*, if I may venture to borrow and apply to a pseudo-corpse this magnificent expression of

Eluard, speaking of a man in the heyday of life. This strength cried out, and words struggled to life in me, tumultuous and irrepressible: words and blood. A corpse does not bleed; but the living man, if he is wounded, bleeds. Suffering—but overcome, integrated within the creative word—is inseparable from the act of living. Only he may speak who receives death and refuses to die—or rather, it is not he who refuses, but the divine dwelling in him.

In the spiritual sphere we all die very early, either because we drive ourselves into a corner of existence, or because we secrete our individual shell of dreams. The divine which is in us does not cease to live, but is nevertheless too weak in most people to break the framework of habit and take up the challenge of being. Either too weak, that is, or insufficiently concentrated: many people have only just enough vitality to keep going at all, to subsist. In a world in which the human substance does not lack reserves of energy, they are relatively happy, since the moral ambience lends them a semblance of personal being, in which the divine is able to breathe. But when the reserves have dwindled, when there is no longer any spaciousness around doctrines and dogmas, they feel a lack of air and a lack of sustenance, and are gripped by a vague, panicky anguish; but they do not understand why, not being equipped to understand. They have dreamed their 'civilization', their machines; they have complacently allowed them to mount up, in the same way as a dreamer buries himself in his dream, without realising that they were thus creating being— in this case, a terribly autonomous being, against which they will shortly find themselves defenceless. For, by fixing their energies on this almost exclusive activity, they were irremediably dividing themselves against themselves: intelligence was merely a technique stripped of all moral considerations, and therefore, falsely free and so facile, with so sure and rapid an acceleration that they were still intoxicated by its giddy impulse even as this began to crush them.

The lament which rises from the world is, for the moment, no more than a voiceless whirlpool. Our gangue is the speed which whips us along, and steadily increases while we become more inert and terrified. But who is to break the spell? A catastrophe, perhaps. Or, perhaps, the divine part of man, that power of renewal which springs from the heart of being, and which, under the appearance of death, in absolute ignorance of its own strength, concentrates and unifies the need of all, ready without knowing it to give to men that language which it lacks in order to pull itself together and reintegrate itself in the universe. Ready, also, to offer man an indivisible universal space, a complex of spiritual scope, in which none of his energies will be lost, whether they be of technique or of dream, whose present abstraction encloses us in the strait-jacket of obsession; but where the different regions of being will correspond organically, through the mystery of an ever closer analogy, of which certain great religious epochs provide us with the example, and perhaps the secret. Then, but only then, will we rediscover our everyday stature at the heart of the universal. And our simplest action, our most silent song, will make even the stars tremble.

Christ au Tombeau was thus not myself alone, but the whole of mankind with me, and in me, in the interminable suspense of Easter. I did not realise this until a short time ago. The fundamental crises of being, collective as well as individual, are only understood on the recoil, when they are half resolved by the labour of substance upon itself. This is true above all of spiritual crises, whose solution borrows nothing from outside, but is carried out, in some way, by a self-restoration of the spirit, analogous to the obscure working of the tissues. The elaboration of the images of salvation eludes at first the light of consciousness: it is a new language which forms *around* the old one, which is blind to or irritated by it, or even suffers by being *excluded* from it. Nevertheless, the old language, the imperfect form of the spirit, feeds upon the new form, and prospers in an unexpected direction. A moment arrives when lucid consciousness assimilates the symbol, and strives to rationalise it; but this happens only after a long time, when the symbolical life, separated from its accidental phantasms, possesses a sufficiently strong coherence to impose its laws on reason. Or rather, one should say, when symbols, chaotic at the outset, emerge as a universe, the reason without knowing has helped to bring it about. But it is only at a late stage that reason is reflected in this universe, and that symbol and reason impregnate one another.

It is possible that new symbols are in the process of being elaborated among mankind, and that thousands of voices have already uttered them, that millions and millions of human souls nurture them obscurely in dream. It is possible that these symbols are merely a new aspect to certain permanent myths of mankind, bound by an interaction whose living law escapes us, and which are the germs, or whose whole is the unique germ, of the spiritual universe. If these symbols, so long scattered like the limbs of Osiris in the shades, group themselves in a symbolic system and become harmonised under the pressure of history, once more will begin the great adventure of thought gradually raised through all the planes of human endeavour, from the womb of symbols to the extreme limit of ideas: an adventure which will be followed by many others, for as ideas become less burdened they will lose sight of the earth, and once more a split will arise, the harmony will be broken, and a new integration will become necessary. There is a particular delight in following, in the personal microcosm, the evolution of human history. A consciousness attentive to the biology of symbols, and which lives them within the situation *hic et nunc*, perhaps contributes, in a modest but decisive way, to that unitary vision of whose coming the world feels a presentiment.

*   *   *

When I wrote *Christ au Tombeau*, I was far from suspecting that this first image bore within it all the others which were to come, and not only them, but my future experience as well as the past: and even more, the experience of every man by analogy, the spiritual Body of mankind. The poems I had written up to then followed the inspiration of the moment. Between them, there was no link except that of external form, and no necessity. But now I was on the threshold of a necessary universe: whence my recoil before *Christ au Tombeau*. Everything is connected in a powerful work: it is a genesis which has its ages, its reigns, its organic stages, its revolutions. An isolated poem is the lament or delight of a moment: it sets ordinary sensibility quivering, and supplies an exquisite nuance to the everyday. A big work has not time to linger over nuances: its strokes of beauty are powerful and untamed, and it must be experienced in its rhythm, the measure of which is difficult to sustain, since it is not traced from ordinary experience. If this rhythm does not possess you deeply, if it does not challenge in you those energies from which you are so well guarded by the social aesthetic, such a work will never be more than a monster for your mind. Forget it, but do not judge it: your rules are not its own, and nothing gives you the right to pronounce against it.

I do not think there has ever existed a great creative spirit which has not been many times overwhelmed by the sensation of its solitude: a solitude in relation to itself, to men, and to its work. For a necessary work always goes against the appearance of facts: and so seductive is the latter, and sometimes so disdainful, that no one is sure of not abjuring himself for its sake. It must be understood that the real problem is to fashion the moral world in its totality, as well as one can, with means that are not always the best, with instruments which sometimes give way under the strain: and, while creating, to forge new tools for oneself, to replace or modify those which cannot bear the wear and tear. It is a question of inventing and adapting at the same time, of advancing no detail which does not contain the whole. One begins from nothing—or rather, one sets out from the unknown, from a massive and, apparently, impenetrable chaos. When a certain image takes shape before me, I know that it contains the whole secret of my life: it is *myself* in the very deepest sense— containing my personal history, that of my generation, of my country and religion, of man to-day with whom I am united, and lastly, of man in all times. All that is held as if emprisoned within a fatality of stone. But within myself, there is something stronger than that fatality: within myself, in that very image, there is a life. I who am astonished by that image, and who believe myself a stranger before it, am already within it, and provoking it into life: this force which is myself, and which at first seems to me blind, illuminates it by its inner progress, and causes it to flower into consciousness and will. It knows itself by acting, and is both creation and knowledge.

Stone, night, and figures of massive density in general have always drawn me. That anguish of being held by and atrociously determined within a matrix, I have known from my childhood, and I see far more in it to-day than a mere adolescent obsession— the eternal condition of man. There is no objective universe: all progress in the universal can only come from within. It is when man lives with the universe, and through the same life, that he is truly free. An excess of abstraction congeals the human universe, whatever the velocity of appearance may be; but under appearance, man lives in the panic inertia of fear. There are few people to-day who have not unconsciously adopted the attitude of corpses. But so long as God is within us, *rigor mortis* cannot seize us. Those three days between Good Friday and Sunday may last a long time—time enough for civilisations to disappear, and new barbarous epochs to emerge, bringing terrors which we thought were of another age but which our own has cultivated to excess; but so long as the Word is given to man—and one *must* believe it is for ever —the Resurrection, however unforeseeable, remains imminent.

I signed *Christ au Tombeau* with a pseudonym which summed up its essential symbolism. A friend of mine, the painter Salvado, had two sons whom he had called Roc and Mithra. I was all the more struck by these names in that they seemed to determine the children's souls. If I had a son, I reflected, I would like these two principles to struggle and reach harmony in him—I would call him Pierre Emmanuel. He would be of stone, but God would live in him. The name is an emblem of love, for in it, word and matter are wedded, lover and beloved are united; but it is also a sign of distress and anguish, for the stone tends always to inertia, and, once possessed, closes up again—to vivify it is an endless undertaking. But surely the two names joined to make one are the image of our life struggling against itself. Surely they are the striking ellipsis of the whole drama of the creation. It was a fine name that I was keeping for my son. But when I had finished *Christ au Tombeau*, this was the name which fell quite naturally into place on the last page. Few mysteries in my life have troubled me as that one did. What else could it mean, except that I was reborn? This new name cut my links with a life which I found hateful. It freed, but at the same time, defined me: it presented me with a command. The Abbé Monchanin had said to me one day: 'You will be the poet of the Holy Ghost'. That I have not become that poet is all too clear. But at least, since I have known the scope of human language, I have wished to be nothing other than the poet of divine speech, the Word given and received. If I fail in this, let me lose my name! For it is both my principle and my judge: it proclaims a faith which I could not abandon without destroying the word within me.

*   *   *

In the poems of *Le Poète et son Christ*, which followed *Christ au Tombeau*, the image of the Resurrection is preceded and governed by another familiar image, that of the Descent into Hell. This image crops up everywhere, even in my recent work. And it is true that Hell exists more than ever among us, more real around us than in our dreams. But we have succeeded, by a frightful forgetting of ourselves, in making that Hell objective. We have consented to accept it as a fact, while it is really a scandalous mystery. With an astonishing rapidity, which would have aroused reflection in other times, horror has become one of the commonplaces of our history. Not only does it perturb us no longer—we are bored by it. Our haste to expel from ourselves all that recalls our fate is merely a sign of our inner vacancy. We no longer possess any moral structures or reflexes. We are no longer able to digest evil, too strong an aliment, only good for an age when man entertained no self-doubts. We have become so feeble that we are only happy in some diversion: novels, radio, cinema, theatres, newspapers, football and bicycle races, all is grist to the mill so long as it flashes *before* our mind. It is a continuous film of disjointed impressions, which devour our time for us: Belsen and the prettiest girl in France, the passengers on the *Exodus* and the return of Sacha Guitry, the atomic bomb and Christian Bérard's beard—or rather, the beard disguises everything, Bikini becomes a bathing costume, and Belsen a family boarding house. As to evil, it is one more object among many, and what is worse, it is literature. It sells briskly, guaranteed harmless: pornography, rape, incest and sadism within the reach of everyone's purse, with (needs must . . . and our epoch is an enlightened one) a solid wrapping of philosophy round it, which the critics supply when the author forgets. Like the bull of Phalaris:* it functioned in the mornings, and in the afternoons its keeper showed it to visitors, on receipt of a tip. Splendid. And it is useless to grow indignant at such indifference, for no one will convert this epoch, least of all Cassandra or Juvenal. For evil is in it, and must develop itself to the end: our *objective* indifference is a symptom of septicaemia.

*Phalaris, tyrant of Agrigenta (565-549 B.C.), was celebrated for his cruelty. He had a bull made out of bronze in which he incinerated his human victims. (Translator's note.)

When an élite group of intellectuals gets to the stage of exhibiting mad poets on a platform,* it is proof that among these 'witnesses' of consciousness, curiosity has definitely got the better of truth: the category of the 'curious' is limitless, and may go as far as unreserved exhibitionism. We must not despair of seeing public fornication become a show for the whole family—what is astonishing is that no one has thought of it yet. It is decidedly not a Juvenal that we need. You can see that these people are already excited by the whip: they have acquired the art of prostituting truth, and making it an instrument of their pleasure. What we need is a Voltaire—or rather, a terrible, cold spectator, but one endowed with a soul, for Voltaire was only a mind. Above all, what we need are saints. They exist—this is beyond doubt—in all circles, all parties, all systems, and it is through them that we 'still hold together': they digest evil for us. That descent into the underworld which the poet contemplates in words they accomplish in reality: not because they want to make an 'objective' inventory, like the great minds of the century, but through their striving towards compassion, which credits evil with a dignity which our exhibitors of monsters ignore. For man, alone in this world, has the power of absolute self-deception; but he possesses a corollary to this freedom, that of hailing the truth. To make evil 'interesting' is a blasphemy against the face of humanity. This is something Dostoevsky did not realise. Evil is tragically evident, and affects us all: it is one of the potentials of our consciousness, which may order itself as it likes.

The objectification of the moral world is the beginning of the end for morality. Once reduced to the status of a phenomenon, an evil action may no longer be judged. For how is one to apply inner criteria to objects which one has agreed to regard in the

*The writer refers to a poetry recital by Antonin Artaud at the Vieux Colombier, in January, 1947, attended by André Gide and many other intellectuals. Artaud died on March 4th, 1948, in the semi-public asylum of Ivry-sur-Seine. (Translator's note.)

same light as an anatomical feature or a Diesel engine? But then, what difference is left between the 'aesthetic' curiosity of the mad poet's audience and the 'scientific' curiosity of Himmler's doctors? The latter, at least, might be claimed to be useful, and in a *realistic* universe is normal and will no doubt become generalised. But 'aesthetic' curiosity? For these gentlemen were not, for the most part, psychiatrists. They had no intention either of effecting a cure or of seriously asking themselves the insoluble question of consciousness and language. If they had, why hire a theatre, to which one paid to enter, and why the crowds round the door, as if waiting to see the Wall of Death? The real show was in the audience itself, and was doubtless not a very pretty one.

Am I straying from the point? Not at all. For I claim that one cannot look upon Hell as a spectator—not even the Hell of others. There is only one Hell, which is common to us all. The madness that you glimpse in this 'interesting' face is only one of the forms of man's evil, which you bear within yourself, and whose grimace is perhaps more frightful, beneath your intellectual's mask, than on the naked, visible features of the poor madman. How do you know that it is not yourself who grimace in this madman? No one knows just where his thoughts are leading. Were there any among the onlookers at this sinister travesty, in which defenceless genius, lashed by 'objective' eyes, contorted itself under the torture, who knew or even sensed that the man had come to this through their own fault? Was there not one who thought of the inner catastrophe which such a diversion threatened to bring in its wake? But of course, this is not literature, gentlemen! It is religion, for which you care not a rap. Nevertheless, I would dearly like to know whether you were not troubled by it in your dreams. I hope that face haunts you, that it may save you thus from damnation. For real damnation begins at the point where even dreams are mute, and no one knows the secret, better than you, of taming dreams.

The saints have dreams so powerful that their monsters emerge from them and become real: they undergo a life-and-death struggle without mercy, which you, being 'objective' intellects, are pleased to label hallucination. I can imagine the erudite terms which came into your heads, as you watched the madman—he who, perhaps, was struggling for your sakes. Saints and madmen are certainly clumsy enough: they see black dogs, or the Pope in a wardrobe, miserable phantoms which don't take you in for a moment. You apply a fine label, which gives you the stiasfaction of understanding without too much effort. Certainly, the life of symbols is poor—it lacks a language, and the fault is frequently yours. But this is poverty in appearance only—a simple insufficiency of expression. With saints as with madmen, obsessional images continually return. But it must be noted that saints struggle against them, liberate themselves, and never succumb to them, while madmen are conquered by them, swallowed up and devoured.

To be obsessed is constantly to run up against some image which blocks the path of inner development. This is an aggressive image, bringing deep-rooted energies into play: in opposition to the unifying struggle of the mind, autonomous mechanisms are created. This may happen as the outcome of social constraint, of a fear which pretends to stabilise life and integrate it within narrow limits: or, on the contrary, in response to some daring operation of consciousness, which has ventured too far, without embracing the rhythms of those energies which it was attempting to discipline. The great danger to consciousness, even at its highest degree, is to become stagnant water, which seems to be sinking in, but merely grows inert. The fault does not lie with consciousness alone, but with the unforeseeable matter which it strives at once to experience and to invest. This double movement of infiltration and approach, however well harmonised, lies ever under a threat which may split it at any moment. It is when the mind no longer controls this threat that the obsessive image appears: having elected either to infiltrate or invest, it finds itself imprisoned within an enormous dream, or face to face with a closed, hostile world. In both cases, it is no longer master of the energies which it has alienated from itself. An excess of anarchy and an excess of constraint produce the same effects. Complexes and strange alliances, the laws of which we do not know, are formed beneath consciousness; and as energy always tends to assume a shape, it instinctively attacks the weakest point of being, whence it erupts in unexpected fashion. The obsessional image is born, whose cohesion depends solely on our lack of awareness of ourselves. By a dramatic movement it makes the need for a life-and-death struggle imperative. The saint faces the black dog, and a thousand devils flee from the beast: the inner complex either crumples or exposes itself to a profound scrutiny. Once more, knowledge becomes possible, but is more difficult than ever.

For the obsessive image, which kept energies pent up in a monstrous whole, did help to preserve a certain equilibrium, a static one, it is true, but almost reassuring. Between obsession and obsessed, a *modus vivendi*, a sly complicity, are sometimes established. Once the energies are freed, the atrocious equilibrium disappears, but life flows all round in confusion: frustrated images everywhere come to the surface, unstable products of partial combinations. The hydra is no sooner destroyed than it seeks to recompose itself. It has created for itself subterranean habits: natural relationships have been sidetracked, giving way to incestuous tendencies. If consciousness quits the field, having momentarily illuminated it, the ancient monster springs to life again, or the monsters issued from its flanks divide its remains. These conflicts, this obscure carnage, take place in regions where personal identity confronts the chaos of mankind, where the former's mission is to inform the latter's density. All that does not reach consciousness, whether rejected or ignored by it, returns to the chaos from which it was perhaps struggling to emerge. Hell is common to us in a double manner—it nourishes our dreams, and our vacant soul nourishes it in turn. There are no personal symbols: or these are merely a mask, the clumsy incognito of universal symbols.

To descend into Hell, in other words to subdue the shadowy life of symbols, is thus an act of knowing of a general character. In order to create the syntax of energy, the mind plunges into the heart of confusion: it puts itself in sympathy with the life force and, in diverse shapes, differentiates its aspects, and tries their articulations, taming it to conscious life. This cannot be done without blunders, nor without danger. Our sense of direction is sometimes weakened among the shades: it can happen that the forest of symbols triumphs, and leaves nothing of the explorer but his bones. But in the absence of a sure method, of a general hypothesis on the functions of the hidden being, a pliable yet unflinching vigilance may furnish references for a method to come, and the approximate form of a future hypothesis. The work created from this effort at vigilance will be alive like an organism, and in it, one will be able to catch symbolic consciousness as it really is. But the author will remember—and those who understand the soul of his work—that this Descent into Hell is a victory for man over fear.

*   *   *

Poetry is a liberation. I lived for a long time under the shadow of fear. One has only to refer back to the opening chapters of this book to perceive what ravages threaten a young man when he is systematically exiled from his living forces. The fact that this fear became crystallised into an image was what saved me. Had it remained latent, and thereby the more virulent, only subterranean pressure could have forced it to reveal itself. But barefaced fear is only able to struggle if it has first reduced consciousness to surrender. My consciousness was on the alert. I was in revolt, but had no foothold, therefore fear became incarnate. To be buried alive is a terrible thing, but the absolute despair of this condition stimulates a fury for life. I was well and truly buried, and my teachers sat on the gravestone. Jansenism, the horror of sex, and all the inferiority complexes which fortify bourgeois prejudices, were a solid cement for my tomb. As to the bonds which held me fast, I myself had put them on. I had thought to concentrate my revolt by condemning myself to silence: and suddenly silence settled over me within. I was immobile, incapable of volition, of making one step to advance. The whole spiritual part of my being had become petrified in a strange refusal to exist: the vital part, the unconscious if you like, being freed by this refusal from the control of consciousness, abandoned itself to the confusion of frustrated appetites for the real.

In the depths of the sepulchre I was obsessed with wild images. For years I was on the verge of a nervous breakdown. Those images were powerful, springing from that very life of which I was so afraid. Barbey d'Aurevilly once produced this brilliant description: 'Hell—is Heaven hollowed out'. Nothing could be more true, when one applies it to the underworld of dreams. A dream is life hollowed out, life condemned. Poetry gave me a grasp on these images: my sole salvation, which I undertook by instinct, was to seize back the life they had derived from me, that, vampire-like, they had stolen from me. I began to reintegrate them, to turn them into a blind synthesis. By degrees, as I lived through them, these symbols became less hostile: their reference to my life became clearer, inverted or negative at first, then slowly fostering energy. My mind was fortified: I felt that the constraints which my youth had endured to the point of death were giving way.

Nevertheless, this inner progress was not without effort or anguish. When I began to control and co-ordinate my movements, the resistance of the symbols imposed itself again in an unexpected fashion. They seemed to elude me, and I had difficulty in circum-scribing them: this was the beginning of a conscious art. I soon perceived that I was gaining in precision what I lost in impulse.

I no longer allowed myself to be dispersed, and accumulated less verbal matter. My monstrous images were replaced by more viable species, and the air around them became less suffocating. But I find it difficult to say with what force I *willed* that I should re-emerge from the depths into the daylight. Over a number of years, each poem meant a struggle against that inner stubborn silence which I am not sure does not still linger on. I lived concentrated upon one solitary object: and it seemed more dead than ever. Even on the day of my marriage I was in the tomb with *Lazare Ressuscitant:* and my wife in the other world, that of the living, where she looked for me in vain. Everything continued to take place on the surface, at infinite distances; but I heard my own voice summoning me to leave the sombre kingdom, and banish the lingering fragments of my past. In reality, I was already free. My everyday existence had been unburdened of its terrors, and the centre of gravity of my consciousness had been brought to a lower level to make a new and durable balance. Personal symbols, thoroughly studied, allowed me to read the drama of being, the drama of history in which I had grafted myself. I was conscious of the totality of human experience, and perhaps I was late in putting it to the test in the images which had represented me—or perhaps those images were valid for me and for all men, for each of us bears within him the essential form of man.

It was during the war that I felt myself begin to live once more in daylight. The unity of human destiny which I had apprehended through symbols was suddenly exposed, the unconscious debate flooded with bright light, and the symbols themselves became identifiable in events. Nothing obliged me further to pursue my subterranean life. The war furnished me with a counter-check to my thoughts. The Christ or the Lazarus of the beginning, the Orpheus of the *Tombeau* searching for his soul, were linked with this Lot of the universal Sodom, the sinner who takes the sin of the city on his back, or rather, understands that the city and his sin are one. From a forgotten failure in love, but one re-sifted in

CHAPTER NINE

THE day war was declared, I was in the Haute-Loire, an austere and melancholy region, of sombre blacks and greens, unwarmed by the sun. My wife and I were coming back from a walk, following the track of the little railway line which runs from Dunières to Yssingeaux. Suddenly, my wife uttered a cry: an enormous toad was blocking our path. I chased it away, but it went only with reluctance, and with ironical hobbling gait. A few paces farther on, we stumbled over a whole family of toads, and the farther we went, the more numerous they became. They were everywhere, on the field paths, on the rails, on the track, in the grass, in the bracken. Was it a sign of rain? But the sky was beautifully clear, and it may be remembered that the early September weather that year was perfect. It was rather a sign of the times. Our hearts were weighed down by an all too definable distress. When we reached the house, we saw the notice posted on the wall.

War. . . . Lacking reference to anything, so terrible in its lack of features, the mere word abruptly destroyed any control we had of the future. A limitless discontinuity separated us both from future and past. The mind was robbed of its yardstick, and even to think became painful, for there was no wisdom and no creative will which could subsist *outside* the catastrophe in which the whole of man was in jeopardy. For how could one contemplate the catastrophe in the very lightning stroke in which it descended? It was like a rain of toads on the world, an invasion of monsters which seemed to have surged out of nothingness. A moment before, there had been that fretful suspense, that presentiment of something giving way, but these had been hidden behind the need

P   225

to entrench oneself, to forget everything, to go on as if . . .
And suddenly, here was the eruption of the secondary reality, of
the latent soul which for a long time had been dominating the
scene.

Here was a vast image of destruction and death, but more
terrifying, infinitely more subtle than any visual image, being
endowed with a ubiquity which vision does not possess. It was an
immaterial image, that of the evil spirit which fills the empty
spaces—a *voice* which seemed to float disembodied, able to do
without the vehicle of language, so self-sufficient were its inflexions
and furies. A literally unprecedented voice, recalling, by its
accents of terror, the tumult of natural forces when abruptly they
are unleashed, and by its accents of allurement, that strange
animal moan which prolongs or revives sensual pleasure. A voice
that drew one like a magnet, and charmed the monsters or
whipped them to fury. This was the symbol of the catastrophe, the
yawning threshold of Hell.

*   *   *

I am deliberately employing, in order to pin down the meaning
of the war, the same images which I used to analyse the Descent
into Hell: one vast, massive symbol, implicitly containing all the
rest—an obsession which must be broken, but at the cost of a
protracted nightmare. The analogy, it must be admitted, is more
than a superficial one. Those who lived the war also in their minds
begin now to glimpse what a deep *catharsis* it produced upon
them, and they on it. Their Descent into Hell, while being real and
peopled with real monsters, was none the less mysterious, nor
confusing to the spirit. The whole significance of man was thereby
wounded in its most intimate certitude, and each word, each
silence, divided against themselves and subtly poisoned. It was
from the excess of this division that there arose that action
properly called the *underground* movement, groping and unsure at

226

first, seeking a framework and a soul, then becoming lucid, more fraternally coherent, the more manifest became the horror.

This cohesion has not survived, I fully realise, and neither has the liberation of the spirit lent its significance to the material liberation. But the real war, the civil war in the soul, is not yet ended. Hitler is within us—this is the title of a book by Max Picard. The psychic nature of the world has been radically altered, and can no longer be measured with what it was: and the reiteration of the old language, either in politics or morals, brings to light a tragic disharmony with a situation for whose true springs we have no name. In one sense—I fully realise how shocking my words are—the open state of war was healthier. Hitler won the war by driving it within. We were alert to this during the occupation, for every fatalistic surrender, every gesture of submission, forced us to confront *our* lie. We finished up by having a feeling in common, modelled on a complex and powerful image of man, of life coursing through us, and decided we would reflect later, if the chance were given us.

It is possible that the external conduct of the war was dictated by considerations of the political balance of power, even accompanied by unavowable reservations. But these chessplayers' tactics overlooked what was essential in the game, the profound chemical changes operating in the soul of peoples. The internal conduct of the war was a spiritual struggle, not against an external system but within a permanent division, which set brother against brother, and idea against idea. Before the war, we were a divided people, too much so, and often through manœuvres in which a foreign power played its part, by bribery or guile. But such divisions did not threaten, did not yet dare to threaten, man himself: the true drama remained latent. Then came the defeat, and the spirit of division was unmasked. Up to then, one had lived after a fashion at least according to a hierarchy of being. There were different planes of action, on which different minds came into opposition, even while remaining in agreement on others. But there was, as a sort of continuous base note which one did not always hear, yet which sustained the whole even in its contradictions—an enduring instinctive respect for the universal in man. It is true that violence sometimes became the order of the day, but this happened sporadically, and not without inner misgivings. Ill-faith laid claim to justice, but did not exalt injustice as an absolute. Though they might be deformed by an unjust cause, values always remained values. It is true that having been abused in this way, and surrendered to extravagances of rhetoric, they had become detached from the deep emotions which gave them life: definitions were lost, and fine phrases remained.

Such an undermining remains unconscious until the day when everything comes crashing down. But a short time ago, such and such a word unified within itself several meanings: it existed at several levels of language, all of which must be borne in mind unless its thought-content was to be warped. But now, division held sway, and changed the meaning of words by a decree, or rather, metamorphosed their being. The word Jew, for example: we had always believed, and even the worst Anti-Semites believed, that the Jew is primarily a man—to which one added a definition of varying characteristics, according to one's perspectives of thought. Now, however, the word Jew received another, absolute meaning, stripped of nuances: it was supposed to mean superfluous cattle, marked for eventual extermination. There could be no illusion on that point, whatever the individual cases might be. Anti-Semitic legislation was merely the rules and regulations of an abattoir.

I might cite other words as examples, such as order, or legitimacy. In a *Letter to François Mauriac,* a sophist tries to condemn the resistance, in the name of Pétain's *legitimate* power. In the author's mind, a legitimate government is one in which constitutional continuity does not cease: as such, it must be obeyed. Legitimacy, however, entails no more than a formal definition: it is a legal investiture. The paradox is, that once received, it becomes a divine right. In the small *Larousse* for the word *legitimate*, I read: having the qualities required by law; but also, just, equitable. Here are two definitions, one legal, the other moral. Up to now, the whole spiritual effort of man has been to make them coincide. But if one agrees that the law is being exalted outside man, or against him, must not one choose between it and man? Is there not a law of man, a biological, psychic, spiritual law, which gives a meaning to the very language which the law of authority uses? Authority receives this higher law in trust, and is only legitimate in virtue of it: if it goes against it, its legitimacy becomes null and void, and gives way to anarchy, or to the tyranny which is a variation of it.

A government which tells me: You thought that Jews were men, but you were mistaken, they are beasts which must be exterminated—commits an arbitrary act against my consciousness and universal consciousness. It may reign through terror, but in no way by virtue of its legitimacy. It can do everything, except demand my acquiescence, and already my refusal becomes a revolt. Still more important, if I remain silent *in my opposition* to it, I make myself a party to its despotism. For it speaks and does violence to the language which unites me with all men: it introduces division into the heart of being, and terror into the essence of words. Many people, before the war, did not know what a Jew was: under the occupation, they uttered the word with a mixture of pity, disgust, and holy terror. I have chosen this word, because in it one comes into direct contact with the substance of man. But one might continue interminably compiling the list of words infected by Hitler or Vichy: and the infection still lingers on. For this regime was only able to exist by perverting words. But whoever does injury to language, also wounds man. Too long a contamination renders impossible even the thought best armed against it. The systematic deformation of language creates intellectual monsters. Plunged into a mental confusion which totalitarian propaganda fosters, the only reflexes they are able to use are artificial ones, created, modified, or extirpated at will, according to the needs of the cause.

The 'realists' in politics, such as the author of the *Letter to François Mauriac,* never take it into their heads to reflect that peoples have a psychic fabric, a secret life, precariously balanced, on which one must act only with respect. When the author in question exclaims—or in so many words, for it is a focal point in his thesis: If Germany had won the war, we would have been in the right—what he intends to say is clear, and justifiable in a materialist conception of France. If one accepts such a conception, the sophist will add: The resistance was not strong enough to exert a material influence over the course of the war; its benefits, if it had any, do not counterbalance its losses, nor the losses it caused among non-resisters; but had France followed solely the policy of Vichy, she would have found herself, by the sheer pressure of events, in the camp of the eventual victors, either Germany, or the Allies. But the sophist does not ask himself whether a French conscience exists, a certain way of contemplating and feeling the universal which, for us Frenchmen, constitutes our very language and soul: a manner of *being*, to sum it all up, which expresses us so totally that its existence and our own are one.

So it is my turn to ask him: If Germany had won the war, and if the German peace had predominated for a thousand years, what would have happened to our conscience? Does he seriously believe that the spirit of division would have laid down arms? One cannot arrest the disintegration of moral life by a decree, and when all share guilt in a lie, it is a struggle for life or death. Has he thought, furthermore, of the massive repressions blindly created by the New Order? Such forces are never visible, and we know nothing of collective psychology. But what is certain is, that handled without restraint, now hurled in advance, now brutally constrained, and kept in perpetual ferment, the forces of instinct reverted to barbarism. What, then, would have happened to

France? What would have happened to man? The question is of interest, for it still arises to-day; for it is not certain, as I have said, that Hitler did not win the war.

But let us now suppose, in company with our sophist, that France, *by the sheer pressure of events,* had found herself in the camp of Germany's conquerors, after having been her ally. It would be a handsome proof, I admit, of the efficacy of 'political realism'. But is it not clear what a danger it would have been for consciousness, and even more, what an unfathomable disease it would have spread in the unconscious? The spirit of division would have been consecrated, and the lie exalted as a virtue: and not only in the political sphere, which some people claim to separate from the moral, but in everyday thinking. For one must not forget that Nazism was totalitarian, and by reducing them to its own image, made sure of the soul of vanquished nations.

With the Allies victorious, would then a dialectical reversal have been sufficient for France, prostituted in spirit and in its deepest sensibility, to rediscover its old equilibrium, and the clear conscience of a nation which has right on its side? Some seem to think so. Yet I am not so sure that our delegates to International conferences would have put such a good face on it, when they met with certain rebuffs that their presence could not fail to attract. But I claim that a people like ours, whose national consciousness has matured under the banner of universality, and has not ceased to draw strength from the permanent principles of morality (let us remember the civic and moral instruction given in the primary schools, the axioms we are given when children as writing exercises, the democratic phraseology, not, admittedly, always sincere, but instinctive, which arises from real traditions, of which something still remains), such a country, I say, could not have tolerated a double *volte-face,* even had it been expounded in the positive language which we sometimes affect. I do not think our people is ripe for such a dialectic, above all so brutal a one. It would quite simply have to have lost all sense of language.

One cannot disorientate the soul of a people with impunity. And when once it has been driven into resentment against itself, nothing can arrest the progress of the obscure despair which torments it.

*   *   *

It may be convenient, in politics, to reason by alternatives, to adopt the alternative position, and see what happens. I do not say that such a position does not involve scruples of conscience. I merely believe them ill-placed, attached to material forms, on which the soul of a people certainly does not depend, but which would die deprived of that soul. Common sense was not deceived when it rejected the alternative, in other words, the division of France against herself. Of all the classes of the nation, only the possessor class (and then not in its entirety) accepted the principle —or the chance—of *playing a double game*. Those who are possessors measure their soul by their possessions, and care of their material inheritance takes the place of a spiritual life. This is not absurd, but even legitimate: major virtues are developed on this basis, but are valid only in a vaster perspective. He who has only his life risks it more readily, as the opacity of possessions does not conceal that perspective from him. What we have to discover is whether France, vanquished and domesticated by Nazism, had anything left besides its life. A live dog is better than a dead lion? The German political prisoner, chained up in his niche in the Weimar camp, forced to bark in salute of his masters, and to lap up his food before them, cannot have been too ready (if he still had the power to think) to dwell on this maxim. If he survived and is still alive, I can well imagine him having developed the head of a dog.

The true alternative, which confronted a whole people, and particularly the *witnesses* for that people, was: either to lose its soul or its life. Common sense, which contains a profound

232

idealism when its instinctive values are at stake, made its choice, with a 'blindness' which shocked the clever. Doubtless it unconsciously recognised the import of that other maxim, whose significance, whatever may be said, is not always confined to the spiritual: 'He that loseth his life for my sake shall save it'. The Resistance, born of the wounded unconscious, of a betrayed fidelity, was first of all a spiritual insurrection. In the struggle against the symbols of death, everywhere present and eternally aggressive, an obscure consciousness was forged, which should vitalise the dense strata of national life, and whose task (still, unfortunately, unfinished) was to bring that life into the daylight. This consciousness existed within history, and was not at all an *a priori* one. It was not detached, but committed. It moved on all planes, and its reactions were so all–embracing that a simple physical gesture was at the same time a cry of spiritual refusal.

It is not my task to discuss the statistical efficacy of these gestures, weighed and balanced in material figures. The therapeutics of the soul are not revealed by such data, their rhythm is not that of appearances, any more than the true rhythm of history is that of immediate events. Hitler died in his underground bunker. But what of Nazism, that imperceptible and fluid thing, whose degree of dilution cannot be grasped by thought? In the spiritual sum of evil and good, which makes up man's unconscious, the range of a moral action is not curtailed by any inertia. But with the exception of certain extreme cases, certain miracles of inner energy (Geneviève stopping Attila), this range is never, and can never be, more than mediate. The moral action step by step innervates personal and collective sensibility, combines with others, becomes articulated within these structures, and at the very end of this slow metamorphosis in space and time, its effect passes unperceived.

Through the interaction and reciprocity of consciousnesses a collective *catharsis* takes place, but of this, our outward-turned world seems to have lost the notion. Yet, though we may be inattentive to this spiritual unity, we are none the less under its sway. By separating ourselves from the destiny of others, by taking appearances alone as law, we provoke an organic response, universally valid, the repercussion of which will only reach us after a long journey around and within us. On the other hand, when wounded consciousness, plunging into the depths of its anguish, undertakes to clean its wound and heal its tissues, it is not alone in this protracted and cruel operation, in which each pressure of the mind starts the bitter wave of suffering flowing to infinity. It undertakes this operation for the sake of all, converging with other souls which are unaware of each other, yet exist side by side in the invisible world of the spirit. Those who have not felt this unutterable solidarity understand nothing of the Resistance, and I deny them the right to judge it. If the Resistance had not liberated people's hearts, if the prudent, the timid, the anxious, the immense mass of this people flung despite itself outside its normal path, and waiting in secret suspense, being unable to do anything else, had not been able to buttress themselves at every moment on those who risked everything for their common sake, France would not have survived—I mean the *person* of France.

Some answer me here by pointing out the faults of the Resistance, and sometimes its crimes—what had these to do with the sense of the universal? Nothing, it is true. But in a period of extreme confusion, consciousness, however vigilant it may be, often becomes entangled in the shadows, and may not so much invent, as cling to, earlier prejudices: which explains much dissension, much mistrust which lingers on. As to the crimes of the Resistance, the least one may say of them is that they were not perpetrated within a system, like those of the Militia. They were local crimes severely repressed by the authorities, with the exception of certain outbursts of popular fury, for which the fault lies more with the repression of instincts than with deliberate incitement. So long as the danger lasted, the Resistance attracted to itself only upright men. When victory seemed assured, volunteers arrived in large numbers, and seized rifles and armbands

234

as a matter of course. One of the faults of the Resistance, which prevented it from continuing its work when peace had arrived, was to lack the necessary authority to screen and discipline the late-comers. It was these late-comers above all who committed the crimes for which the Resistance had to share the blame, whether it punished them or not. But it did not wish these crimes, from which it was able to learn a lesson. One must not forget that if criminal psychology became widespread during the war, and if sadism grew richer for a new repertory of experiments and observations, this was due in the first place to the Gestapo, and then to the Militia. The tortures inflicted by the Militiamen became a legend in both town and countryside. And as the latter did not always follow the Duce's maxim: 'Kill them, the dead tell no tales', there was no lack of direct or indirect witnesses. The fact that the example of these brutes was followed by other brutes does not mean that the Resistance must bear the whole opprobrium.

This invasion of non-Resistants, of elements lacking all moral qualifications, was only one of the numerous dangers that the Resistance had to overcome in its difficult operation of *catharsis*. But it was a significant danger, the symptom of a redoubtable test whose amplitude the Resistance was unable to measure: the test of life above ground once again. Neither peoples nor individuals have an easy time emerging from the catacombs. In the work of symbolic reintegration, one of the most difficult moments is when the symbol and the reality meet on open ground. Having achieved the unification of symbols, the mind has still to transcribe them into the swifter script of events, and penetrate into their everyday existence, without either weighing it down or plunging it in shadow. And reciprocally, a freer, lighter air must circulate within the symbols, eliminating those which crumple up in the sunlight.

The Resistance was not able to adapt and convert itself to the daylight: and it must be said that its allies were not anxious to see this happen. The spirit of division had not capitulated, if it had transferred its seat to the camp of the final victors. In the quarrel between the two powers, one forged in the shadows, the other, just as legitimate, born on the outside, was demonstrated once again the tragic duality that both sides had struggled to resolve. It was all too clear that French unity, however deeply rooted it might be in ordinary sensibility, would remain unstable and fortuitous so long as it was not codified by the mind. But the abstract authority held the lead. The Resistance was diffused through the body of the nation. It can happen, in the life of symbols, that the mind opposes to fertile images the wall of its categories: the intelligence willingly dwells on the past. The head held the central power: it used it to create division, rather than to inform itself, to coordinate impulses, and to bring them to consciousness. Automatically, it rediscovered the old cadres. The Resistance, in order to survive, had no other outlet but anarchy, against which the soul of the people was aroused. It would have meant betraying itself. It preferred to dissolve itself, leaving the letter of the law for its spirit. The movements towards unification disintegrated, and were stabilised by parties. The old troop of politicians, having strayed momentarily, were back on their former paths, peopled with familiar shadows.

But the Resistance was not dead. It had overturned old notions, and given life to many a dead image. It had reawakened the vigorous universalism which slumbered in the French soul, and unmasked the Protean nature of certain threats which had placed it in mortal peril, and may still do so again. One may well regret that it had neither the time nor the necessary tranquillity in order to teach its followers to think in common: at least it taught them to feel, suffer and act in common. Finally, its failure was only apparent, for the sense of historical solidarity is more acute than ever among many people: and we do not know the true value, for the spiritual equilibrium of our people and of the world, of the presence among us of those who lived through the supreme horror, there meditated on the mystery of the Communion of the Saints, and rose again to testify to it among the living dead that we still are. When I see a Martin-Chauffier or a Jean Cayrol, to cite only my friends, I know that the Resistance has not said its last word, and that it is the imperative for all durable creation. All the energy that certain men were able to concentrate within themselves has been neither lost nor disbanded. Spiritual urgency is still great, and the crisis of man acute: they feel it, and are prepared for it. *To resist* that which wishes to destroy him—this is man's only law. And he who resists, creates. This biological truth may be stated without reservations, were it in the midst of barbarism itself.

*　　　*　　　*

I had no intention, when I began this book, of writing an autobiography. If at times I have expanded on certain decisive moments in my life, I did so only in order to reveal more clearly the progress of my inner development. Now that I am nearing the end, and the future already looms before me, is certainly not the moment to deviate from my plan. For all that, it is not without regret that I leave in shadow the details of four years of suffering, hope and joy. There is no lack of monographs to serve the future historian, and help him to understand the misery of our people, to measure how high man may rise when he defends his naked truth. But each one of us feels it a duty to pay tribute to the memory of those who were his fellows. If my homage is brief, I hope they will pardon me: it dwells tirelessly in the secret depths of my heart.

Nevertheless, I cannot come to an end without evoking that admirable French village, whose name in itself is a promise, and which was, among the extreme division of consciences, an image of the unity of the homeland: I am referring to Dieulefit, in the Drôme. I arrived there in July, 1940. Jouve had taken up residence there, and I proposed to spend several days with him. I was to stay in Dieulefit for four years, leaving it only for brief trips to Lyons, Avignon or Paris. It lies thirty kilometres distant from the

237

Rhône, a large market-town clinging to the arid earth, surrounded by a fan-like range of hills. It belongs neither to the Dauphiné nor Provence, but is a closed-in region, contained within the hairpin curve of the Miélandre, resembling the crupper of a powerful beast, behind which rise the large suns of summer. However coarse the earth may be, it is everywhere under man's dominion. The air is pure, the light clear: no detail escapes the eye, but everything is visible. There is little shade. The trees are sturdy, but the struggle to grow has stunted them. Twenty kilometres away the olive trees are even more squat. But the chestnuts have had the same struggle, and the dwarf oaks of the mountains. Sometimes, in the distance, one sees a line of poplars, whose slender height captures and deepens the space beyond. The wind never stops blowing, and one has difficulty in getting used to it. But it is of the essence of light, and sharpens the clear contours. Here, in most austere mode, the law of the French countryside is verified: severe, but almost musical, imposing to the mind, but giving a harmonious inflexion to the emotion. It is a landscape of deep and reserved sensibility, profoundly invested by consciousness, contemplative, impressing itself on memory, to the point of merging indistinguishably with thought.

Perhaps it is not without significance for the landscape itself that Dieulefit is Protestant: or the old stock is at least, even if the newcomers are Catholic. On the neighbouring heights, one may still find what are called *déserts*, sort of natural amphitheatres, majestically situated among the trees, far from the roads, and near to God. Pursued by the king's dragoons, the Protestants, with a Biblical instinct for grandeur, chose these high places for their worship. Here, the Bible and the landscape are in harmony. Generations of the hunted took up their stand in this impasse where the valley closes in. They put up fortifications there, turned to fight, and never accepted defeat. Like that Protestant heroine,*

*Marie Durand, who was imprisoned in the Tower of Constance. (Translator's note.)

they carved upon the mountain the word: *Resist*. The recollection of those persecutions has never disappeared from Calvinist memories. To-day, as in the days of the dragoons' incursions, the Protestant heart is on the side of the outlaw.

Dieulefit gave clear proof of this, becoming a place of refuge and reconciliation. Of its two thousand inhabitants, the more unstable half is Catholic: a sign of division, of which the French genius has suffered so many examples, but here overcome, almost imperceptible, and stimulating rather than destructive. When a group has managed to triumph over a radical division, without destroying its diversity, its sense of the universal emerges the greater for this trial. The differences which but yesterday seemed irreconcilable have discovered their common basis of truth. They reflect the whole from different aspects without betraying the living unity. This is a unity without egoism, quite the opposite of the *status quo*, hailing the universal wherever it appears, and recognising it as its own. In Dieulefit, no one is a stranger. He who has just arrived, aching all over from a ghastly bus drive, famished, perhaps hunted, and living in terror of glances levelled against him, may be reassured. For here, peace will greet him at last: he will find himself among his own people, as if at home, for he is the neighbour for whom there is always a place at table.

The village saw its population doubled during the war, without ceasing to be homogeneous, and without losing its *identity*. And I am not talking of the thousands of refugees of all kinds who passed, rested for a moment, broke bread with their brothers, and set out once more with the certain knowledge that here at least they were loved. In the whirlwind of an exodus which for many lasted four years, those who had felt the whole earth slipping away under their feet, who had neither possessions nor homeland left, thought they were dreaming when they found themselves on solid earth again. It took them weeks to get used to their new freedom, to adapt themselves to the sincere goodwill on the faces of those who hastened to meet them. But sooner or later they surrendered to the sensation of well-being, and relaxed. Their pariah's hostility vanished, they merged within the fraternal ambience, and became everyday faces. I lived for ten years in my native region, and every summer for ten years more: but Dieulefit is my little homeland.

I am sure that many others feel just as I do, among the hundreds of wanderers whom the village adopted. Some were fleeing from the four corners of Europe—Alsatians, Belgians, Poles, Germans. Others were English or Americans, caught in the trap, and threatened with P.O.W. camps; old offenders (against the Vichy regime) who preferred to look on Vichy justice from a distance; people with a past, a lamentable millstone at a period when informers with official approval were continually raking over their memories; and finally, Jews, some of them French, the rest in their hundreds from anywhere. They were so terrified that their race could be read in their eyes, but those around them refused to see it, in order not to humiliate their distress. In all, there were almost two thousand newcomers. Almost all of them, if they had not already got false papers, were given a complete set by the mayor's admirable girl-secretary.

The above is a material indication of the village's power of assimilation, or rather, of its power of unification. Dieulefit, during those four years, consciously illustrated the lesson of the Epistle to the Romans: For there is no difference between the Jew and the Greek: for the same Lord over all is rich unto all that call upon him. Here is a single definition of man, which must be defended everywhere and in every man in whom it is threatened. I do not know whether my neighbour, the Communist electrician, or Mademoiselle Marie, the old Protestant dressmaker who came to mend our linen, would have been able to formulate such a definition. But could I do so myself? When Madame Peyrol, who was perpetually being infuriated by the radio, which she would switch off in a rage and immediately switch on again, exclaimed with her *midi* accent: 'All men are human, after all!' it was a simple and self-sufficient equation. A equals A, and can never, will never, be non-A.

We are an old people, who for long have known what man is: so long, indeed, that this knowledge is entirely instinctive, swifter than words, even swifter than the mind itself. And it never errs. The proofs of instinct are the singular privilege of the poorest. It never enters their heads (and for a good reason) to judge themselves by virtue of their possessions: they are thereby the more expert, through the naked sense of value, at getting at the man beneath the skin. The soul of the Dieulefitois was clear like the surrounding landscape: both tender and firm, delineated by simple outlines, yet whose curve was able to modulate all the heart's nuances. They found it impossible to live in confusion. This inaptitude for lying is one of the dominant features of the people, and particularly of these people, who credit others with a candour equal to their own. When they are deceived, or feel themselves deceived, they cannot tolerate the imposture: not that it wounds them, but it strikes at their inner humanity. July 1940 had no sooner arrived than three-quarters of the Dieulefitois had detected the lie: and thenceforth nothing would alter the verdict they had once passed upon it. Nothing was able to prevent them clearly testifying that truth has only one face. They were Protestants, nourished on a Word which accepts no compromise. Even a Communist, if he comes of Protestant stock, naturally employs the commanding accents of the Bible: such a Communist is not a phenomenon produced *ex abrupto* by ideology alone.

These humble people, proud of their constancy, never went back on their word. They formed the image of the French community, of the French universe. They achieved that *catharsis* whose operation was to preserve our country from moral disintegration. But, through an act of grace of which there were few examples at that period when horror confounded thought, Dieulefit, without ceasing to share in the sufferings of the world, remained full of light and joy. Such a paradox is the virtue of great souls, at the end of a long struggle for integration which has rejected nothing, even absolute evil. Here, the integration was made instinctively, and the whole of life was summoned up, without any weighing of pros and cons, or any undue astonishment at evil. Which is proof that vital health is one with the highest spiritual equilibrium.

*   *   *

This virtue of the people was the virtue of great souls, possessing the same language and the same faith. Among those whom I loved during the war, and whose companion I was, none stands higher than my old teacher, the Abbé Larue. When July 1940 came, I received several letters from him, which left me in no doubt as to his violent reaction. Subtle as he was, he showed himself entirely single-minded. His irony stimulated his anger, for those who practise true irony have only truth as their idol. Being a mathematician, he was able to appreciate a situation which gave him proof of the insane mechanism of certain minds. But he was far-sighted, and saw right through the problem. He saw the enormous initial error pile up its consequences: and his familiarity with history allowed him to preserve no illusions. But this man of action, who had been made sceptical by a long exile in contemplation, to the point where he sometimes wondered whether conscience is not a monstrous canker on life, recovered, when faced by a tragic paradox which others surmounted only slowly, that swiftness of decision which gives proof of inner discipline, but even more of an instinctive choice in favour of the wounded conscience. He realised that conscience is life itself, or rather the supreme adventure of life. The latter runs an absolute risk, which we are already able to sense through our power over matter. But the risk cannot not be run, for life keeps going only by transcending its limits. It strains towards total consciousness, against and within the inertia with which its past confronts it.

It was at the moment when man became entangled within his insoluble contradictions that the Abbé Larue staked everything on him. He was not a priest who vaticinated, and he detested the Apocalyptic tone. But he perceived the major rhythms of history, and did not exclude the possibility of a new barbarism—a barbarism which would obtain for a set period, a momentary aberration of the mind succumbing to the excess of its own forces. For the risk of the world blowing up depended in the last resort on the mind, and perhaps, at a time when the mind was losing control of its potentials, there was no other salvation against suicide except a barbarian slumber, a breathing-space in dispersal. Whatever the immediate future, the Abbé Larue nevertheless believed that consciousness cannot be lost. It may perhaps be swallowed up, but only to reappear elsewhere, changed, no doubt, but also retaining what it already was. There are thus no two choices for the mind: at the moment of extreme danger, not only must it not submit to being placed in jeopardy (Vichy, adhering to the opposite alternative, encouraged the intellectuals to make their *mea culpa*, and one has only to read the things Jouhandeau wrote on his return from Weimar to understand how far such a denial could go), but it must concentrate all its strength, all its diamond-like lucidity, in the act of thinking the universal. It must pass beyond the shadow of death.

With this certain knowledge (and perhaps a foreboding of a tragic end), the Abbé increased his activity tenfold. Without any apparent change in his life, while continuing to behave like a peaceful professor happy with his pipe and his books, he became one of the leaders of the military resistance in the south-east. But heavy as this task was, it did not absorb all his time. He read everything, assimilating all the most recent currents of thought, detecting the point where they converged, and their significance in the spiritual drama which was being played out. From then on the thought of historical evolution continually occupied him. Having to come into contact with Communists, and appreciating

243

them as man to man for the integrity of their ideal, he worked his way through the enormous theoretical literature with which the doctrine is encumbered. He procured the complete works of Marx, and annotated Lenin pencil in hand, soon gaining a detailed knowledge of the cross-currents, the crises of conscience, the struggles against heresy, all contained in the Bolshevik Revolution. He began to think that Communism, unsatisfactory as it might be in its definitions of the individual and of freedom, opened up a vista of a new humanism, to which the Communists whom he met seemed to him to offer indisputable proof. And this humanism, still imperfect, but bold and fed with sacrifice, was the only one which seemed to him coherent in a world in which Christians were digging their own graves. He clearly perceived what this humanism owed to Christian humanism, but without recognising it in passing Christian forms and even dogmas, misunderstood by Christians, which now emerged in secularized dress, revealing both the need of the epoch and the prophetic boldness of the minds which had conceived them. In the eclipse of Christian thought (but not of *all* Christians, nor of the truth of Christ) he saw no more, after all, than a transitory phenomenon. an apparent disappearance of the great river whose alluvium had fertilised the West. No one could foresee in what form this river would spring forth again, nor even whether it would be identifiable after its underground journey. But in any case, one thing was only too clear: the insolvency of the religious organism in man's struggle for his life. The bishops had the mentality of sub-prefects, and the priests, with the exception of a few that the administration did not know what to do with, were emasculated from youth onwards, and had no grasp of the terrible problems which men are called upon to face every day. The Word of God, weakened, tarnished, almost ashamed of itself, no longer had currency. Amidst general indifference, and before an audience which bewailed its own end, the services celebrated their funeral rites round the remains of a dead God. We had come to the

Easter Friday of the Church. But had not Christ said: 'Let the dead bury the dead'? The Abbé, in his priestly heart, must have mourned: he refused to separate the fate of Christ from that of the Church. And doubtless he foresaw that the Church of Easter Sunday would have nothing in common—or rather, Christ only—with the Church of Easter Friday.

But there were more urgent questions, which, besides, conditioned this one. When a building threatens to fall, one begins by rescuing those whom it may bury. If they, at least, remain alive, they will rebuild it if they take any heed. It was a question of saving conscience first, the true tabernacle of the living God. There exists one universal truth for man, dazzling in its clarity, and which has no need of compromise. Whoever rejects it makes an attack on man. Christians possess this truth—but not only Christians, for it has penetrated humanity for centuries: only, they should possess it more clearly than others. The Church repeats it from habit, without knowing fully what it says, and they themselves feel a proprietary right in their souls, although they scarcely pause to consider the real nature of this truth which belongs to them. They are no longer able to produce it before the demands of the century: and the century cries its needs out aloud. The century knows the rigorousness, and points the consequences, of this truth which Christians poorly appreciate. Both ironical and pitiful, it brings to light all the contradictions, and Christians can only rub their eyes and say: 'Is that my truth?' They feel that it is impossible to live this truth as it is, above all in such a period of upheaval. That is why they have no wish to see it naked, but rather adorned with those material possessions and the social consideration which attach themselves to ideas when they grow complex. In former days, the Christian truth was proud and unyielding in its purity: growing old, it becomes lax, through fear of being soon abandoned. It is true that it is still paid court to; but will this last much longer? Nothing could be less sure. It has already abandoned much: and its splendid remnants, which barely hold together any longer, will soon betray it. Christians feel themselves falling into the grip of fear. Is the century wholly wrong? Must not truth follow with the times? They temporize and conform with self-interest and common sense. They make excuses. Nothing irritated the Abbé more than his archbishop's palinodes, an ex-lawyer, to whom he had given the name *my client Jesus Christ*.

There was another way of looking on the Christian witness: a way which the archbishop did not approve, as he discreetly made it clear, in his funeral oration. But His Eminence put it aptly: the Abbé was not always prudent. Yet he certainly had every reason to be, he who loved so much his own den, good tobacco, a good brandy, a rare book, and well-cooked dishes prepared in the Lyonnais manner, in which he excelled. (He liked to do his own cooking, a habit retained from old army days, but he went about it with the application of an artist who leaves nothing to chance: it was a sight to see him in his kitchen, wearing a white apron, singing, reciting suitable jingles, weighing everything meticulously, and admiring his labours with the indulgence of the gourmet.) That also was a part of his world, and was his truth, the truth. It was all part of the risk, and not at all an irrelevancy, an amiable little weakness. The Abbé Larue knew how to be fully *aware* at every moment of his life. He liked living, and did not conceal the fact, which, for certain Christians, seems rather shocking. The day came, however—I am sure he was expecting it—when, on his way home to his comfortable fire and his pipe, he was picked up by two individuals, before he could even throw a final glance at his books and his pictures. Several more gentlemen arrived later, and turned all his treasures upside down. It is fortunate that he was not present, for he would have trembled with impotent wrath at seeing them smoking his cigars and drinking his precious cognac.

He was put in the best company: in the cell with those who had been condemned to death. There were two youngsters there, almost children, who were to die at dawn. The whole prison went through the double agony, communing with these youngsters in their despair. It is well known that the collective soul, in the prisons, is quick to share suffering: it has abandoned the churches, to take up refuge in places of affliction. Suddenly, the sound of singing rose from the cell, a triple chant: happy, avenging, free. The others heard them singing all night, war songs, old folk songs, romances—victory, love, faith, and the immense joy of youth. In the morning, the two boys went out steadfastly to meet death. The veterans of Monluc recall that the news flashed round immediately, by the mysterious prison telegraph, that an extraordinary curé had just arrived. Each day of his imprisonment was a replica of the first.

That will suffice to show the power that emanated from this man who, in four years, had developed an unutterable strength of humanity and love in himself, without ceasing to be ironical and reserved in his relationships. No one, to my knowledge, more perfectly integrated the meaning of this war, no one desired so ardently to understand the mechanism of history in evolution, and no one was able more constantly to express his knowledge in his actions. The Abbé Larue managed to fulfil his destiny by concentrating together in one secret and sublime form all the positive values of man, even including that death which, in the words of Claudel, is our 'precious patrimony'. For that death is a gift of life. He died in the massacre and blowing up of Saint-Genis-Laval. Nothing could be found of his mortal remains, but his spirit no longer had need of that transitory support. That was on the eve of the liberation of Lyons. The following day, *my client Jesus Christ* was already scattering his benedictions over the ruins.

*　　　　*　　　　*

The *catharsis* achieved by the Abbé Larue was the gradual revealing of a vast historic horizon, in which the ignominy of modern man found its law and its perspective. Faithful to his passion for intelligence, the Abbé rejected all explanations of man other than by the ways of reason. But he loved the powerful structure of myths, in which his mind liked to discern a formidable concentration of the human future. He read them in rational terms, at the same time quivering with that strange tenderness towards man which inspired Henry Michaux to say: 'He whom a pebble causes to stumble had already been walking for two hundred thousand years, when he heard voices of hatred and menace, which tried to strike fear into him'. We came into contact on every plane, but never, never more intimately than within that tenderness.

I often complained to the Abbé that we lacked a great historian: someone capable of achieving the synthesis of man. Two hundred thousand years of existence, perhaps more, and seven thousand years of reason: the laziest imagination cannot help reflecting on these figures and this mysterious ratio. It may still plunge back into the past to the extreme fringe of consciousness. But faced with the future, with the possible, the imagination grows the feebler the more agonising becomes the danger to man. Pedestrian history, which goes from one nearby cause to an immediate effect, satisfies the mind only in periods of calm, when the pressure which drives man towards the unknown is relaxed. These are periods when much is learned about man, but they finish in pure abstraction: they are periods with a brief and measured rhythm, underneath which, underground, the major rhythms pursue their course. In the constitution of the earth, one might doubtless find many analogies which might illuminate the constitution of history, and explain how a break occurs between a perfectly explicable past and the unforeseeable future. By studying those 'great tidal waves which we call a great love, a great unhappiness, or a religious conversion', whose astonishing effects Claudel evokes in La Peinture Hollandaise, perhaps one might achieve an image of the radical metamorphoses which humanity sometimes undergoes.

But the history of civilisations is a subject yet to be born, and comparative psychology must give way to a simultaneous vision of all times: successive civilisations are the generations of mankind, and the crises of man are the crises of each generation. At the time, I still knew nothing of Arnold Toynbee, one of the first men of universal genius who have dared to transcend the narrow Western perspective of history, and resolutely place themselves at the centre of the human psyche: or, otherwise stated, who conceive history as the spiritual genesis of man, a genesis which has barely begun. To reverse the whole meaning of historical research, to project the future from within the past, to initiate vast parabolas whose path, while taking full account of the single event, may express a movement whose energy goes beyond the centuries—by no other method could we be saved from the false impasse into which we had got ourselves.

Thus, I complained that man no longer has a history. The Abbé replied that man has poets, whose role is to invent the future. At that time I was reading Holderlin, whom I set out to discover in the light of these words. From the *Archipelagus* to *Patmos*, the anguish of genius grows steadily greater before the historic mystery of man. I do not always feel in agreement with the syncretism of the poet of Hyperion, and for this, I have worked out the explanation elsewhere, in fairly long articles. But I can never grow tired of admiring the degree to which he was able to assimilate the whole drama of the species, and prophesy the divine within it. The history through which we were living assumed the form of a myth. All that I have said above on the personal experience of symbols applied also to mankind generally: there was no break in continuity between the individual struggle and that other one whose setting was the universe.

Since the Spanish War—which affinities of blood made me feel in my deepest being—I had come to understand that man to-day, even when driven solely by the need to deepen his inner life, cannot withdraw from history, in which the stake, hidden beneath vast material changes, is nothing less than the perenniality of the spirit. It becomes impossible for us to take part in the least event without our emotions, feelings, ideas, all that sustains our singular identity, being set in motion. All this takes place in the worst confusion: our loftiest certainties have been battered from all sides, and rent within by ambiguity; we do nothing which does not bear the mark of division, and yet we have no stronger aspiration than towards the unity of the world within ourselves. Yet, scattered in our effort, protecting ourselves clumsily against a multitudinous adversary, we live in a whirlwind of blows given and received. Everywhere delusion assails us, and our truth is no longer any more than a faceless instinct, too overwhelmed and often too discouraged not to let itself be tricked.

The war at least was clear-cut, as we experienced it from the inside. It expressed itself in rough and massive forms, easily recognisable, which called forth a direct reaction. All the good on one side, all the bad on the other: it was a simplification, but clear. But these massive forms blocked the view, and in addition, few people perceived, or wanted to perceive, the amalgam of which they were made. For it was not only from the adversary that they borrowed their elements, although it was perhaps better in the immediate sense that man should believe he was fighting against an enemy from without, while he was really fighting within his own monsters. Nevertheless, there was a risk that he would stiffen with pride in his clear conscience—the most dangerous of his monsters, and the last. Intolerance was a weapon of war: it might become a system when peace returned. Then it would seek out enemies in the ranks of those who had been brothers, and mankind's civil war would be pursued in other spheres. The remedy was to re-establish the perspective, to centre the war within consciousness, and to spare the best from the natural temptation of pride. *Hitler in uns*—these three words dispelled the ambiguity of any facile freedom of mind. A common share in evil was not something circumscribed and invested by a common share in good: these two were superimposed, and interpenetrated to their extreme limits. It was necessary to abandon the fable of the naturally good man, if one wished to define the true nature of man, and restore to him the autonomy of his destiny.

But then, who had taught us that consciousness is a tragic duel? Who had offered us vast symbols for man's struggle against himself? It was Christianity, first and foremost. In this period, when the Church remained silent, when faith was merely a dead letter, the Christian myth acquired a significance unknown since the centuries of belief. It became the embodiment of history—whether to become history's swan song, or to discover at the appointed hour the material for a higher incarnation. In a mind nourished by Christianity, through which still coursed the life-blood of the ages, the central images of Christianity, the mysteries as we call them, to stress their undefined symbolism, took shape with the event, and ordered it in a quasi-liturgical drama, from the Incarnation to the Last Supper, from the Last Supper to Golgotha, from the spurned and wounded Christ to the Christ of Easter. Christ became man himself, who dies through man, and rises again, to save even his executioners. Hitler also was man who kills man in order to become God.

In times of spiritual torment, when man no longer recognises his countenance, he becomes enamoured of his own chaos. A genius of chaos has only to arise, anonymous and shapeless as itself, and his voice enters into the instincts, activates them by stirring them to the point of vertigo, and launches them off on a purely arbitrary path, on the conquest of the void. Each time that instincts thus given a body, and made incarnate in human masses—and the mass-individual is no longer *a person*, but part of the mass in action—meet on their path the true visage of a man, it acts upon them like an exorcism in its primary stages: it drives them to extreme fury, which are turned against him and tear him to pieces. 'Why are you looking at me?' the torturer asked his victim, and began to beat him until he lost all control, in order to forget himself. For instinct cannot bear to be seen, and thus immobilised within its nothingness. A penetrating gaze divides it, and aggravates its latent anguish. Pure anguish is unstable and distressed, able to subsist only through movement. Christ's serenity before his judges called forth their wrath: and when they delivered him up to the torture, it was to break down the majesty of his countenance, and to confront him with himself in the grimace of agony.

Thus, in the same way as other myths, but providing the loftiest with their full sense—even more, divested of the trappings of fable, a part of the universal everyday, become almost a casual news item—the Christian mystery took man at his source, and identified him, in one act of recognition, with Christ and his executioners: regarded him as for ever divided internally, and at the same time sustained him in unity. Because the story of Christ is infinitely *banal*, capable of being repeated in any man, or through his fault: hence it follows that his significance can only be absolute. In *Combats avec Tes Défenseurs*, in which Christ appears on every page, it was not as a votary of the suffering Christ that I invoked his example and his name. No other image but his (which by no means all Christians accepted as orthodox) was sufficiently common and total to embrace the suffering and the hope of the universe. I have said, in an earlier chapter, that the figure of Christ established universal fellowship. Each of us carries within him the countenance of his God: or, to use terms more easily grasped by those who believe in God without knowing it, the universal from of man. Our common basis of existence is also our supreme end. Whoever tries to diminish me, to disfigure me in such a way that I become ashamed of what I am, outrages human nature in me, the countenance which we have in common: he disfigures himself at the same time, which is really what he wants to do, whether he is aware of it or not.

These symbolic truths can be better expressed by images. While

I am attempting to transcribe them in a language which is not their own, I am constantly aware of the narrow limits of prose and the limits of understanding. I know, nevertheless, and it is a knowledge which I have acquired with difficulty, that they await a language which will make them familiar to the mind: the language of communion, the Word which gathers men together, no longer in that external fellowship which the politicians offer us, but one of spiritual design. It is not by working on chaos from without that we will manage to give it a form: all we can hope to do thus is to create isolated systems, petrified within their profound divisions, and ranged against one another in struggles which will only perpetuate chaos.

Whatever my belief in the destiny of man, and my conviction that nothing, not even the desperate efforts man makes to destroy himself, excuses us for despairing of him, I am inclined still to think that chaos has not yet produced all its progeny, and that the Descent into Hell is not yet over, for our pseudo-civilisation, by increasing its mechanisms, gives birth to more spiritual monsters than it is able to absorb. The irrepressible future is no longer balanced by any permanence. The most active philosophies offer us as a dogma the vision of an indefinite metamorphosis: an accelerated cancer-like growth of appearance which has no more to do with the mind than the inverse process of petrification. The two become one and the same, besides: and one may conceive a tyranny Protean in form, bristling with all kinds of constraint, which imposes on its slaves the regime of the perpetual volte-face, and keeps them in a motionless agitation, to prevent them from thinking. The tyranny of fashion bears witness to this. But politics are not excluded from the danger, at a time when people no longer think except under the sway of contradictory stimuli which continually harass them in various forms of propaganda. Babel is the city of the confusion of tongues, as it is of extreme tyranny: within its invincible walls reigns total disorder—a disorder which ends in stubborn silence.

Of all the images I have used in my poetry, the one of which I am most keenly aware is the symbol of the Dove rising slowly from chaos. This came to light in the middle of the war, in a very short poem whose significance struck me:

Ce sont toujours les mêmes mots
Qui hasardent le monde
C'est la même colombe
Qui surplombe
Les eaux.
[It is always the same words
Which venture into the world
Still the same dove
Which hovers
Over the waters.]

In the confusion of tongues at the very heart of Babel, there are very simple words whose sense has become lost because it demanded continual reflection. I might cite some of these words with their inexhaustible symbolism: Christ is one of them, and also bread, earth, love. Whoever reads the Gospel of Saint John will find them all there in their eternal light. They speak to us of things we have forgotten. It is useless to forge new words, or to dismember the old ones under some philosophic pretext. Man is in evolution upon himself in the interior of these primitive words, which in all ages have signified his very life. After all, however impoverished they may be, these words still retain their power over men: opposing systems seize upon them, less for their meaning than for the force of attraction which they represent. They will outlive all systems, as the seed survives the frost. And it is from them that will be born the future forms of language, when, from the depths of barbarism, men endowed with inner sense have meditated on them long enough.

In the beginning was the Word. The insemination of the world by the Word began with the instinctive needs of man, but continually aspiring upwards, towards the spirit. I am convinced that the Holy Ghost, the creative Dove, waits in profound words, and that it was not at all by chance that Christ chose bread as the sign for universal communion. If one reflected sufficiently long on the nature of bread, from the germination of the wheat to its final assimilation by the spirit sustained by the body, if one meditated on the division created by its lack, and the harmony which reigns when it is fairly shared, one might write around that single word the whole history of man. And perhaps it is the poet's task, not so much to seek out rare satisfactions in a fastidious use of words, but to restore to these simple words, which everyone has almost forgotten, their integral, everyday, and sacred meaning. It is a task which will never end, for it embraces the whole range of the universe, and the whole system of relationships which link man with his neighbour and with the world. But it is perhaps in a period of absolute disruption that these words have the best chance of being meditated upon on all planes, and unified by a need for certainty which brings us back to the root of being. It is possible that revolutions frustrated and turned into barbarism may leave man lying for a long time fallow, and then make him turn in himself and feed upon his own corruption. Meanwhile, the imperishable seed, like that Egyptian wheat which lived on in the tombs, awaits its hour of growth, to spring up from an earth renewed by death, the grain aspiring towards the light.

*   *   *

And now I find myself like a man who has spent a long night of vigil, thrown more and more into anguish by the silence, ever more deeply invested by the Presence which has no name. The arid soliloquy of the soul has grown quiet: the further I advanced in my weariness, the more intimately it merged with the patient dream of the earth. Now it is morning, and the house still sleeps. I open the window, and feel the dawn breaking on my heart.

Lord, how good it is in this still solitary world, which men will soon fill with their sounds. The apple-tree with laden arms bends towards me in its morning greeting, and I greet it in turn. Whatever the world's distress, one certainty at least is left me, which I feel as I bite into an apple. And there are so many others, just as simple, that the apple reminds me of. For thirty years I despised them, because they were banal and within my reach. Thirty years I spent, searching for truth in the mind alone. Those thirty years lasted no more than a night: and this morning, while on my palate still lingers the bitter savour of an exhausting battle, the unity of the world is revealed to me in an apple. But how many sufferings, how many deaths have strewn the path to this truth! There are men who have died—my friends—in order that I may, on a summer morning, stretch out my hand to a branch and choose the handsomest fruit. I think of that impossible miracle: an apple-tree in a concentration camp. It is true that happiness exists in the moment; but not in that moment which one hastens to seize and empty, in order to pass on to others. It is a solemn moment, heavy with experience, which sums up within it immense sacrifices and boundless struggles. Boundless? Between the child who eats an apple and the grown and suffering man who tastes a universe in it, the difference is a world. We only find simple, spontaneous life again after having gathered all things up, and when we are able, in full awareness, to assure ourselves that all is contained in all. Life remains not the less simple for this, but in the manner of a symphony wherein each bar contains the rule. In this gesture of taking up an apple and sinking my teeth into it, I confirm my presence in the world: an act of love, in which I am no longer alone, but unconsciously in harmony with all my brothers. I have only to glance within myself to feel their thronging presence.

Paris and Le Mesnil-Guilbert
(March–August, 1947).